The Authority of Experience

The
Authority of Experience
Essays in Feminist Criticism

Edited by Arlyn Diamond and Lee R. Edwards

The University of Massachusetts Press

Amherst, 1977

All new material copyright © 1977 by
The University of Massachusetts Press
All rights reserved
Library of Congress Catalog Card Number 76-8755
ISBN 0-87023-220-7
Printed in the United States of America
Designed by Mary Mendell
Library of Congress Cataloging in Publication Data
Main entry under title:
The Authority of experience.
1. Women in literature—Addresses, essays, lectures.
2. English literature—History and criticism—Addresses,
essays, lectures.   3. American literature—History and
criticism—Addresses, essays, lectures.   I. Diamond,
Arlyn, 1941–   II. Edwards, Lee R.
PR151.W6A9   801'.95   76-8755
ISBN 0-87023-220-7

Copyrights & Acknowledgments

ite and Rainbow; Mrs. Dalloway; and "Defoe" from *Collected Essays,* Volume I.

Houghton Mifflin Company for material from A. B. Guthrie, *The Big Sky.*

Michael Joseph Ltd. for material from Doris Lessing, *The Golden Notebook.*

Louisiana State University Press for material reprinted by permission from *The Complete Works of Kate Chopin,* Volume II, edited by Per Seyersted, copyright © 1969, Louisiana State University Press.

Macmillan London and Basingstoke for material reprinted by permission from Mary Ellmann, *Thinking about Women.*

The New American Library, Inc., and José Ortega Spottorno for material from *On Love,* by José Ortega y Gasset, translated by Toby Talbot. Copyright © 1957 by Toby Talbot. By arrangement with The New American Library, Inc., New York, N.Y.

Penguin Books Ltd. for material from M. Dorothy George, *London Life in the Eighteenth Century.*

Routledge and Kegan Paul Ltd. for material from Frank Kermode, *The Romantic Image;* and for material from Ivy Pinchbeck and Margaret Hewitt, *Children in English Society,* Volume I, published by Routledge and Kegan Paul (London) and the University of Toronto Press.

Charles Scribner's Sons for material reprinted by permission of Charles Scribner's Sons from "Fathers and Sons" from *Winner Take Nothing,* by Ernest Hemingway, copyright © 1933 Charles Scribner's Sons; and for material reprinted by permission from *A Farewell to Arms,* by Ernest Hemingway, copyright © 1929 Charles Scribner's Sons.

Simon and Schuster, Inc., for material from Doris Lessing, *The Golden Notebook.*

Stein and Day/Publishers for material copyright © 1968 by Leslie A. Fiedler, from the book *The Return of the Vanishing American.* Reprinted with permission of Stein and Day/Publishers.

The Swallow Press for material from *D. H. Lawrence—An Unprofessional Study,* by Anais Nin. Copyright © 1964 by Anais Nin. All rights reserved. Currently published by the Swallow Press, Chicago. Reprinted by permission of the Author's Representative, Gunther Stuhlmann.

Contents

Foreword

As an introduction this essay might better be called an 'afterword' since, in writing it, we are accounting—after the fact and on theoretical grounds—for material collected practically and intuitively. Our initial boundaries were broadly drawn, aimed at including rather than excluding material or points of view: we desired only that authors should address themselves generally to the problem of defining feminist criticism and/or deal in some declaredly feminist way with significant English or American texts. Diverse by design then, rising out of particular critics' concerns with particular authors or problems, the sixteen essays which follow do, nonetheless, participate in certain fundamental assumptions about the nature of both literature and criticism.

Sharing a common philosophical perspective, they demonstrate that literary material can legitimately be understood in terms of its wider social and moral context. All our authors see art as the product of a particular cultural milieu, sometimes embodying a society's most deeply held convictions, sometimes questioning these values, sometimes disguising an artist's own ambivalence with regard to these matters, but never disengaged from the claims of time or social order. Marcia Landy, in one of the trio of theoretical essays which open this collection, describes feminist criticism as one among several "critiques of literature and criticism which have at their core the inclusion of views of oppressed groups, that probe the mythology about women and other minority groups perpetuated in the stereotypes and attitudes which are a mirror of prevailing fantasies and conscious social norms." As Annette Barnes similarly suggests, Matthew Arnold's eternal world of art and culture bears a striking resemblance to Never Never Land.

Although many critics and many schools of criticism share a belief in the interrelationship between society and art, feminist critics, obviously, are distinguished by virtue of their particular concern with society's beliefs about the nature and function of women in the world, with the transformation of these beliefs into literary plots, with the ways in which artistic and critical strategies adjust and control attitudes toward women. When Maurianne Adams points out that "to rethink *Jane Eyre* requires a new orientation, not to the dilemmas of the male, to whom the male critics have understandably shown themselves duly sensitive, but to Jane herself," her voice strikes the major chord of this collection.

A simple shift of attention, however, is not enough; the critics represented here do not rest with the description of an author's techniques or the stance of a particular work, but instead point constantly to the need to measure literary reality on the one side against historical and personally felt reality on the other. This is not an easy task. Imagination and informed seeking are required in order to justify our discomfort with what we have learned about ourselves through literature. The search begins with a willingness and ability to ask the right questions, and therefore our three critical essays are in some sense prolegomena, indications of the critical tools and disciplines available to those engaged in rediscovering and recreating personal and public history.

The works of Chaucer, Shakespeare, Lessing, Chopin and others become, at least in part, indices and models for our own experience of life. Adjusting our visions to see these writers and their works anew, we are calling for a similar readjustment of perspective in viewing the world at large. It follows, then, that most feminist critics—for the time being at any rate—are women, for to us the question of our 'true' nature and place in the larger scheme of things is not merely academic. The parts we play in literature are not unconnected to the parts we are permitted to play in life, and the attitudes that critics, predominantly but by no means exclusively male, have taken toward both female characters and women writers, hedge us all around. But feminist criti-

cism should not be considered important only for women. Mary
Cohen says of Doris Lessing that "the anger that the feminist label
rouses in [her] most probably comes from the fact that what has
seemed to be special pleading for women has been only a part of a
larger plea, that humanity re-examine its directions." And this plea
—both Cohen's and Lessing's—is echoed in Barbara Carson's essay
on Katherine Ann Porter's women; in Lee Edwards' discussion of
Clarissa Dalloway; in Priscilla Allen's dissatisfaction with a so-
called rehabilitation of Kate Chopin's *The Awakening* which
begins and ends in the assumption that Edna Pontellier's humanity
is defined and confined solely by her sexuality. The authors they
consider realize that women no less than men are fitting symbols
for the aspirations, desires, victories, and failures of the whole of
the human species, not just an isolated fragment.

These convictions mesh with a love of literature to produce a
criticism which is ultimately positive. Freeing the works from the
prison of too narrow a critical focus, the discussions which follow
make apparent new ways of reading which are illuminating for
an audience not drawn by any pre-existent ideology. Barrenly attacking literature for the attitudes it shares with its environment
has seemed to us and to the critics assembled here less fruitful than
attempting to understand it. Sometimes, however, as Judith Fetterly and Coppélia Kahn both indicate, this may require adjusting
our perspectives in order to deal with the disparity "between what
is overtly stated and what is covertly expressed," within a particular work. Although Shakespeare's Kate "seems to be the most
vocal apologist for male dominance, she is indeed its ablest critic."
Catherine's fate in *A Farewell to Arms* reveals the suppressed
hostility toward women that stands behind so much that has
been celebrated as romance in Western literature. Dawn Lander,
finding herself alien from the traditional image that, we are told,
American literature gives of American women, examines many
works to point out the danger of assuming, as so many critics have
done, that the male view of the female view is identical with the
female view itself, or that the female view cannot be found in our
written past. Patricia Barber playfully turns Melville's male scrivener into a feminine Miss Bartleby, using the critical essay as a
means of imaginatively grappling with the notion "that the supposedly 'masculine' or 'feminine' traits can be possessed by both
sexes . . . and if one is to believe that we are all able to experience

and understand the concerns of both men and women, one [may]
explain this ability with the idea that we all share in an androgynous universality of human experience." Thus, Katherine Rogers
and Miriam Lerenbaum caution us to remember that a male author
can himself be "an acute observer of women ... sympathetic to
their plight," seeing them not as 'moral Models," but as beings
who, like men, are "created out of every day fact and human
psychology. . . ."

The anger that our critics feel finds in their essays its proper
target: not the literature itself but the misconceptions of past
critics, the received evaluations about literature which, rooted in
bias, have for too long passed for disinterested impartiality. Thus,
many of these essays begin, necessarily, by clearing away false
visions before they can proceed to articulate what is truly new.
The words with which Lynn Sukenick concludes her essay might
serve as an epigraph for this volume in general: "Art has a life of
its own, and an awareness of injustices toward women is not going
to make a bad book better; yet it is criticism that evaluates and
preserves that life, and criticism which is sexually, as opposed to
intellectually, discriminating, will hide and withhold a significant
portion of the life of a book. Elements in women's writing which
have been unappreciated or denigrated by male critics may appear in a different light once the prejudices of these critics have
been named as such. Sexual neutrality in criticism may be impossible or even undesirable; sexual hostility, however, is not inevitable. Until that hostility disappears, women will have to keep
speaking of it ... making of the freedom to speak with authority
a tradition and a norm rather than a history of exceptions."

The insights yielded by our re-examinations of familiar material
are validated by the discovery of other works which have been
consistently under-rated or neglected in the past. "Eve Among the
Indians" opens up a rich vein of American materials simply waiting to be mined and minted into critical coinage. Katherine Rogers suggests that feminists might do well to have a second, or even
a first, look at Samuel Richardson's monumental novel, *Clarissa*,
and in so doing might be provoked to shift in their own minds the
relative weight they give to his works as against those of Henry
Fielding. Barbara Carson and Priscilla Allen, examining Katherine
Ann Porter and Kate Chopin, imply that these authors too are

worth more space than is generally accorded them in the usual critical hierarchy.

Furthermore, although the obvious material for contemporary feminists to consider belongs to our own time, this collection demonstrates that it is equally fruitful to survey the entire range of our traditionally defined literary inheritance. The danger here, of course, is that of distortion, of demanding that the past not simply share, but prove the truth of an awareness that we ourselves have only recently and painfully achieved. Satisfying the claims of historicity is, however, not so difficult as we might fear initially. Writing about medieval literature, for example, both Maureen Fries and Arlyn Diamond indicate that "an approach to Chaucer inspired by feminist concern is not an historical perversity ... but a very natural way of examining him given the lively, even obsessive interest the later Middle Ages took in the problem of female nature." Far from being a recent invention, feminism is as old as anti-feminism, and anti-feminism, for good or ill, is a most ancient attitude. Similarly, Miriam Lerenbaum's essay on *Moll Flanders* corrects what amounts to a twentieth-century sentimentalizing of Moll by showing that her attitudes, particularly those toward motherhood and children, were not the aberrations that most modern critics have seen them as being, but were, in fact, typical of her time and the result of a general set of social, economic, and medical conditions. To see Moll in isolation from these conditions is, therefore, not simply to view her too narrowly but finally to distort the book which bears her name. The weight of feminism does not unbalance criticism, but stabilizes it.

The suspicion that feminist criticism is parochial and negative is rooted in a misplaced fear that those writers we profess to admire will somehow be diminished if we look too closely at what they were really saying about women—or men, or society, or the relationships among them. But the essays we have selected demonstrate the contrary is true, that Chaucer, Shakespeare, Defoe, Richardson, and Melville are finally more and not less humane than we have perhaps been willing to think them.

Although in terms of most of the views held by Western culture, a literary critic who is both female and feminist is an anomaly, we do have a heritage to which this volume makes a contribution. We ought to remember, for example, Christine de Pisan's assessment of *The Romance of the Rose*, Mary Wollstonecraft's comments about Milton and Rousseau, Virginia Woolf's criticism. These women, like the ones who follow here, were attempting to enclose precise literary commentary within a more abstract and theoretical framework, to set up a dialectic between the truths that literature suggested and what their own lives had taught them to see and to accept. That there is as yet no universally acceptable, definitively formulated feminist aesthetic is neither surprising nor particularly depressing; in a world which still argues about what Aristotle meant, such purported critical monuments disappear like Ozymandias' tomb. If our aim is more modest, we also think it is more useful. By asking new questions, providing new contexts, scrutinizing new material we hope to provide a criticism that will be fresh, accurate, compelling and suggestive. If feminist literary criticism does not connote a school of criticism with a rigidly defined methodology, the term does imply a general orientation, an attitude toward literature which can turn a wide variety of existing techniques to its own ends. Like Annette Barnes, we accept as minimal criteria for feminist literary theory the assumptions "that women are not automatically or necessarily inferior to men, that role models for females and males in the current Western societies are inadequate, that equal rights for women are necessary, that it is unclear what by nature either men or women are, that it is a matter for empirical investigation to ascertain what differences follow from the obvious physiological ones." And, like her, we would close our introduction with the wish that the hypotheses these essays cause the reader to formulate in his or her own mind may themselves remain open to question, revision, expansion.

ARLYN DIAMOND
LEE R. EDWARDS

"Experience, though noon auctoritee
Were in this world, is right ynogh for me
To speke...."
The Wife of Bath

As for the critics whose task it is to pass
judgment upon...books,...let them look
indeed upon the writers as if they were
engaged upon some vast building...being
built by common effort.... Let them...
scan the horizon; see the past in relation to
the future; and so prepare the way for masterpieces to come.
Virginia Woolf, "How It Strikes a
Contemporary"

Female Criticism:
A Prologue

ANNETTE BARNES

If the critic's function is to expose, yet speak with balance, to kiss thought up another notch,[1] does it matter what sex performs these feats? Do Matthew Arnold's critical demands, "a disinterested endeavor to learn and propagate the best that is known and thought in the world," "to see the object as in itself it really is," [2] not make gender irrelevant?

The disinterestedness Arnold seeks requires the critic to put aside "practical" considerations, to forget political or religious motives, and speak in the vacuum of Truth. Unless one has a truly misogynous soul, it seems unlikely that women would automatically be ruled out of the enterprise. Even if one thought it likely that many women would find the starkness and lack of frills intolerable and hence fall with the weaker men into the muck of bias, surely one would leave room for the probably plain, hence explicable woman.

If it weren't for the fact that Arnold's notion of criticism is confused, we might have found a place for a female critic, a place of spartan equality. But the critic, like the author of the work criticized, cannot come to the task as an ideal spectator devoid of culture, history, political perspective—a Venus off the halfshell dripping with innocence. Though virgin productivity is a seductive myth, the critic has been formed by contact with the world. If one is a Socialist, Democrat, Christian, woman, feminist, this conviction or state can cause one to be a biased or limited critic, fitting the material at hand into one's framework, whether the fit is Cinderella-like or not. Though there is always this danger of doctrine, the remedy is not shedding one's cultural inheritance. We are weighted creatures, whether creators or critics or silent spectators. Like any mortal a critic lives within a given age, and is at most and at best human.

If myriad influences affect one's critical faculties, can one ever be in a neutral position, can one ever give an unbiased or impartial review? Yet aren't critics expected to do just that, to transcend particular ideologies? Calling a critic an ideologue, a "figment of the Zeitgeist" [3] is momentously pejorative. Are we perhaps more like Jeremy Bentham than we care to acknowledge, advocating a policy of what people ought to do, while nevertheless believing in a theory about what people were capable of doing which rendered the prescriptive theory useless in the ordinary world. Can we tell critics that they ought to be objective, disinterested, when in point of fact we believe that objective criticism is impossible, given that critics are, after all is said and done, humans?

To put the question in another way: if critics approach the work with questions they want answered, questions asked at a certain time and place with some expectation as to what would count as an answer, can critics nevertheless get at the object in itself as it really is? Or are critics destined to carry their world view with them, a world view which does not get at how things really are?

I suggest that a critic is not able to escape some classificatory schema, some way of perceiving the world. The schema may be modified, adapted, changed for better or worse, but a critic is always wedded to some framework of alternatives. If it doesn't make sense to suppose that we can rid ourselves of all frameworks, that we can have those innocent eyes of which Ruskin, among others, was so fond, does this mean we distort what we see, that we are forever locked in with ourselves; the work as it really is secure from us?

> They said, "You have a blue guitar
> You do not play things as they are."
> (Wallace Stevens, "The Man with the Blue Guitar")

Given world and time enough, I would argue that to work within a classificatory system does not bar access to a way the object is. Without some framework one has no access at all to what James described as the booming, buzzing confusion. What we do not have access to is *the* way the object in itself really is, for there is no one way it really is. Trivial as it may sound, the object (in this case the work being criticized) is many ways, no one of which eliminates all others.

Critical exposures, to be sure, do often claim finality. If a critic believes his or her answer to be the true and correct one, this suggests that other critics must acknowledge it, cannot but yield to it to the exclusion of all others. Yet the complexity of even the simplest world most often permits of an overlay of readings. Even a fairy tale is an intellectual's gold mine.

Though the work is not "one way" this does not mean it is "any way" an ingenious interpreter can come up with. Satiric in intent, *The Pooh Perplex* amuses because Crews applies various critical approaches so outrageously to the Pooh world. The claims to exclusiveness are ludicrous, as are the claims to truth. *Winnie-the-Pooh* is no more about Christopher Robin's recent "destruction and repression of his Oedipus complex" than it is about "dialectical materialism, scientific socialism, the spirit of the Commune, democratic cooperation between peoples, and the necessity of the revolution." [4]

But if what I say above is true, if the framework of alternatives we bring to experience determines our reading of it, how can we ever claim some interpretations are true and correct, others amusing by their very absurdity? Are there any independent standards, impartial criteria we can refer to, which would allow us to evaluate the claims of correctness or truth made by a Freudian critic, a Marxist critic, a feminist critic? Are we really in a Hobbesian state of war with rival viewpoints elbowing each other aside in the race for survival? If an overlay of readings is possible for many works, how distinguish the true, correct ones from the sheer fantasies?

Having raised such weighty questions it would seem appropriate for the author of this piece to answer them. But I confess to inadequacy. In any given instance, I can try to show why I would claim one reading is plausible, insightful, while another distorts, but I can not get at any general theory which would allow me neatly to separate the profound from the perfunctory. I want to maintain that good critics' claims are objective, disinterested, that readings make sense independently of who offers them, that the

authority of a critic is in a very important way irrelevant. But I
know of no standards common to all critical approaches that will
enable me fully to do this.

Is the reading consistent, coherent, comprehensive, simple,
powerful, fecund? But these criteria seem to let too much in,
not to allow me to rule out some readings. For example, I read
the case study of Little Hans, awed by Freud's imagination yet
reluctant to see Hans's crumpled giraffe as his mother, or the "*sitting* down on top of" in terms of "possession." [5] The study is coherent, consistent, only too fecund, and yet wild. It is not that
Freud cannot bring reasons in; it is that I must buy a whole appara-
tus of covert sexual symbolism. Freud can of course explain why
there is this reluctance on my part just as Christianity explains the
non-believer, but these explanations do nothing to convert a dis-
sentient.

Though consistency, completeness, simplicity . . . do not guarantee that a reading will be satisfactory, the absence of these features can make a reading unsatisfactory. If one is judging an
interpretation of a work against its rivals one might profitably
begin by determining whether any of the interpretations lack
these features. For example, Stanley Cavell interprets King Lear's
motive in the opening scene of the play as Lear's "attempt to avoid
recognition, the shame of exposure, the threat of self-revelation." [6]
Others have spoken of Lear's senility, or puerility, or how the
scene is ritualistic rather than naturalistic. One might begin evaluating these interpretations by asking—do the theses that Lear is
senile or puerile account for his behavior during the rest of the
play? Does Cavell's analysis have the necessary scope and simplicity, does it raise and answer significant questions? Simplicity,
scope, power, as I claimed, are not sufficient since there may
be hypotheses that satisfy these criteria but which are nevertheless unpalatable. These features, however, are among those required for a satisfactory interpretation. The difficulty arises when
an interpretation has these features but does not seem to get truly
or correctly at the work. [7]

If it can be argued that even in science the truth of a hypothesis
is a "matter of fit—fit with a body of theory, and fit of hypothesis
and theory to the data at hand and the facts to be encountered," [8]
then confronted by several critical hypotheses all purporting to
fit the object at hand, how is the weary reader to proceed? With

one of Cinderella's sisters the shoe did not fit no matter how much of a radical adjustment, short of chopping off the excess, was tried. When does a reading fit, or when does it fit because you are predisposed to its fit? In her article, "Psychology Constructs the Female," Naomi Weisstein asks whether "psychiatrists ever learn anything different than their theories had led them to believe?" [9] She makes a case for distinguishing between clinical experience and empirical evidence, claiming that the bias of the experimenter —expectations of how, for example, females and males will behave—does influence how in fact these people do behave.

But surely, you might say, we know what people mean when they say that a critic "should see the object exactly as it is"; that sometimes critics "may have seen (in the wider sense of 'see') more than there is to be seen; and the only test of whether the qualities are really there must be some agreement among careful and disinterested observers." [10] "The judgments of a skilful, sympathetic, widely experienced critic are better than those of one without these, and other appropriate qualities." [11]

But who are the careful and disinterested observers, the skilful, sympathetic, experienced critics? Can we go any distance toward finding them? If, for example, a museum director cannot tell by looking at two paintings that one is a forgery, the other not, if x-rays are required; then is the careful disinterested observer the x-ray operator rather than the museum director who bought the forgery? The director has had practice and training, but can't a desire to buy a great painting affect discernment?

Johnson, in his life of Milton, does not "pretend to speak as critic," of some of Milton's Italian pieces, though he had "heard them commended by a man well-qualified to decide their merit." Some minimal knowledge is required for competency. Music critics must know something about music; critics of Einstein's theories of relativity, physics. But how much knowledge is required? Can your knowledge of one field preclude your having knowledge in another; can it make you a biased critic? I am thinking of the Western art critics who saw African art through the limiting lenses of their own culture, or the academic painters who were not able to recognize innovation, however good it subsequently was shown to be.

Suppose one believes that all works of art are subsumable under some universal principle; for example, all works of art appeal to the libidinous fantasies civilized people repress. When confronted with any particular work—be it *Macbeth* or *Winnie-the-Pooh*, *Mourning Becomes Electra*, or *Through the Looking Glass*—on the above view, a critic's task would be to show how the particular work substantiates the general claim. For example, a critic claims that *Pooh* provides its readers with a substitute satisfaction for unfulfilled desires—Christopher has resolved his Oedipal conflict. It would be reasonable to protest, however, that though Oedipus may live out the incestuous and deadly fantasy men nourish, it is absurd to burden Christopher Robin with the resolution of his Oedipal complex. This is not to claim that *if* Freud were correct and Christopher were a real boy, he would not face the Oedipal situation. Rather it is to say that the work is not about that situation.

A critic who believed that all works of art should be analyzed in feminist terms might point out that *Pooh* is really *about* the inadequate female and male role models existent in Western society. A similar protest is appropriate here. Even if female kangaroos do behave remarkably like some of their human counterparts (as mothers and housekeepers), *Pooh* is not about those role models though one might agree that Chopin's *The Awakening* is.

Whether the universal principles are psychological, religious, sociological, or political, it often happens that in individual cases the shoe fits only if the foot is literally cut to the requisite size. Starting life as an empirical thesis, a universal hypothesis about the nature of art can get calcified into a necessary truth. When it becomes such a truth, evidence is no longer relevant. If someone plausibly argued that *Pooh*, for example, did not deal with any repressed libidinal wishes, the psychological critic who replied that the work had not yet been adequately analyzed would be dangerously close to defending a nonfalsifiable position, a position arbitrarily made secure from attack.

Though Freud's theory about art is advanced as part of a larger empirical hypothesis it could be claimed that many theories about art are never empirical. When Tolstoy demands that an art work be infectious—"it is a means of union among men, joining them together in the same feelings"—any work lacking that feature is by his account, not art. But if theories about art are each similarly insulated against attack, how does one choose among them? Why isn't art, contrary to Tolstoy's claims, "the manifestation of some mysterious Idea of beauty or God," or "a game in which man lets off his excess of stored-up energy," or "the expression of man's emotions by external signs"? [12]

One could argue convincingly that all art does not do any one particular thing exclusively, so that all works would not conform to any one principle or set of principles. This would allow for the possibility that some art works did the particular thing in question. If no theory about art in general is adequate for all works, in individual cases one might still debate whether the work at hand was or was not covered by a theory. How we know when a work fits a theory or when the work is squeezed into the theoretic parameters is not something one can give a general account of, though one can in particular cases make a convincing case for or against an imputed fit.

We have been discussing difficulties inherent in criticism, whether the critic be a Freudian, Socialist, or Christian. Is there a special group of critics who by virtue of their sex make up a significantly distinct class? We can recognize Freudian and other critics by the doctrinal company they keep. Do women critics share some gospel? Are there doctrines that women adhere to either by choice or by nature?

If one were to argue that there is some natural difference between men and women which is reflected in their criticism, that the male critic is intellectual, the female intuitive, perceptive, emotional, I would counterclaim that though training in society encourages men and women to value different mental functions, it does not follow that the emphasis (for men on intellect, for women on sensitivity) is a natural one, nor that such emphasis is unchangeable. Moreover one could point to many male and female critics who clearly challenge the truth of any such general rule.

If it is unclear whether there exists any grounds for talk of men and women being this or that by nature, is there some position women do choose which would affect their critical performance? If what I claimed earlier is the case, if critics cannot divorce themselves from their nurture, then their beliefs about possible relationships between men and women will color their readings of a great many works. If one believes that a woman's purpose is motherhood, that belief will affect one's reading of *The Doll's*

House, Medea, Family Happiness, or even *The Republic.* If one believes that models of womanhood are possible which provide alternatives to either eccentric spinsterhood or mindless marriage, this belief will influence one's critical comments.

Recently, a young male student of mine characterized masculinity as "virility, independence, strength, bravery, aggressiveness, and insensitivity (to a certain degree)"; femininity as "gentleness, docility, dependence, sensitivity, beauty, meekness, and weakness." Men are "active creatures whose chief function is to ... forge their own path." "Women are supposed to be passive creatures, whose main concern is taking care of the appearance of their homes and of themselves (... for the benefit of their husbands ...)." [13] The traditional doctrine about the implications of sexuality for behavior allows, of course, exceptions or additions to motherhood and housewifery. Chorus girls, intellectuals, prostitutes, and other career women of all sorts exist. Men and women who accept this traditional doctrine about sex-linked behavior are ideologically compatible. The doctrine prescribes distinct but complementary functions for each sex.

Adherence to these traditional beliefs about roles frequently means giving male and female audiences different paps as well as assigning male and female critics separate domains. The female literary critic's proper assignments, for example, might include children's books, cook books, gardening and craft books, and those novels and biographies romanticizing the world in "marmalady circumlocutions." Exceptions, as we noted, did occur in this best of all possible worlds and the literary "ladies," Woolf, Parker, McCarthy, Hardwick et al. have digested the hardier stuff.

If this dichotomy is rejected, if what I designate a feminist perspective is adopted, then those who adhere to its doctrine will form a distinct class. In order to determine whether only women will choose to be members of that class, it is necessary to offer a characterization of feminism.

Currently people are challenging the established models of human behavior—models which have been naturalized in the arts, sciences, religions, as well as in the media, the present day molder of public awareness. A grim night was prophesied for those "unnatural hags" who perverted their roles. Unless one had wings, a phenomenon surprisingly lacking in most women, those who attempted flight ended badly. The university psychiatrists who, when confronted by female patients having scholastic difficulties, advised them to stop worrying about success in masculine endeavors and learn to love the inevitable—matrimony and maternity—are not impressed by protests about inadequate role models. But suppose these role models are man made, patterns humans must fit if they expect any share of happiness. A large area becomes available to critical inquiry. Are the theories which prescribe what is natural behavior as opposed to what is determined by social enclosure satisfactory? Are any guilty of the "interest" Arnold deplored? What patterns of behavior are pictured for men and women in literature, paintings, films, in sociology or psychology texts, in dances or operas?

Though there are internal disagreements within most perspectives, nevertheless just as all Freudians believe in the unconscious, in infantile sexuality, in neurotic behavior as a form of purposive behavior; so all feminists, I argue, would agree that women are not automatically or necessarily inferior to men, that role models for females and males in the current Western societies are inadequate, that equal rights for women are necessary, that it is unclear what by nature either men or women are, that it is a matter for empirical investigation to ascertain what differences follow from the obvious physiological ones, that in these empirical investigations the hypotheses one employs are themselves open to question, revision, or replacement. I have adapted what I take to be the minimal criteria for feminism. I acknowledge that in so doing I avoid by fiat questions which some proclaimed feminists consider crucial.

If one understands feminism as I have characterized it, does one need to be a woman to criticize from a feminist perspective? Theoretically, no. Plato in his ideal state allowed men and women the same tasks, firmly convinced that men would always do them better. Given the present state of awareness I would propose that though the perspective is open to both sexes, women have the decided advantage of seeing better with it. I draw no firm line here—there are both male and female dullards and ideologues, as well as male and female imaginative geniuses.

Though the adoption of feminist beliefs would presumably benefit both sexes in the long run, it is a rare bird (male or female) who gives up a feathered nest. The strays, who either by choice or circumstances, have no nest, or discover the hazards in their own, are the ones who frequently speak out. That many women consider themselves strays in this society, that they therefore have vested interests in change, is not a telling objection against their position. All parties in the dispute—female chauvinists, male chauvinists, feminists—have vested interests.

I am not claiming that a feminist perspective is appropriate to all critical endeavors though it may have results in areas which seem initially sex-proof. In some disciplines the critic is asked to make predominant use of the intellect on the asumption that being male or female, white or black, Greek or Persian, is irrelevant. If, for example, one is criticizing Aristotle's advocacy of a slave state on the ground that such a state is unjust, if one is evaluating the claim that formal systems if consistent are not complete, it makes prima facie sense to suppose the mind is housed indifferently. The concept of justice seems sex-proof—how ludicrous the idea of a justice for men distinct from justice for women. Absurdity, however, is no guarantee of abstinence—there is a need for an equal rights amendment for women in twentieth-century America. Though it seems plausible to suppose that in some disciplines the only qualification for a critic is the ability or capacity to understand the claim and understand what evidence is, or what good arguments or reasons are; sometimes what one takes to be a good reason relies on certain unquestioned beliefs about the nature of men and women. Aristotle's belief that slavery was just, rested on his belief in the natural intellectual superiority of certain men over other men and all women. Women are not to be equated with slaves, though their position in society is restricted by their male rulers. With an aplomb that numbs, Aristotle tells us to look in nature where we shall find the rule of the superior over the inferior in effect. A clear and obvious case, men ruling women, for "the male is by nature superior, and the female inferior." [14]

Though a feminist perspective enables one to see the arbitrariness of Aristotle's dictum, and having such a perspective brings results in some unlikely areas, there are cases when the perspective is inappropriate. There are some who write and talk as if logic or arguments themselves were sex-linked—male or female logic, masculine or feminine argument. I am puzzled by this kind of talk. Is the counter-example, an argument which is quick, neat and destructive, male or masculine? Would a helpful, charitable construction be female or feminine? That is, is the difference between saying, "Jones is wrong, his account can't handle this case," and saying, "Jones is unclear, he wants to say such and such which he can if he modifies his position in the following way," the difference between a masculine and feminine argument? The only sense I can give to the modifiers "masculine" and "feminine" here relies on my accepting the traditional distinction between masculine and feminine—a distinction a feminist critic must question, not accept.

Arguments are valid or invalid, good or bad, premises true or false. Whether the arguments are used pugnaciously or patiently may be a matter of sexual conditioning, but intrinsically arguments are neither warlike or pacific. An Abzug wields an argument with as much ferocity as a Mailer. (I would bet on Bella in an alley confrontation.) It may be true that the approach one takes to a discussion, the kind of arguments one utilizes as well as how they are utilized, is influenced by one's adherence to the socially prevalent masculine and feminine standards—the aggressive male, the conciliatory female. Women have preferred certain fields to others, English and Art to Philosophy and Physics. But Physics and Philosophy are no more male or female than is the number three. When one begins to argue that, to the contrary, the number three is female, curvaceous, round and odd, as it is, then one has brought into the discussion assumptions which need to be examined. To make the example less fanciful, consider the remark, "For there is in Romaine Brooks's painting a force, even a vehemence, that can only be described as masculine." [15]

Many words are written about women. Criticism has not been idle, nor has it been disinterested. Are feminist critics especially prone to bias as some would have us believe? "He did not know why a lack of such literary niceties as fair quotation and measured attack should bother him more in women. Was it because a male critic who practiced such habits could not go far—the stern code of professionalism in other men was bound to cut him down...?" [16] Or does the interest of the critic, whether it be male chauvinist, feminist, or female chauvinist, make arguing in this area specially delicate and precipitous?

The following examples are intended to show both that female critics (in particular feminists) are neither more nor less partisan than their male counterparts, and that much of what goes under the guise of impartial criticism about women is in fact partial and bad criticism.

In a recent *New York Review of Books* where women were predominantly an issue, Irving Singer (a male philosopher) reviewing Mary Jane Sherfey (a female psychiatrist) finds many of her arguments unsatisfactory. For example, he says:

> Sherfey asserts that "the early embryo is not undifferentiated; 'it' is a female." She argues that without a great deal of androgen after the first five or six weeks no embryo would become a male, but that the female does not require additional hormones of any sort. She presents us with the image of a female development in the early embryology of all human beings, who would continue to be females if the androgen bath did not deflect some of them into becoming males.[17]

Singer suggests that her conclusion is reached only by a "crude sleight-of-hand." He says that "genetic or chromosomal sex is determined at the moment of fertilization"; if so, the fact that male embryos develop due to their androgen bath does not show that the embryos were female prior to their bath. They are male when they are given certain chromosomes. But one looks in vain in Singer's review for the crucial support he needs for his claims. One wants to know what being male or female at the moment of fertilization comes to. If all chromosome "males" developed into females without baths, then in what sense are they "males"? Would a chromosome female given an androgen bath become male? Do chromosome males without baths actually become females as seems suggested by Sherfey? If chromosomes determine the reproductive capacities of an individual, while an androgen bath would allow a reproductive female to function actively as a male, what becomes of the notion of sexuality? Is it tied to reproduction or characteristics like voice, hair, and breasts? These are questions that need to be answered and if they have been answered, the answers stated before, one can ascertain who is right.

In the same issue, Adrienne Rich (a feminist poet) reviewing a book by Midge Decter (a non-feminist writer) comments about Sherfey: "To think as a feminist means trying to think connectedly about, for example, the science of embryology as it may connect with sexuality (what does it mean, for example, that in the fetus, male differentiation occurs only after several weeks?)." Rich has accepted Sherfey's contention that the embryos become male at a time later than fertilization. Again, in order to assess whether she is correct, one must answer the questions raised earlier.

In the same review Rich claims that "we can no longer afford to keep the female principle—the mother in all women and the woman in many men—straitened within the tight little post-industrial family, or within any male-induced notion of where the female principle is valid and where it is not." I do not understand why there is a female principle, why there is a mother in all women, what having a mother in you involves. Rich sounds suspiciously as if she is bringing in through the front door, adorned in metaphysical garb, what she has thrown out the back. The female principle as a heritage of all women and some men, since they have "women" in them, is dangerously linked to characteristics of motherdom, characteristics cultivated and associated with the "maternal" influence in certain societies.

Irving Howe in his critical review of Kate Millett's *Sexual Politics* demands that a critic adhere to certain standards which he accuses Millett of failing to achieve. To award Ph.D.'s to intellectual featherweights, he asserts, is a serious devaluation of the educational degree. Yet consider some of Howe's own attempts at argument. Howe claims that Millett holds Freud responsible for rationalizing "the invidious relationship between the sexes." [18] The implication is that by so doing Freud caused these same relationships to continue and indeed justified their continuation. Howe asks, "[H]ow could the Freudian theories of which Miss Millett approves have left their mark on modern thought and experience without also profoundly affecting for the better—as in fact they did—'the invidious relationship between the sexes'? Could the current concern about sexual roles even have begun without the contributions of Freud?"

The suppressed premise of Mr. Howe's argument is, I take it, that the only way the problem about sexual roles ("the current concern . . .") could be stated is in Freudian terms. If the problem could only be stated in Freudian terms then of course it follows that Freud's theory was necessary in order for this concern about sexual roles to have begun. But it is false that this is the case. Was Freud not explaining a phenomenon in existence rather than creating one? Why couldn't someone ignorant of Freud but not ignorant of the situation in our culture see that the sexual roles of men and women were different and question whether there were factors that justified that difference?

Simone de Beauvoir raises the problem in a very different, non-Freudian context. She claims that women are defined nonreciprocally in relation to men. Women are defined as the other, the inessential. Each man defines himself as a subject and opposes himself to other men, but as each man makes the same claim, there develops a reciprocity among men's claims. She tries to show why this definition occurred and why women have accepted it even though it makes them an inessential yet necessary sex. Couldn't one raise the question about sexual roles in countless other ways?

Howe, in the same paragraph, claims that "Miss Millett keeps employing Freudian concepts as if they were the merest axioms and specifically notes her approval of the 'theories of the unconscious and infantile sexuality.' (Apparently, as Freud himself notices once or twice, there are times when too great an awareness of what one is doing can be burdensome.)" Now suppose Millett believes that parts of Freudian theory, the theory of the unconscious and infant sexuality, are insightful, and she accepts them. Why does this show that she is unaware? Can't one accept parts of a theory and reject other parts? Suppose I believe that children do have sexual fantasies, do have sexual desires and experience sexual gratification. If I acknowledge this am I unaware if I reject, giving good reasons, Freud's theory of penis envy? If criticism is to be more than polemic, critics must investigate their own houses.

The feminist critic, the male chauvinist critic, the cat-loving critic, all have beliefs which are emotionally charged. When such beliefs enter into the critical discussion the danger of bias, as I have shown, is great. Mill notes at the beginning of *The Subjection of Women*:

So long as an opinion is strongly rooted in the feelings, it gains rather than loses in stability by having a preponderating weight of argument against it. For if it were accepted as a result of argument, the refutation of the argument might shake the solidity of the conviction; but when it rests solely on feeling, the worse it fares in argumentative contest, the more persuaded its adherents are that their feeling must have some deeper ground, which the arguments do not reach.

A feminist critic, as I have defined the creature, cannot but challenge a male chauvinist critic. Their frameworks are not compatible. In order for the opponents to do more than feel and counterfeel, good arguments, however tedious, must be given. Despite Mill's grim and probably accurate picture, despite the falsehood of slogans like "the pen is mightier than the sword," creatures of words—critics, who plan on enlightening us, indeed on changing us by changing our heads—need to assume that intellectual capacities are compatible with feelings.

The self-blindness of critics is notorious, not necessary. One can only hope that if the evidence is overwhelmingly against the male chauvinist, eventually he or she, like Humpty Dumpty, will have a great fall. The feminist critic must therefore rationally shove.

The Silent Woman:
Towards a Feminist Critique

MARCIA LANDY

In trying to come to terms with the problem of feminist criticism, it quickly became clear to me that I was going to become
involved in central questions such as "What is literature? What is
criticism, and what is the relationship between art and society?"
To immerse oneself in the women's movement—any movement
concerned with social change, for that matter—is to raise fundamental issues about all aspects of contemporary society, about the
nature of performance in a capitalist society, about the nature of
work, about roles, social, domestic, and personal, and about prevailing values. Specifically in relation to art and criticism, such
an examination entails a total reassessment of the mythology of
women as it has been conveyed up to the present time in the
literature and criticism which we have chosen to affirm and thus
study, as well as that which we have chosen to neglect. This
means also that we examine attitudes which we have regarded as
essentially extrinsic or irrelevant to our traditional areas of competence, the most striking being the relationship between day-
to-day existence in the society and the role of the artist, the work
of art, and the interpreters of that art.

Let me state, first of all, that I do not believe that there is a
feminist criticism, just as I do not believe that there is black
criticism or any other criticism of the oppressed which is an um-
brella. I do believe that there are critiques of literature and criticism which have at their core the inclusion of views of oppressed

groups, that probe the mythology about women and other minority groups perpetuated in the stereotypes and attitudes which are
a mirror of prevailing fantasies and conscious social norms.

A further look at literature, a look which goes beyond the
uncovering and acceptance of the basic mythology of female
subordination to the male and which questions its existence, should
provide more information about the social reasons for the myth,
how it functions, and about the kind of world it portrays, a world
which may have seemed inevitable or necessary to the writer and
his society but certainly not to the contemporary reader, not to
women, and perhaps not even to men.

Literature, up to now, has expressed our deepest fantasies, our
capacity to create through the word a world which need not be
in thrall to the world of hard work, time, death, and mute suffering. We expect pleasure from a work of art, even though the
pleasure is derived from the confrontation of pain and we expect
affirmation. By affirmation, I do not mean that the work gives us
a satisfactory resolution to pain, that it gives us a pragmatic solution to our petition "Let me be pleased" and "Let the world be
different," but that the language affirm our experiences, that
through the word there is a validation that what we fear is fearful, that what we love is to be loved, that for what we only dimly
perceive, there is a word or gesture which can clarify. Most particularly in its articulation of dream, play, and gesture, it validates, even in its most negative moods, the human enterprise of
symbolizing and constructing. If literature can no longer celebrate
communal ritual, if the writer has "ceased to be a witness to the
universal," if literature "is no longer felt as a socially privileged
mode of transaction," it can still "affirm the existence of a formal
reality independent of language." [1]

Milton, for example, believed fully in his mission as upholder
of the domination of humankind by a male God, male language,
male power in art and in society. In giving play to his imagination, he succeeded in weaving together a magnificent edifice of
classical and Christian mythology which legitimizes male supremacy. His mythology reflects traditionally idealized religious
and social values as he assimilated them with his own personal
modifications. An examination of the ways in which he portrays
power, the role of knowledge, kinship ties, love, marriage, divorce, and poetic creativity in his prose and poetry can provide

a more concrete understanding of the past attitudes governing the role of women as transmitted through the works of one of the great literary artists in Western culture. To read and to understand Milton's mythology and to articulate its scope and limitations can point to a more specific understanding of the nature of the historical exclusion of women from great affairs and high art as well as the nature of the linguistic power which has created, perpetuated and reinforced this situation.

One dimension, therefore, of a feminist critique involves a careful and critical examination of the mythology embedded in the art of the past—of Homer, of Ovid, of Milton, of Shakespeare, of Pope, Keats, Joyce, and others. This examination entails an understanding of the social structure which produced these works of art. It involves an understanding of kinship, the role of property and power, the role of ritual, particularly the role of marriage as a central ritual. It involves an understanding of the nature of language and myth, particularly in terms of questioning whether the mythic patterns which we discern in the works are innate and unchanging.

Perhaps, the methods of structural myth analysis which reveal synchronic structures, but allow for considerable diachronic differentiation, will prove very helpful in understanding the mythology of women and the way myths function in literature. A more precise way of charting and analyzing the social and literary use of mythology, the content of the myths, and the variations in and deviations from basic patterns may provide feminist critics a richer set of tools for analysis, criticism, and projection. Possibly critics might better delineate basic roles of women as well as changing roles. The female artist's role in particular needs to be considered. Even here, however, it is important to distinguish carefully among changing circumstances, such as the different modes of representation selected by women artists in different periods from the Renaissance to the present. There will be differences in the availability to women of art forms, aside from what severe limitations in terms of the content, range, quality, and quantity of the art may exist. Equally significant are the changing presentations of women within literature.

In a tribal society, for example, the role of art has been interpreted as collective representation through song, dance, and music, a collective representation which is not differentiated from the work patterns of the society but is an integral part of the total social performance. And the mythology will reflect, as seen for example in Lévi-Strauss' study of the Asdiwal, the basic tensions or oppositions in the social fabric which are successfully mediated. Thus it may be possible to have a sense of the continuous structural elements in myth and also a basis for comparison with other cultures and other eras. One would not expect a high degree of alienation in such societies, because the *gemeinschaft* (community) system of relationships describes "real and organic" relations among members of the group; a "lasting and genuine form of living together." [2] Therefore, in examining the role of women under that type of arrangement and the creative expressions of such a society, which are its reflection, one would expect to find different assessments of relationships, different linguistic representations, and, above all, different forms of art. It may be that the views of women will vary from group to group insofar as women play dominant or subordinate roles in the major activities of the group.

In an urban society, one where there is division of labor, a *gesellschaft* form of relationships predominates: "Gesellschaft (society) exists in the realm of business, travel, or sciences." Such a society is "transitory and superficial," and should be understood "as a mechanical aggregate and artifact." [3] Accordingly, under such a system there is "a movement of poetry away from concrete living, so that art appears to be in opposition to work, a creation of leisure." [4] The role of art and of the artist changes, but then so do all institutional forms and practices. In modern society this change also took place for the woman artist, and yet there was still a wide difference in the quantity and quality of her work compared to that of the male artist. Women who have been segregated and powerless, have not had full access to language, and have not had access to the larger society beyond the domestic arena have continued to fulfill the myth of the silent woman in one form or another. The silent woman has often been the domesticated woman, and a reader of *Epicene* or *The School for Wives* can see this equation exposed. Women must fight against the idea of the virtue of silence. However, a very serious problem is posed for the woman writer and the female literary critic who tries to break this barrier. She has been socialized—certainly in America—to believe that she is an aggressive, loud bitch if she talks too much. And the image of herself in literature she has been asked to appreciate, is that of silence, receptivity, and responsiveness to the needs of the man.

This image also raises questions about how women have assimilated the portrayals of them presented in literary works. While it is true that one need not have shared the same background and experiences as the artist in order to respond to a literary work, it is certainly necessary to begin to question the nature of the identification that women have made. Do they respond in the same way as a man to works? Some women claim they do not feel that their responses are different from men's. Others claim that they read and teach works differently. We need to explore further to discover whether or not such a difference exists, and if so, we need to develop ways to concretize these differences. One might conjecture that there would inevitably be distinctions—and these distinctions are beginning to emerge more and more as women articulate their situations independent of male perceptions, and as they begin to explore their history in literature and society.

From the Bible to Renaissance literature, the Christian view of women, Protestant and Catholic, has been articulated and adhered to in literature, providing the basis for the most idealized—as well as the most degraded—views of women. However, the modern world, formed out of the contradictions inherent in the Protestant views of the self, of marriage, of economic life, produced new forms of social life and of literature. We have noticed how the *gesellschaft* relations characterize arrangements under capitalist society. In literature, the novel, in its portrayal of bourgeois society, its emphasis on romance and sentiment, on psychology, paved the way for a closer examination of social relations, particularly of male-female relationships. The biography and autobiography, the journal and diary are inevitable counterparts of the novel. All of these forms have contributed to the idea of a private life removed from collective behavior and ritual. Walter Benjamin in his essay, "The Storyteller," affirms:

> The earliest symptom of a process whose end is the decline of storytelling is the rise of the novel at the beginning of modern times. What distinguishes the novel from the story (and from the epic in the narrower sense) is its essential depen-

dence on the book. The dissemination of the novel became possible only with the invention of printing. What can be handed on orally, the wealth of the epic, is of a different kind from what constitutes the stock in trade of the novel. What differentiates the novel from all other forms of prose literature —the fairy tale, the legend, even the novella—is that it neither comes from oral tradition nor goes into it. . . . The novelist has isolated himself. The birthplace of the novel is the solitary individual, who is no longer able to express himself uncounseled, and cannot counsel others.[5]

In the novel tradition, we do find the female artist playing an important role. It is no accident that an art form like the novel or the lyric, which abandons historiography, should be most congenial to women. In Benjamin's view, "any examination of a given epic form is concerned with the relationship of this form to historiography. In fact one may go even further and raise the question whether historiography does not constitute the common ground of all forms of the epic." [6] And since women have played subordinate roles in the direct shaping of history, the epic form, the form most dependent on history, has been inaccessible to them. But even within the novel tradition, one must examine why for the most part, although women have been novelists, the majority of significant novels have been written by male writers. In part, this situation can be attributed to the male guardians of "the great tradition," perpetuated in critical studies and in university curricula, so that the kinds of works we study are at the expense of other forms of literature and art in the culture, and we automatically accept standards of literary excellence on the basis of pre-existing social bias, in terms of legitimating the traditional social order and its values. The more significant explanation resides, it seems to me, in the persistent exclusion of women from significant historical events, in their limited education, in their general socialization, in their internalization of restricting views of their creative potential. This state of affairs is inevitably reflected in the nature and kind of literature and criticism they produce. Their use of language must, no doubt, suffer.

Some critics assert that great art has always been bi-sexual, polymorphous. Perhaps women writers, restrained as they have been by restrictive notions of women's role, have not had the freedom to explore and give expression to the masculine consciousness, as male writers have to female consciousness. It might be added that such an imbalance exists in many American male writers who have been restrictively concerned with cultural notions of male dominance over nature and over other men, busily preoccupied with conquering the wilderness, war, and the big kill safari. Nevertheless, it would be helpful for the feminist critic to explore the nature of the bi-sexual in the writings of men and women.

Another problem for the feminist critic to explore is whether fictional language and structure must reflect the sex of the creator. Are there linguistic consequences if the female writer, in order to write, identifies herself with the opposite sex? An examination of form might yield information about how the female writer organizes space and time. The "blocking" and physical movement might present considerable differences in approach from that of the male writer. Responses to nature, to objects, and, of course, the image patterns may reveal a great deal about a male and female perspective. Studies of the forms female and male writers choose may yield further information, as should comparative studies of European and American women, European and American men and women.

The formalist attention to technique is necessary to feminist studies. A careful analysis of form should yield information about the nature of language, image, sound, rhythm, diction, and rhetoric. Boris Eichenbaum's looser union of formalist and historical method can provide a mediating link between analysis of function and historical and sociological phenomena. Eichenbaum in "The Theory of the Formal Method" describes the evolution of the formalist approach and speculates on its function as a bridge to historical consideration:

> From the ascertainment of a single device applicable to various materials we proceed to differentiate techniques according to function and from here to the question of the evolution of form—that is, to the problem of historical-literary study.
>
> .   .   .
>
> Examples of how life becomes literature are shown, and, conversely, of how literature passes into life.[7]

In the case of a feminist critique, it is essential to examine language and form very closely in order to discern all of the distinctions in language and form cited earlier and to relate them to life situations, to history, to social and literary change.

A mode of critical analysis which will certainly prove helpful is that of Kenneth Burke. In his analysis of the strategies of art and of ritual enactments is to be found a close conjunction between artistic function and social behavior. He creates a mode which allows for more integral relationships between literary form and life, the psychology and sociology of art, and between personal behavior and social institutions. While not eschewing the advantages of formalist carefulness about a text, Burke's classifications of the strategies inherent in form

> ... would consider works of art ... as strategies for selecting enemies and allies, for socializing losses, for warding off evil eye, for purification, propitiation, and desanctification, consolation and vengeance, admonition and exhortation, implicit commands or instructions of one sort or another. Art forms like "tragedy" or "comedy" or "satire" would be treated as *equipments for living*, that size up situations in various ways and in keeping with correspondingly various attitudes. The typical ingredients of such forms would be sought. Their relation to typical situations would be stressed. Their comparative values would be considered, with the intention of formulating "a strategy of strategies," the "overall" strategy obtained by inspection of the lot.[8]

Burke's categories, his "situations," based as they are on epic, tragedy, comedy, and satire, have not been utilized in "naming" female strategies, since he has mainly applied them to activities and strategies governed by the world of masculine-dominated situations—the self-murder of a Samson, the rhetorical gestures of a Mark Antony.

Nonetheless, his criticism is very revealing of "what the poem is doing for a poet," which Burke asserts may result "in generalizations as to what poems do for everybody." [9] He does not suggest that the symbolic enactments are determined and unalterable aspects of human behavior. For example, in his essay "The Nature of Art under Capitalism," he finds that different periods require different kinds of art. The pure art, the classical art which leads

to passivity and acceptance may serve to become a social measure insofar as it assists us in tolerating the intolerable. The *"corrective* or *propaganda* element in art ... must have a definite
hortatory function, an educational element of suasion or induce-
ment; it must be partially *forensic*." [10] Applying these few ideas
from Burke to a feminist critique can serve the feminist critic in
uncovering and naming strategies, both male and female, which
help to clarify the work of art and also the situations which have
their counterparts in the world. His view of corrective art can
give heart to the female writer who is often judged by the
standards of pure art, written most often by male writers. Out of
this corrective role can come the nucleus for a purer art in which
the female writer may play a greater role.

Another area of exploration for a feminist critique is that of
signification. So many problems need to be examined: sound, syn-
tax, the nature of speech and language, the sociological deter-
minants of language, the nature of the sign, the signified, and the
signifier. Structuralist activity, in general, aims to identify systems
or rather a metalanguage, a conceptual structure which may provide an understanding of, and key to, potential alteration in communication.

The analysis of signs and systems of language perhaps provides
a further key to the social legitimations of particular kinds of
speech and language in given periods of history and can perhaps
afford assistance to the feminist critic in her attempt to understand past and present problems relating to the general function
of language, literary form, and style.

It is particularly important to understand what new possibilities are available to the writer—male and female—in an attempt
to create more satisfying forms of communication. At present, the
female writer suffers in two ways: from the problem of conversion to language out of her traditional silence, and from the
problem which most writers face of experiencing language as
silence (as seen, for example, in the modern theatre). Roland
Barthes describes the dilemma of the modern writer thus:

> Every writer born opens within himself the trial of literature,
> but if he condemns it, he grants it a reprieve which literature
> needs to use in order to reconquer him. However hard he
> tries to create a free language, it comes back to him fabri-

cated, for luxury is never innocent: and it is this stale language, closed by the immense pressure of all the men who do not speak it, which he must continue to use. Writing therefore is a blind alley, and it is because society itself is a blind alley. The writers of today feel this; for them, the search for a non-style or an oral style, for a zero level or a spoken level of writing is, all things considered, the anticipation of a homogeneous social state; most of them understand that there can be no universal language outside a concrete, and no longer a mystical or merely nominal, universality of society.[11]

If Barthes' description is accurate, it offers hope to the female writer in that it frees her from the constraints of the past and enables her to be part of the reconstruction process. It also provides the female critic further encouragement to see the present state of writing and standards of value and taste as favoring more inclusive social and literary assessments. Furthermore, while holding directions open for new forms of communication, Barthes also reveals the gravity of the opposition and the contradictions: "Like modern art in its entirety, literary writing carries at the same time the alienation of History and the dream of History; as a Necessity, it testifies to the division of classes; as Freedom, it is the consciousness of this division and the very effect which seeks to surmount it." [12]

It is especially important, too, that a feminist critique, whether literary or purely sociological, take into account the impact of technology on literary art—the art of printing (Butor, McLuhan), film (Benjamin, Robbe-Grillet), modern music, and television, as well as the role of the automobile, architecture, and urban styles of living. Without an understanding of these phenomena, women, in general, and the woman writer, in particular, will exist in traditional and limited modes of expression.

In addition to the explorations of the nature of language and literature, of technology, we might also add a few other areas of concern for the feminist critic. For example, the nature of editing might be expanded to include a wider array of textual concerns. Other than citing conventional sources from the writer's immediate literary environment—quotations, allusions, word borrowings, phraseology, etc.—one might cite, as well, the non-literary or extra-literary sources. The sociological environment specifically, as it relates to other influences, might be expanded in order to have fuller possibilities for formal analysis and comparative kinds of study.

As for teaching, the broadening of criticism to include all of the problems cited relating to female consciousness should produce changes in the classroom, undergraduate and graduate, as well as a change in kinds of research. The student's perceptions about language, literary structure, and modes of response to literature can probably be expanded through the introduction of these complex critical problems. The question of the female artist and critic has already begun to cause many of us to examine anew many traditional assumptions about the literary artist. The excitement and concern about the crisis of modern art and language is not that of the solitary literary researcher and the isolated artist, but belongs to the culture. The classroom should be a major vehicle for exploring these concerns.

A sense of unalienated language, of anticipation, of invention is something which, as students of literature, we all should or do share, and the inclusion of women in this project, which signifies a basic change in the consciousness of Western art and society, is intellectually and socially fruitful, necessary and legitimate.

An historical examination of the role of woman as writer and as critic clearly reveals that woman has been peripheral in this enterprise of art as "a socially privileged mode of transaction." Inspiration she has certainly been acknowledged to be, but the domain of the creator, the divine role, has been exclusively the man's —he, the *sacer vates*, she his Urania. In the creation, the word was in the beginning through the agency and power of the male divinity and this power has been transmitted to men. One may, of course, think of exceptions, and so there are—not women epic poets, but portrayals of heroic women, female lyric poets, novelists, and tractarians. But women as epic writers, as writers of great tragedy and comedy, where have they been? They have been constricted in the social fabric, their dreams articulated by men, their roles defined by men, and their scope of pleasure described through male desire or aversion. And the male fears about woman's power are also deeply embedded in the myths. Why has there been but little reaction against this state of affairs? Some of the reasons lie in illiteracy in earlier periods; but even more fundamentally one must conclude that for the most part women have concurred, have accepted the male images as their own or have created accommodations satisfactory to them within the given power structure—a Virgin Queen, an Amazon, a Wielder of Power over Children and Lovesick Men—or women have agreed to see themselves as witches, demons, and deceivers. The consequences of straying from legitimized social norms were obviously too costly to entertain—deprivation of God, of man, of sociability, of economic sustenance, of biological needs.

Given the possibilities women are beginning to explore for themselves, it can be anticipated that the old myths and attitudes will finally disintegrate and that new modes of social and artistic creativity will slowly emerge. Through social action, social criticism, and experimentation with language, women will play a different and significant role in art and criticism.

On Women and Fiction

LYNN SUKENICK

There is a special consciousness with which women setting out to write have been automatically afflicted—a consciousness of gender. Whether this comes as a result of social restriction, literary isolation, or critical attack, and whether it issues in anonymity, self-censorship, or a flawed artistry—or none of these—the fact is that the awareness of gender is almost consistently present in female writers. Georg Simmel, the sociologist, put the problem in these terms:

> If we express the historic relation between the sexes crudely in terms of master and slave, it is part of the master's privileges not to have to think continuously of the fact that he is the master, while the position of the slave carries with it the constant reminder of his being a slave. It cannot be overlooked that the woman forgets far less often the fact of being a woman than the man of being a man. Innumerable times the man seems to think purely objectively, without his masculinity entering his consciousness at all.[1]

Like the minority writer, the female writer exists within an inescapable condition of identity which distances her from the mainstream of the culture and forces her either to stress her separation from the masculine literary tradition or to pursue her resemblance to it. In either case, like the writers who belong to ethnic or racial minorities, she carries with her a special self-consciousness. As Mary Ellmann explains, "commentary upon themselves may be easy for women to disbelieve, but it carries the obligation of notice. . . . Their self-consciousness grows with their reading. . . . They are not allowed to escape the sense of species, they are like giraffes reading Lamarck every morning before they stretch their necks." [2]

The nature of this awareness of species has varied, of course, from writer to writer. George Eliot confronted the fact that she was not—as a writer—of neuter gender, asserted that it is' "an immense mistake to maintain that there is no sex in literature," and concluded that "a woman has something specific to contribute" [3] at the same time that she maintained her masculine pseudonym. Anaïs Nin enlarged the sense of species into a positive credo, urging that "the woman artist . . . fuse creation and life in her own way. . . . She has to create something different from man. . . . She has to sever herself from the myth man creates, from being created by him; she has to struggle with her own cycles, storms, terrors which man does not understand." [4]

But not all awareness of gender in women writers has been so positive. Sarah Fielding, in the preface to *David Simple*, apologized for being a woman.[5] Charlotte Brontë raged against her limitations as a female and marred the balance and proportion of her work.[6] Virginia Woolf wrote two full-length feminist tracts[7] in order to exorcise, without distorting her fiction, the sense of injustice she felt, believing that women had been inordinately crippled in their contribution to literature by the discouragement and hostility they had faced over the centuries.

Although women have faced support and encouragement as well, a rapid collage of critical excerpts will show that gender has often been an important factor in critical points of view, and that evaluation has frequently therefore been negative. While the female author cannot anticipate with any certainty that her sex will be held against her, neither can she assume that it will be left out of any appraisal of her work. The general perspicacity of the critic is no guarantee against sexual bias, and Ellmann warns that "with a kind of inverted fidelity, the discussion of women's books by men will arrive punctually at the point of preoccupation, which is the fact of femininity." [8]

As sensitive a critic as Hazlitt, for example, could write of Fanny Burney:

Madame d'Arblay is a mere common observer of manners and
also a very woman. It is this last circumstance, which forms
the peculiarity of her writings and distinguishes them from
... masterpieces. She is a quick lively and accurate observer
of persons and things; but she always looks at them with a
consciousness of her sex, and in that point of view in which
it is the particular business and interest of women to observe
them.... The difficulties in which she involves her heroines
are too much "Female Difficulties"; they are difficulties created out of nothing.[9]

A contemporary critic, intending to give a more favorable estimate of the same writer, remarks that "the talk of Miss Burney's
cads and eccentrics [bears] no painfully feminine stamp." [10] In
both cases, the references to gender are meant to speak for themselves: one censures the female author for yielding to her own
interests and her own point of view; the other commends her for
resisting them; but in both cases "female" and "feminine" are
pejorative.

In some instances, the very fact of female gender is a disquali-
fication in the eyes of the male critic. Anthony Burgess writes,
"But now having formed my sensibility a different way, I recognize that I can gain no pleasure from serious reading (I would
evidently have to take Jane Austen seriously) that lacks a strong
male thrust, an almost pedantic allusiveness, and a brutal intellectual content." [11] Hugh Kenner makes no such forthright generalization about his tastes, but in a rather vicious scrutiny of a
novel by the late Susan Taubes in the *New York Times Book
Review*,[12] he uses her gender as a weapon against her. "Lady
novelists," he states, "have always claimed the privilege of tran-
scending mere plausibilities. It's up to men to arrange such things.
... Your bag is sensitivity, which means, knowing what to put
into this year's novels." Kenner ends the review with the phrase,
"The with-it cat's cradling of lady novelists," and thereby leaves
the reader in no doubt as to how much the author's sex is responsible for her failure.

The fact that ephemeral reviews seem most susceptible to sexual
pejoratives shows, perhaps, that denigration of the feminine is
commonplace enough to function as a standby or substitute for
more thoughtful evaluation. An early review of Anaïs Nin's *Lad-*

ders to Fire may represent only the usual insignificant irritations of a book reviewer, but the form his irritation takes is instructive: "Actually, after serious critical appraisal, this novel seems no more surrealist, imagist, or 'modern,' than any woman in a permanent tantrum, from the Middle Ages, or from the Renaissance, or any other period; any woman in fact who had grown up and had lived too long in the art colonies of the world; and had too little to do with children, cooking, and the garden in the backyard." [13] If the silliness of this appraisal tends to disqualify it from being what one can consider an "intellectual climate" surrounding the female writer, still, it suffices as an example of the degree to which the critic is tempted to see a woman's work through the grid of gender, or through whatever aspect of that gender is most prominent for him.

Yet it is not necessary to rely only on the negative statements of male critics to show that the female writer is affected by a consciousness of gender. Praise, too, has come in the package of sexual terminology, and female critics have also used the parameter of gender to convey their impressions of other female writers. Mrs. Gaskell, for example, saw the Brontës in the light of sex: "They did everything they knew how to do in order to throw the color of masculinity into their writing. They were spiritually sincere, but on account of this desire to appear male, technically false. It makes their writing squint." [14] On the other hand, Kate Millett, a feminist critic who ordinarily insists on minimizing sexual differences, finds in the very same Brontës a femininity which she is ready to praise: "Mill had remarked that most of what women produced when they began to write was but sycophancy to male attitude and ego. . . . Yet, inasmuch as the first phase made possible the emergence of a truly feminine sensibility, one can find in the Brontës the real thing." [15]

It would appear that the idea that the mind has gender is, if not inescapable, at least habitual, and that even critics who are intent on collapsing generalizations about gender give way to them in phrases such as "truly feminine sensibility." The assumption which floats behind the criticisms quoted above is that there *is* a feminine sensibility, or at least something called feminine interest, or at the very least certain qualities which can assuredly be described as feminine. Even given the fact that each critic may imagine a different scenario behind the curtain of that word, what are the elements that contribute to a shared definition of it, what are the connotations that have attached themselves to the word "feminine" when it is applied to the accomplishments, minds, or sensibilities of females?

Before attempting to clarify briefly the nature of the word "feminine" it is necessary to note the obvious: that the ascription of femininity to a person or thing represents a tendency toward or effort of dualization. The existence of two genders constitutes the first appearance of dualism in the world, and these genders have come to stand as analogies for other, more lately constructed dualities. Thus, if we posit an opposition between soul and body, feeling and reason, our metaphorical thinking tends to make one the masculine and one the feminine counterpart. Leslie Stephen, for example, defined a whole train of literary activity in terms of gender: "The modern sentimentalism may, perhaps, be defined as the effeminate element of Christianity. The true sentimentalist accepts all that appears to be graceful, tender, and pretty in the Gospels, and turns away from the sterner or more masculine teaching...." [16] And if sentiment is "effeminate," then "sense" is masculine. Bate lumps the latter two qualities together when he writes of Dr. Johnson that "upon almost all occasions Johnson both informed and reminded with a masculine honesty and with an inimitable and trenchant good sense...." [17]

The preceding passages draw on one of the most ubiquitous commonplaces with respect to gender, the notion that sentiment is feminine and sense masculine. Variations on this particular duality abound: intuition is feminine and intellect masculine, feeling is feminine, reason is masculine, sensibility is feminine and sense, again, is masculine. The expectation that women will be more likely to present the nerves rather than the mind of experience, that women tend to be the custodians of feelings rather than of facts or ideas, is perhaps so careless a notion that it would seem to have no place in a serious study of literature. We may perhaps dismiss Diana Trilling's statement that "in our own century certainly, from the time of Dorothy Richardson right down to our present-day women writers for *The New Yorker*, the female self has been the locus of all the sensibility presumed to have been left us by modern life," [18] as easily as we pass over Ashley Montagu's bland assertion that "women are more emotional than men. It is an incontestable fact." [19] But whatever the quality of this notion itself—and it is not my intention to attempt to determine the accuracy of the generalization—it has been a sociological and literary given with which women authors have, by their own admission, been forced to deal.

Mary Wollstonecraft, for example, in writing one of the first defenses of women's rights, argued that a better education for women would eliminate those tendencies which prejudice men against them. The tendency which she cited repeatedly as most characteristically "feminine" was that of "sensibility," which she defined variously as susceptibility to "enervation," [20] susceptibility to "sensation" (p. 105), a predilection for extremes (p. 115), a predilection for love (p. 147), a disposition to "flights of feeling" (p. 196), and finally, in Dr. Johnson's words, a "quickness of sensation; quickness of perception; delicacy" (p. 108). None of these manifestations of sensibility was, as she put it, "to be confounded with the slow, orderly walk of reason" (p. 196).

George Eliot later took a parallel position. Implicitly echoing the lines from Meredith's *Modern Love*,

> Their sense is with their senses all mixed in,
> Destroyed by subtleties these women are!
> More brain, O lord, more brain!

she wrote: "Women have not to prove that they can be emotional, and rhapsodic, and spiritualistic; every one believes that already. They have to prove that they are capable of accurate thought, severe study, and continuous self-command." [21]

Eliot's plea for remedial intellect was not so much a defense of her own intellectual disposition as it was a plea that women begin to rebut the generalizations which had encouraged their one-sidedness. Her remark was founded on centuries of dismissal of women's intellect, a dismissal in which some of the best and most important minds had participated. For a number of thinkers, the word "feminine" evoked a creature who could not—and should not—think.

One can cut into the history of literature, philosophy, and even science, at random points, and find evidence of this dismissal of women's intellectual capacities. Milton's influential version of the Fall, for instance, a sharpening of the bland misogyny that has prevailed throughout the development of the Judaeo-Christian tradition, was based on the idea that Adam represents Reason, Eve, Passion; Passion theoretically subservient but actually subversive, Reason rightfully sovereign. The notion that man is the contemplative animal, woman the irrational, persists even in the twentieth century; among other places, it appears in the writings of Ortega. Ortega stated that "the more of a man one is, the more he is filled to the brim with rationality. Everything he does and achieves he does and achieves for a reason, especially for a practical reason." Lest we assume that by "man," Ortega means "humanity," he continues, "a woman's love, that divine surrender of her ultra-inner being which the impassioned woman makes, is perhaps the only thing which is not achieved by reasoning. The core of the feminine mind, no matter how intelligent the woman may be, is occupied by an irrational power. If the male is the rational being, the woman is the irrational being." [22]

This sort of distinction and bias became ripe, at the end of the nineteenth century, for "scientific" support; the belief in male intellectual superiority was freshly perpetuated by the observation that man's brain had a greater physical weight than woman's. Viola Klein explains: "It was emphasized by brain anatomists that the frontal lobes—believed to be the seat of logical thought and of all higher intellectual processes—were distinctly more developed in men than in women." [23] Just how much such scientific observation was coloured by sexual prejudice was acknowledged by Havelock Ellis: "It was firmly believed that the frontal region is the seat of all highest and most abstract intellectual processes, and if on examining a dozen or two brains an anatomist found himself landed in the conclusion that the frontal region is relatively large in women, the probability is that he would feel he had reached a conclusion that was absurd." [24] Even that ardent and persuasive defender of women's rights, John Stuart Mill, had admitted that "a woman seldom runs wild after an abstraction." [25]

If it is true that women have been regarded for centuries as creatures who have no relation to the rational, it is also true that they have often been endowed with substitute gifts. Love, empathy, pity, or simply the absence of analytic intellect—often replaced by intuition—have been cited as women's particular strengths. Intuition has, in some quarters, been respected as an alternate manner of perception; and women's sympathy has traditionally been regarded as a mollifying and spiritually nourishing factor. In Montagu's view, "women . . . are more interested in human relationships, in which they can creatively love or be loved. As long as this remains," he continues, "the true genius of women, the world will be safe for humanity." [26]

It is useful, in a discussion of characteristic, or supposedly characteristic attributes of women, to dwell briefly on the uses and felicities of feeling in order to determine the opportunities available to "feminine" identity as well as the obstacles already suggested. Given the assumption that women are creatures of feeling, what advantage of viewpoint, if any, does their emotional approach create? And how consistently, and in what way, is this viewpoint respected, both by men and by women themselves?

The derivative of feeling most commonly esteemed as both creditable and innate in women is intuition. Generally thought of as an immediate perception made without preliminary reasoning, and defined by Bergson as "intellectual sympathy," intuition is at once a feeling and a mode of cognition. Helene Deutsch, the Freudian analyst, thought that "the most striking feminine characteristic, intuition," made woman "an ideal life companion." She explained: "What we see in intuition is . . . the other person's mental state . . . emotionally and unconsciously 're-experienced,' that is, felt as one's own. The ability to do this will naturally depend on one's sympathy and love for and spiritual affinity with the other person." [27] John Stuart Mill saw women's intuition as a means of original and freshened vision. He wrote:

> With equality of experience and of general faculties, a woman usually sees much more than a man of what is immediately before her. Now this sensibility to the present, is the main quality on which the capacity for practice, as distinguished from theory, depends. To discover general principles, belongs to the speculative faculty: to discern and discriminate the particular cases in which they are and are not applicable, constitutes practical talent: and for this, women as they now are have a peculiar aptitude.[28]

Intuition, then, is an insight, not necessarily verbal, into something outside itself; it is a means of knowing.

Feeling as a means of knowing has been, particularly since the decline of religion and the rise of science, a subsidiary mode of cognition in Western culture. In a culture where the rationalism of science and technology prevails, an equal valuation of intuition and analysis is not likely. Some philosophers, however, Bergson most notably, have been willing to award the non-rational a respectable place in our perception of the world. Philosophers, he said, tend to agree

> in distinguishing two profoundly different ways of knowing a thing. The first implies that we move round the object; the second that we enter into it. . . . The first kind of knowledge may be said to stop at the *relative;* the second, in those cases where it is possible, to attain the *absolute.* . . . It follows . . . that an absolute could only be given in an *intuition,* whilst everything else falls within the province of *analysis.* By intuition is meant the kind of *intellectual sympathy* by which one places oneself within an object in order to coincide with what is unique in it and consequently inexpressible. Analysis, on the contrary, is the operation which reduces the object to elements already known, that is to elements common both to it and other objects.

Analysis, then, must forever multiply its points in order to perfect the reduction, but "intuition, if intuition is possible, is a simple act." [29]

Karl Stern makes the same bifurcation. For him, the division is between the poetic and the scientific, which parallel the intuitive and the rational, the absolute and the relative, spoken of by Bergson. "The poetic relation to nature," Stern explains, "is one of imbeddedness, the scientific one is that of confrontation." [30] The poetic relation, intuition, intellectual sympathy—all are a function of entering into and feeling with the object. The fact that intuition depends on union with the object brings it close to the feeling of love. As in the mode of knowing which Herbert Feigl characterizes as "internalization," [31] sympathy is a means of knowing; it is a feeling with, a union with the knowable. Its contrary is "externalization," or the knowable experienced as object, outside of the self. To "comprehend" means to "take into": the intuitive form of knowing brings things closer together rather than creating distances between them ("detachment").

Stern tells us that Georg Simmel had remarked that for woman " 'being and idea are indivisibly one.' " "This creates the impres-

sion, so often expressed in popular psychology, that women have
no logic. This popular view expresses, according to Simmel, a *lack
in man*: for him the idea can be conceived only as an outside and
an above; it is not immanent. . . ." [32] Germaine Greer takes up this
thread as it passes, more negatively, through Otto Weininger's
thought, and reminds us that "women today might well find that
what Weininger describes as defects may be in fact *freedoms*
which they might do well to promote." [33]

In a study which touches on the dissociation of sensibility,
Frank Kermode describes Yeats's quest for images and his related
conception of women, a conception in which body, thought, and
feeling are indistinguishable and inseparable. Yeats, he says, sought
images which were "unyielding to philosophers . . . ; an organic,
irreducible beauty, of which female beauty, the beauty of a
perfectly proportioned human body, is the type. . . . She . . .
must have no intellectual content that is not appropriate to her
form, and expressed by her form; there must be no division of
soul and body, but an 'uncomposite blessedness.' . . . In women, as
in poems, the body as a whole must be expressive; there should be
no question of the mind operating independently of the whole
body. In a sense the body does the thinking." [34] Not just "sheer
being," but in this case, beauty, is the proper activity of woman.
Intellect, a divisive faculty, sullies it.

Whereas, for Yeats, woman's value lies in her "sheer being" and
her beauty, that is, in the simple radiance of her bodily presence;
for others, the value of woman's bodily presence has been linked
with one of her biological functions; it is often remarked that
woman's creativity lies in her body, that because of her capacity
to give birth, to deliver by virtue of her labor a completely new
thing into the world, she is innately a creative being. Stern affirms
this ancient and contemporary view: "woman's *specific* form of
creativeness, that of motherhood, is tied up with the life of nature,
with a *non-reflective* bios." The rhythms of woman's biology tie
her more deeply "to the life of nature, to the pulse beat of the
Cosmos." [35]

The description of woman as non-reflective bios is the far—
though not necessarily inevitable—end of the continuum which
begins with woman as the receptacle of feeling. From being a non-
analytic, intuitive, and empathetic being, but presumably still with
the powers of speech, woman becomes all body, undivided by the

particulars of language. She may express a wisdom *through* her body, but she is not, since she is non-reflective (cannot, in effect, mirror herself) capable of perceiving that wisdom. Because she is not a composite being, any imaginative rearrangement of self—i.e., composition—has to be accomplished from outside.

Such an idea is directly inimical to any creativity in women other than the biological, for if woman's essential nature, if it exists, is one in which being and idea are one, her creation is ephemeral, a power which only the immediate witness can appreciate; it is not a gift which can be left in a storehouse of culture. She cannot, in effect, record herself because that capacity is not part of her gift.

The capacity to reflect, to stand back, to be detached is requisite to the act of writing; to contribute to the texts of the culture, one must subordinate the living-out of the moment to the summing up of the moment. Not only has this capacity been regarded as not innate in women, it has been seen by some—by those who posit an opposition between mind and "sheer being" and who feel that the former easily defeats the latter—as a distinct threat to woman's "basic" nature. Thus the desire to keep woman free of the educational mill has sometimes been based on a wish to preserve her as pure being.

Yet if woman functions as pure being she will necessarily be relegated, in the written evidence of a culture, to object, and her point of view will not be recorded except insofar as man can imagine it. Women authors, by definition, by the very fact that they engage in the occupation of writing, escape this limitation; yet the picture is attractive enough in some respects to catch, and perhaps confuse, their attention. For the image of woman as pure being carries with it the glamor of the archetypal, the gratifying harmonies of mind-body unity, a feeling of immediacy and surety of identity, and the connotation of positive affect. As Norman O. Brown puts it, "Eros is the instinct that makes for union, or unification, and Thanatos, the death instinct, is the instinct that makes for separation or division." [36] To venture into the analytic, then, is to make (gentle) partnership with the death instinct; to rest with non-reflective bios is to assure oneself of a closer connection with Eros.

The views of Yeats, Stern, and Weininger are extreme in that they locate woman's core in an area which is untranslatable. The role of woman as an intuitive being, as opposed to "pure being," is a more moderate one, yet it presents its own problems. For instance, Bergson's description of the two modes of knowing suggests that the analytic mode will have more to say; intuition is a simple and absolute experience which will have, presumably, little to relate, particularly of a sequential nature. Schlegel stresses the simultaneous and unitary nature of the mode of feeling when he says, "Conception can only comprise each object separately, but nothing in truth can ever exist separately and by itself; *Feeling* perceives all in all at one and the same time." [37] It is enough to suggest here that the advantages which have been ascribed to feminine sensibility in themselves engender possible obstacles to creative effort, and make a closely-woven combination of attractions and impediments which the female writer must untangle in order to find her point of view.

The premise accompanying many of the generalizations about women is that women's tendencies are innate and, as a result, whether constructive or destructive, resistant to change. Two thinkers who took a position against the innateness of women's attributes—Mary Wollstonecraft and John Stuart Mill—took exception to that comfortable doctrine precisely in order to stimulate the hope of change in women and to encourage improvements in their social and legal status. For the possibility that women possess a special capacity for intuition suggests that there is already a knowledge within women which does not have to be instructed; this particular virtue, like Shaftesbury's conception of benevolence, is innate. Whether for good or for ill, she allegedly possesses a form of knowing which precedes reason, a form of knowing which is not necessarily susceptible to further education. Her "non-reflective bios" equips her to know things through her sympathy with them, and offers an excuse to those who think women's education unnecessary.

The argument about whether the human personality is formed by inborn traits or acquired experience has had particular relevance to the fate of women, insofar as they were rarely regarded as innately possessing reason—most especially when they were seen as the polar opposites of men. It was only when their *sameness* was stressed, often to emphasize the bonds between all man (and woman) -kind, that reason was seen as a principle present in both sexes, a faculty universal to all.

In thinking about women, writers have tended either to enlarge the differences between the sexes or to diminish them. Plato did the latter and Aristotle the former. The few early writings by women, with their emphasis on education, tended to stress the sameness of the sexes so that women might be brought to the level of man, since the idea of inferiority was implicit in that of polarity. Yet the idea of similarity of mind did not take exclusive hold in the general consciousness, and Havelock Ellis, for example, the first crusader for a scientific study of sex, wrote in the late nineteenth century, "So long as women are unlike in the primary sexual characters [sic] and in reproductive function they can never be absolutely alike even in the highest psychic processes." [38]

The argument about whether or not women are the same as men in their mental and spiritual functions despite their physical differences continues into the present. The relevance of this argument to a literary study of women authors lies in the fact that the two sides of the debate form a Scylla and Charybdis which flank every female writer; a choice, though it need not be an extreme one, is inescapable. For wherever the female author establishes her voice, her point of view, it is bound to be somewhere along the continuum between sameness of mind and polarity of mind. Such a choice is, no doubt, not always willed; but it will set off a series of literary decisions which can, in fact, be studied in retrospect and in light of the clichés and criticism which have helped to determine it.

It might be argued that the male writer's identity will also fail at some point in a sexual continuum, and examples easily come to mind: Fielding, Kipling, and Hemingway are "masculine"; Richardson, James, and Proust are "feminine." The difference, however, between the male literary tradition and the female (as opposed to the "masculine" and the "feminine") is that the female tradition has been far more vexed by notice of its sex than the male. Rarely has a male writer received criticism which describes "masculine interest" as inherently incriminating; for women writers, on the other hand, there exists always the risk that their work will be considered "feminine" in the negative sense.

If this indicates a social imbalance between the sexes, it also reinforces the hunch that the female writer will have a sense of obstacle, as well as, perhaps, a temptation to transcend those characteristically "feminine" traits which seem to make her vulnerable to attack or categorization. Particularly in fiction, a form which has been regarded by many as congruent with women's particular talents, a number of women writers have taken pains to show that their gifts are different from what is expected. For example, one of Doris Lessing's female characters in *The Golden Notebook* comments that the heroine is not "someone who writes little novels about the emotions," but writes about "what's real." [39] Virginia Woolf, who outlined the constraints on the female imagination in *A Room of One's Own*, was at least partly correct when she envisaged the hypothetical contemporary woman writer as reflecting her self-consciousness in a terseness which "might mean that she was afraid of something, of being called 'sentimental' perhaps." [40]

Even Jane Austen, coming before the full burgeoning of feminism by half a century, was wary of the faculty of emotionality which was often attributed to women of her day. Although she was more eager to delineate the differences between moral stupidity and moral excellence than the differences between the sexes, she made as pungent an attack on the behavior of sensibility in *Sense and Sensibility* and *Northanger Abbey* as did her contemporary Mary Wollstonecraft in *A Vindication of the Rights of Women*. Indeed, Austen's cool and balanced style might have been praised in just the way Wollstonecraft praised Catherine Macaulay's work, when she remarked, "In her style of writing, indeed, no sex appears, for it is like the sense it conveys, strong and clear." [41]

It was precisely Austen's cool skillfulness that irritated her first serious successor. Charlotte Brontë wrote with vehemence that "the Passions are perfectly unknown to her; she rejects even a speaking acquaintance with that stormy Sisterhood. . . . Miss Austen being . . . without 'sentiment,' without *poetry* . . . cannot be great." [42] In her own work Brontë recruited from a life as secluded as Austen's a great deal of passion, and the surface of her novels is as chafed as Austen's was smooth. Yet Brontë, skeptical enough about the common valuation of women writers to take a pseudonym, was attempting, in spite of her open presentation of intense emotion, to present more than a woman's point of view. "I wish you did not think me a woman," she wrote to G. H.

Lewes after his review of *Shirley*; "You will, I know, keep measuring me by some standard of what you deem becoming to my
sex. . . . It is not on those terms, or with such ideas, I ever took pen
in hand." [43] Yet those terms were forced on her: intending to
stand in the middle of that continuum of gender which would
make the author's sex irrelevant, she had to face more conventional conditions of acceptance.

Unlike Charlotte Brontë, George Eliot lived to see a full political crystallization of feminism in England, yet her attitude to
feminism was not without its conservative side. In her novels she
allows for no innate sexual distinctions at the level of intellect;
on the other hand, her ideology of feeling orbits primarily around
her heroines, and she held closely for a time to the Comteian view
that women are the prime receptacles of feeling in the culture.
Although her rational style has prompted critics to view her writings as commendably masculine, her characterizations and manip-
ulations of plot depend for their significance on the value of
feeling. As opposed to Brontë's spurting alternations between
obedient restraint and anarchic ecstasy, exemplified in *Villette*,
Eliot's wide canvas is one in which thought and feeling are woven
evenly into a uniformly moral texture.

Clearly, any report of success in women writers tends to under-
mine the argument that they are hampered by a general negative
estimate of their capacities. Only deeper biographical studies—
which are doubtless going on at this moment—can finally prove
the extent of consciousness of gender and the literary choices it
prompted in the writings of the exceptional women—the Brontës,
George Eliot, Mrs. Gaskell, Olive Schreiner, and others. And only
a study of twentieth-century writers as well will ascertain
whether obstacles of gender have survived modern advances in
the understanding of the psyche, of society, and of literary form.

With respect to women and writing, the twentieth century has
not been as different from the nineteenth as one might imagine.
Feminism, which could have been expected to remove the burden
of reform from the serious writer, in some cases exacerbated it,
most notably in the case of Virginia Woolf. In *A Room of One's
Own*, gracious and anecdotal compared to the bitterly ironic
Three Guineas, she made passionately clear how the practical obstacles faced by women writers combined with the absence of a
feminine tradition constituted a deprivation and a temptation to

embrace a false identity. Explaining in *A Room of One's Own*
that not to think specially or separately of sex is "much harder
... now than ever before," she declared that "it would be a thousand pities if women wrote like men," [44] envisioning an ideal
in which a woman wrote as a woman but as a woman who had
forgotten that she was a woman, writing without grudges or
apologies.

This same ideal, put to different but not completely dissimilar
fictive uses has been espoused in more recent years by Anaïs Nin.
In contrast to those women writers who defy the clichés about
women's emotionality and lack of interest in the abstract, Nin
transforms these generalizations into constructive guidelines for
personal development. In a critical book on D. H. Lawrence she
quotes a passage from a story of his which serves as a formulation
of her own attitude: "women are not fools.... they have their
own logic. A woman may spend years living up to a masculine
pattern. But in the end the strange and terrible logic of emotion
will work out the smashing of the pattern, if it has not been emotionally satisfactory." [45]

It was Lawrence who named the two basic possibilities for
women the hensure and the cocksure. The former is close to the
undifferentiated non-reflective bios whose wisdom is immanent
and passive; the latter is more aggressive, differentiated, and intellectual. Lawrence, a rebel in matters other than this one, preferred the former. Such a distinction is alive in the minds of
many women writers, too, as their diaries, letters and fiction show,
and few women can escape a knowledge of what is generally considered feminine, since they are so often reminded of it. Yet that
at times it is best to resist such reminders is made clear by the
example of Charlotte Brontë, to whom Robert Southey wrote:
"Literature cannot be the business of a woman's life, and it ought
not to be. The more she is engaged in her proper duties, the less
leisure will she have for it, even as an accomplishment and a
recreation." [46]

This essay has attempted to condense some of the attitudes towards women which have formed women's ideas about themselves and to explain in part why women are, if not perpetually,
then habitually, conscious of their gender. The pejoratives off-

handedly applied to their intellectual capacities and the compensating references to their ability to love are woven into the texture of the culture, and suggest that women are supposed to do
best what they need not express. The emphasis on innate differences between men and women tends to reinforce women's voice-
lessness or impose at least a separate decorum on their speech.

A woman declaring herself not significantly different from men
tends to make a special plea for her own rationality and ability to
speak. A woman accepting the designated polarities is more likely
to turn toward emotion as a rule of response, and to stress the
difficulties of utterance, the higher bliss of speechlessness. Women
writers like Woolf and Nin have found a style or styles which
accomplish this, and it might be argued that intuition is no dis-
ability in the works of, say, Keats, or the French Symbolists, all
of whom sing of speechlessness with unhampered articulation.
Yet for the male writers these wrestling matches with silence
come out of a tradition of verbal strength; they are metaphors
that emerge from a context of sophistication, metaphors enacted
to make a dent in or difference to a tradition of speech which is
considered rightfully theirs. For women writers, silence has greater
relevance and danger, for it is all too congruent with their alleged
destiny.

An awareness of a special consciousness in women and of disabilities which they have faced is not a substitute for but a prologue to literary study, not only as a *sotto voce* accompaniment
to biography, but as soil and context for the works themselves.
Art has a life of its own, and an awareness of injustices toward
women is not going to make a bad book better; yet it is criticism
that evaluates and preserves that life, and criticism which is sexually, as opposed to intellectually, discriminating, will hide and
withhold a significant portion of the life of a book. Elements in
women's writing which have been unappreciated or denigrated
by male critics may appear in a different light once the prejudices
of these critics have been named as such. Sexual neutrality in
criticism may be impossible or even undesirable; sexual hostility,
however, is not inevitable. Until that hostility disappears, women
will have to keep speaking of it, withdrawing perhaps as muses
and amanuenses, and making of the freedom to speak with authority a tradition and a norm rather than a history of exceptions.

"Slydynge of Corage":
Chaucer's Criseyde as Feminist and Victim

MAUREEN FRIES

Chaucer's characterization of Criseyde has called forth a great deal of controversy, including several defenses besides the exculpatory verses he added to the poem.[1] However inconsistent her actions may be, his Criseyde is, by almost universal agreement of critics and readers, the most subtle and attractive created by any artist who has told her story.[2] Before and after his version, in the hands of Benoît de Ste.-Maure, Boccaccio, Henryson, and Shakespeare, she is little other than the Bad Woman, as opposed to the Good Women whose *Legend* Chaucer composed perhaps to atone for his own ambiguous rendering of Criseyde.[3] That ambiguity has been much admired; for Charles Muscatine, "her ambiguity is her meaning." [4] In an attempt to make that ambiguity less dense, I want here to examine Criseyde in two simultaneous roles in the *Troilus*: as would-be feminist, and as victim of her actually medieval, supposedly classical society. Such an interpretation is no modernist heresy: feminism is not a recent movement, but—as Francis Utley reminds us—as ancient as anti-feminism itself.[5]

Any consideration of Criseyde's feminism must begin with her "speech on liberation," as Ann Haskell has perceptively called it:[6]

"I am myn owene womman, wel at ese,
I thank it God, as after myn estat,
Right yong, and stonde unteyd in lusty leese,

Withouten jalousie or swich debat:
Shal noon housbonde seyn to me 'chek mat!'
For either they ben ful of jalousie,
Or maisterfull, or loven novelrie."
(II, 750–756)[7]

From this declaration of independence, Criseyde turns to a consideration of accepting Troilus as a lover, momentarily deciding that if she can

"kepe alwey myn honour and my name,
By alle right, it may do me no shame."
(II, 762–763)

But, with the mercurial swiftness that characterizes her musings,

A cloudy thought gan thorugh hire soule pace,
That overspradde hire brighte thoughtes alle,
So that for feere almost she gan to falle

That thought was this: "Allas! syn I am free,
Sholde I now love, and put in jupartie
My sikernesse, and thrallen libertee?"
(II, 768–773)

This part of Criseyde's soliloquy is one of the striking alterations Chaucer made in Boccaccio's *Il Filostrato*, where the heroine is most concerned with the delights of illicit love:

"And now is not a time to take a husband; and even were it, to keep one's freedom is by far the wiser choice. Love that comes from such a friendship is always more welcome to lovers; and let beauty be as great as it wilt, it is soon stale to husbands for they are ever lusting after some new thing. Water got by stealth is a far sweeter thing than wine possessed in abundance; so the hidden joy of love quite surpasses that of holding a husband ever in one's arms. Therefore welcome eagerly thy sweet lover, whose coming has assuredly been ordained for thee by God, and satisfy his hot desire." [8]

Criseyde's brooding upon her threatened freedom, her return to the subject even after she has begun toying with the idea of accepting Troilus, differentiates her from Boccaccio's Criseida; the former understands, as the latter does not, the necessary subjection of women to men in a paternalistic society.

Criseyde's "feere" from which "almost she gan to falle" is understandable if we look at the position of women in the laws of the period, in the didactic works addressed to women, or even in medieval romances. Summarizing the husband's power to chastise his wife, Blackstone states:

> For, as he is to answer for her misbehavior, the [common] law thought it reasonable to intrust him with this power of restraining her, by domestic chastisement, in the same moderation that a man is allowed to correct his apprentices or children, for whom the master or parent is also liable to answer. But this power of correction was confined within reasonable bounds, and the husband was prohibited from using any violence to his wife *aliter quam ad virum, ex causa regiminis et castigationis uxoris suae, licite et rationabiliter pertinent* [except insofar as he may lawfully and reasonably do so in order to correct and chastise his wife]. The civil law gave the husband the same, or a larger authority over his wife; allowing him for some misdemeanors *flagellis et fustibus acriter verberare uxorem* [to give his wife a severe beating with whips and clubs]; for others, only *modicam castigationem adhibere* [to apply moderate correction].[9]

As Margaret Gist notes, didactic works of the period "were based on the idea of woman's submission, meekness, and obedience, not on her sharing with man." [10] Commenting for his daughters' benefit upon a knight's breaking his wife's nose for arguing with him in public, the Knight de la Tour Landry complacently sums up, "And therefor the wiff aught to suffre & lete the husbonde haue the wordes, and to be maister, for that is her worshippe." [11] Such teachings, derived from the Christian Fathers' opinions of women,[12] had their effect upon the courtly literature itself: "That a wife was a man's chattel, subject to bodily injury at his hands or those of another, if the husband willed it, is seen in several romances," notably *The Seven Sages of Rome, Amis and Amiloun,* and *Athelston* (in which the pregnant Queen is viciously kicked by her King, who then piously mourns the heir of which he has deprived himself).[13] St. Thomas goes so far as to say "a wife is bound to pay the debt even to a leprous husband." [14]

Seen in this context, Criseyde's desire for freedom is a sensible one. Having endured marriage with an apparently unkind husband, she almost swoons at the thought of once again subjecting herself to male domination. While Boccaccio's Criseida is represented as at least superficially sorry for her husband's death— " 'since my husband was taken from me my desire has always been far from love, and my heart is still sad over his grievous death' " (p. 45), Criseyde's becoming weeds—"widewes habit large of samyt broun" (I, 109)—seem to be her only concession to her former marriage. Chaucer never represents her as thinking of her dead husband, and when she speaks of him (to Diomede, V, 975–976), it is in the midst of lying about her love for Troilus. The scene with Pandarus in her garden which precedes her speech on liberation shows her happily presiding over "an urbane and serene household" [15] of young girls. Since from "very early times the law has continued to put the single woman of mature age on practically a par with men so far as private rights are concerned," [16] Criseyde at this point of the poem seems indeed her "owene womman."

But Chaucer sees more clearly than Criseyde does as yet the social obstacles to her liberation. The most serious of these is the necessity for male protectorship, which arises from the concept of woman as chattel of some man.[17] We might remember in this context that ownership of the characters Briseis-Chryseis, for whom Criseyde was variously named by Benoît and Boccaccio, precipitated the initial crux of *The Iliad*.[18] Chaucer emphasizes the need for male protectorship early in the poem:

> Now hadde Calkas left in this meschaunce
> Al unwist of this false and wikked dede,
> His doughter, which that was in gret penaunce,
> For of hire lif she was ful sore in drede,
> As she that nyste what was best to rede;
> For bothe a widewe was she and allone
> Of any frend to whom she dorste hir mone.
> (I, 92–98)

Boccaccio's heroine is merely frightened by the consequences of her father's flight, in particular the Trojan's threat to burn his house (p. 32); Chaucer's is both more terrified and more alone. Indeed, Criseyde's isolation and her fear[19] are a recurrent rhetorical theme of the poem, not only in this initial situation in which she appeals to Hector, but also in Book II, as Pandarus plays on her emotions and she debates between her freedom and the acceptance of Troilus' love:

> Criseyde, which that wel neigh starf for feere,
> So as she was the ferfulleste wight
> That myghte be
> (II, 449–450)

> But as she sat allone and thoughte thus
> (II, 610)

> Criseyde, whan that she hire uncle herde,
> With dredful herte
> (II, 1100–01)

By changing Pandarus from cousin (as he had been in Boccaccio) to uncle, Chaucer emphasizes his position as the male relative who should assume protectorship of Criseyde in her solitude and fear. Chaucer's longest addition to the poem, the intrigues of Pandarus at Deiphebus' house and at his own, in which "almost a quarter of the whole poem" is "devoted to this final stage of the wooing," [20] cannot but emphasize to an extraordinary extent Pandarus' failure as male protector, a failure Criseyde cannot but recognize:

> Allas! what sholden straunge to me doon,
> When he, that for my beste frend I wende,
> Ret me to love, and sholde it me defende?
> (II, 411–413)

But this is not the only dereliction of male protectorship in the poem. Criseyde has first been betrayed by her father's defection —he seems never to give her a thought until he belatedly bargains for her exchange in Book IV—and will afterwards be betrayed by both Troilus and Diomede, each of whom claims, initially, to have honorable intentions. The people of Troy *en masse* will also betray her in a scene probably drawn from Guido delle Colonne's *Historia Trojana*, in which the Trojans object to Criseyde's exchange but are overruled by Priam.[21] In Chaucer's version, the people favor the exchange and Hector becomes Criseyde's defender for the second time in the poem:

"Syres, she nys no prisonere," he seyde;
"I not on yow who that this charge leyde,
But, on my part, ye may eftsone hem telle,
We usen here no wommen for to selle."
(IV, 179–182)

The populace, however, know well the value of a good fighting
man (as opposed to an idle woman) to a besieged town:

"Ector," quod they, "what goost may yow enspyre,
This womman thus to shilde, and don us leese
Daun Antenor—a wrong wey now ye chese—

That is so wys and ek so bold baroun?
And we han nede of folk, as men may se.
He is ek oon the grettest of this town,
O Ector, lat tho fantasies be!"
(IV, 187–193)

Hector's "fantasies" regarding the protection of the widow Criseyde were mandated under both church and chivalric codes. "At
the time of the proclamation of the First Crusade, a general in-
junction was issued that every person of noble birth from the
age of twelve should take an oath before the bishop that 'he
would defend to the uttermost the oppressed, the widow and the
orphan; and that women of noble birth should enjoy his special
care.' " [22] Ramón Lull, in The Book of the Order of Chyvalry,
notes, "Th'offyce of a knyght is to mayntene and deffende wym-
men / widowes and orphanes." [23] Summarizing what had for centuries been the code of Arthurian romance, Malory also singles
out widows and noblewomen. [24] In her capacity as both, Criseyde
was entitled to special protection rather than repeated betrayals.

But such ideals were honored, as Chaucer and his audience well
knew, more in the breach than in the observance. Women were
"often the victims of [the] misfortunes [of battle], helpless suf-
ferers from its brutality, or pawns passed between opponents." [25]
Ironically, Criseyde's sole disinterested protector, Hector, is not
only unable to save her but even reproved by a society which
should have closed its ranks around her. Nor can her father, whose
interest in her seems to vanish once he has regained his chattel,
keep her safe in the Greek camp:

> Upon that other syde ek was Criseyde,
> With wommen few, among the Grekis stronge
> (V, 687–688)

While this passage follows Boccaccio rather closely,[26] Chaucer's substitution of "strong" for "armed" is more suggestive of the ever-present possibility of rape. In medieval romances, "knights knew the physical weakness of women and were willing to risk the penalties imposed for attacking them. . . . Women constantly gave utterance to their fear of attack from men who were forcing attention upon them or even from their avowed lovers."[27] Diomede's feigned offer of protection, " 'And that ye me wolde as youre brother trete' " (V, 134), once he has determined to seduce Criseyde, is not unparalleled in romance. "The extension of hospitality with the opportunities it offered was another factor in overstimulating sexual desires. When beautiful women were received as guests, their host or his followers often sought sexual intercourse with them. Examples are numerous in the Arthurian stories, where kings themselves were frequently the offenders."[28] Diomede, the son of a king, pursues his advantage with full knowledge of Criseyde's weak social position:

> And shortly, lest that ye my tale breke,
> So wel he for hymselven spak and seyde,
> That alle hire sikes soore adown he leyde,
> And finaly, the sothe for to seyne,
> He refte hire of the grete of al hire peyne.
> (V, 1032–36)

Nor was this betrayal of the responsibility of protectorship unknown in real life; Froissart cites King Edward's entertainment of the Countess of Salisbury at London after he had been unable to seduce her in her own castle, which she had held alone and of which he had relieved the siege.[29]

Not even Troilus is guiltless in the widespread male victimization of Criseyde, as Chaucer emphasizes during the central love scene of the poem:

> What myght or may the sely larke seye,
> Whan that the sperhauk hath it in his foot?
> (III, 1191–92)

Troilus echoes the sentiment:

> "O swete, as evere mot I gon,
> Now be ye kaught, now is ther but we tweyne!
> Now yeldeth yow, for other bote is non!"
> (III, 1206–08)

I do not mean here to imply that Troilus' guilt is of the same degree as Diomede's; Diomede has no Pandarus constantly to manipulate his affair, nor does he feel anything beyond sexual desire for Criseyde. What I do suggest is that, even in the midst of the beautiful central love scene Chaucer added to Boccaccio's tale, the poet shows full awareness of the extent of Criseyde's powerlessness. Just after the lines comparing Criseyde to a lark seized by a sparrowhawk, he suggests the bittersweet quality of their lovemaking: "To whom this tale sucre be or soot" (III, 1194). The very verb with which he describes Criseyde's reaction to Troilus' first embrace is also suggestive of her position:

> Criseyde, which that felte hire thus itake,
> As writen clerkes in hire bokes olde,
> Right as an aspes leef she gan to quake.
> (III, 1198–1200)

In spite of this pseudo-maidenly *frisson*, Criseyde replies to Troilus' command to yield in terms suggesting acceptance of her assigned societal role:

> "Ne hadde I er now, my swete herte deere,
> Ben yold, ywis, I were now nought heere!"
> (III, 1210–11)

In her affair with Troilus as well as her affair with Diomede, Criseyde suffers not only from her lack of "the protective power of the husband's presence" [30] but also from what Utley has called the eternal theme of the Easily Consoled (because sexually initiated) Widow.[31]

But Criseyde's liberation is impeded by her own inculturation with the so-called womanly virtues as much as by the societal realities and clichés which surround her. "Expediently but almost compulsively, she submits herself to male dominance: Hector, Pandarus, Troilus, Calchas, Diomede." [32] In her first appearance in the poem,

> This lady, which that alday herd at ere
> Hire fadres sheme, his falsnesse and tresoun,
>
> On knees she fil biforn Ector adown
> With pitous vois, and tendrely wepynge,
> His mercy bad, hirselven excusynge.
> (I, 106–107, 110–112)

Criseyde as much as the people of Troy sees herself not as a separate person but as a projection of her nearest male relative. As Calchas' daughter, although "unwist" of his betrayal, she feels involved in it and must beg forgiveness of and protection from the most powerful male she knows. Hector, in turn,

> Saugh that she was sorwfully bigon,
> And that she was so faire a creature;
> Of his goodnesse he gladede hire anon.
> (I, 114–116)

One wonders what Criseyde's fate might have been had she not been "tendre" and "pitous," had she not used the womanly weapon of tears, had she been foul instead of fair!

Having received Hector's assurance of his protection, Criseyde "hym thonked with ful humble chere" and "toke hire leve, and home, and helde hir stille" (I, 123, 126). Chaucer emphasizes, as had Boccaccio before him (p. 32), the desirable female virtues of quietness and humility, as prescribed by the Fathers of the Church.[33] "A woman oweþ to lerne in silence, wiþ alle obedience & subjeccioun," Wyclif admonishes.[34] Taking the passage in *Il Filostrato* which reads, "her face was adorned with heavenly beauty, and in her look there showed forth womanly pride" (p. 34), Chaucer elaborates:

> that creature
> Was nevere lasse mannyssh in semynge.
> And ek the pure wise of hire mevynge
> Showed wel that men myght in hire gesse
> Honour, estat, and wommanly noblesse.
> (I, 283–287)

These were qualities admired in medieval women in real life as well as in fiction; we may compare Boccaccio's dedication of his *De Claris Mulieribus* to the Countess of Altavilla: "your gentle

and renowned character, great honesty, lofty womanly dignity." [35] Criseyde is also more modest than Criseida, who takes
"the mantle from before her face" and makes "room for herself
by moving the crowd a little aside" (p. 34), actions deleted in
Chaucer's version, where the heroine stands:

> ful lowe and stille allone,
> Behynden other folk, in litle brede,
> And neigh the dore, ay under shames drede.
> (I, 178–180)

As Constance Saintonge has noted, Chaucer's Criseyde, "in proper
medieval obeisance to the will of society, never forgets that its
forms require of her a constant tact." [36]

Nowhere is such tact more apparent than in her long dialogues
with Pandarus. She flatters his male wisdom:

> "And but youreselven telle us what it is,
> My wit is for t' arede it al to leene"
> (II, 131–132)

She emphasizes her submissiveness to his masculine superiority:

> "Youre friendshipe have I founden evere yit;
> I am to no man holden, trewely,
> So much as yow, and have so litel quyt;
> And with the grace of God, emforth my wit,
> As in my gylt I shal yow nevere offende;
> And if I have ere this, I wol amende."
> (II, 240–245)

She even graciously forgives his violation of the responsibilities of
male protectorship, as she entertains him on the morning after
he has bedded her down with Troilus:

> And ner he com, and seyde, "How stant it now
> This mury morwe? Nece, how kan ye fare?"
> Criseyde answerede, "Nevere the bet for yow,
> Fox that ye ben!"
> (III, 1562–65)

Similarly, she not only forgives her father his desertion but immediately reassumes her obedience to him:

> Hire fader hath hire in his armes nome,
> And twenty tyme he kiste his doughter sweete,
> And seyde, "O deere doughter myn, welcome!"
> She seyde ek, she was fayn with hym to mete,
> And stood forth muwet, milde, and mansuete.
> (V, 190–194)

Of all the males in the poem, only with Troilus does Criseyde seem capable of being her "owene womman," and even here, because of her subtle conditioning by society, her attempts to act against it are doomed. R. E. Kaske has suggested that, in the central love scene, the rhetoric and actions surrounding the aubes of Troilus and Criseyde indicate a reversal of sex roles,[37] with Criseyde emerging as dominant. Pandarus seems to recognize Troilus' weakness and Criseyde's supposed new strength as he discusses with her the problems posed by her projected exchange:

> "I mene thus: whan ich hym hider brynge,
> Syn ye be wise, and bothe of oon assent,
> So shapeth how destourbe youre goynge,
> Or come ayeyn, soon after ye be went.
> Women ben wise in short avysement;
> And lat sen how youre wit shal now availle."
> (IV, 932–937)

But Criseyde is so completely a creature of the masculine establishment that she has already accepted the necessity for her exchange:

> "My goyng graunted is by parlement
> So ferforth that it may nat be withstonde
> For al this world, as by my jugement."
> (IV, 1296–99)

Rejecting Troilu's plan for flight (IV, 1506–26), she shows herself in accord with the patristic view of women as "evil temptress bent upon man's destruction":[38]

> "But that ye speke, awey thus for to go
> And leten alle youre frendes, God forbede,
> For any womman, that ye sholden so!

They wolden seye, and swere it, out of doute,
That love ne drof yow naught to don this dede,
But lust voluptuous and coward drede.
Thus were al lost, ywys, myn herte deere,
Youre honour, which that now shyneth so clere."
(IV, 1555–57, 1571–75)

Chaucer commends her sincerity in making her own desperate, alternate proposals (IV, 1345–1407). But, once in the Greek camp, she not only never attempts to trick or bribe her father, as she had told Troilus she would, but shows herself "milde and mansuete" with Diomede as well as with Calchas. Her proposals for escape, like her earlier liberation speech, are brave verbal shows, feminism of the *word* rather than feminism of the deed. "Even in her betrayal, she embodies the traits which men have traditionally desired in women: she is soft, amorous, sweet, timorous and mysterious." [39]

Indeed, Criseyde's much noted "ambiguity" arises partially from this conflict between her doomed inner strivings for independence and the constraints which her society places upon her. "Constant tact and poise impose a secret inner life," making Criseyde "on occasion aloof and self-sufficient. She has no intimates." [40] This ladylike aloofness makes her withhold herself even from Troilus' long ecstatic confession of his love after their first lovemaking (III, 1254–1302):

"But lat us falle awey fro this matere,
For it suffiseth, this that seyd is heere,
And at o word, withouten repentaunce,
Welcome, my knyght, my pees, my suffisaunce!"
(III, 1306–09)

To aloofness she joins stubbornness. Pandarus' intrigues over Criseyde's seduction emphasize a stubborn refusal to be pushed into a love affair which Boccaccio's heroine, easily won, had not shown. To maintain this same stubbornness with Diomede, she must resort to lies:

"I hadde a lord, to whom I wedded was,
The whos myn herte al was, til that he deyde:
And other love, as help me now Pallas,

There in myn herte nys, ne nevere was."
(V, 975–978)

and to half-promises:

"If that I sholde of any Grek han routhe,
It sholde be youreselven, by my trouthe!"
(V, 1000–01)

Stubbornness, aloofness and lies are traditional fictional female weapons[41]: Criseyde "is powerless to carry out her promise to return, not through circumstance, but through her own nature. Open defiance is not for her." [42] Nor, we might add, for many sensible heroines of the Middle Ages. Chaucer seems to recognize her position at "dulcarnoun" in his final verses absolving her:

For she so sory was for hire untrouthe,
Iwis, I wolde excuse hire yet for routhe.
(V, 1098–99)

Criseyde's speech on liberation, then, is a brave but untenable gesture. No matter what indignities (and she withholds details of them as completely as she withholds herself) she has suffered in her marriage, she cannot do without male protectorship, which she either seeks or accepts from each of the main male characters of the poem in turn. Inculturated with all the virtues—tenderness, modesty, submissiveness, forgiveness, and above all beauty and amiability—expected from a person of her sex, time, and class, she cannot escape, any more than Troilus, from "double sorwe." Tact, aloofness, stubbornness and deceit are alike insufficient to save her from the fate she prophesies for herself:

"Allas! of me, unto the worldes ende,
Shal neyther ben ywriten nor ysonge
No good word, for thise bokes wol me shende,
O, rolled shall I ben on many a tonge!"
(V, 1058–61)

As a would-be feminist both in her liberation speech and her desperate verbal intentions to return to Troy, she is a tragic rather than a heroic figure, betrayed by the sexist nature of her nurture as she attempts to cope with circumstances for which that nurture had not provided. Boccaccio had noted, in his preface to *De Claris Mulieribus*: "how much more should women be extolled (almost all of whom are endowed with tenderness, frail bodies, and sluggish minds by Nature), if they have acquired a manly spirit and if with keen intelligence and remarkable fortitude they have dared undertake and have accomplished even the most difficult deeds?" [43] Criseyde has no "sluggish" mind; but she is betrayed by the tenderness and lack of fortitude which was the almost inevitable result of a culture which, both in the experience of its daily life and in the "auctoritee" of its books and laws, continually emphasized the physical and mental weakness of women.

Criseyde survives in that culture, "unfaithful and discredited as she is," [44] because she accepts that "auctoritee," as indicated not only by her submission to male dominance throughout the poem but also by her rejection of Troilus' plan for flight from Troy. Her characterization of herself as "any womman," and her correct surmise that "they" (the males who govern her culture) would see Troilus' actions as arising from "lust voluptuous" rather than from love, indicate acceptance of a system in which the male bond of *comitatus* (Troilus' "trouthe" to Troy) was far more sacred than any bond, particularly outside of marriage, to a woman (Troilus' "trouthe" to Criseyde). Yet, in spite of her acceptance of this precept of "auctoritee," because Criseyde betrays her *own* "trouthe" to a male, Troilus, she becomes the Bad Woman, whose reputation even Chaucer's pity (V, 1095–99) could not save— especially since Henryson's *Testament of Crisseid*, in which she is punished by leprosy, was regularly included as the Sixth Book of *Troilus and Criseyde* for many years after it was written. [45]

As Pat Overbeck has noted, in contrast to Criseyde the Bad Woman's acceptance of "auctoritee," Chaucer's ironically named Good Women of the *Legend of Good Women* (including Medea and Cleopatra) are "uncontrolled and uncontrollable,... living libido[s], in the Augustinian sense" who defy their societies' norms and "act precipitantly, rashly and thoughtlessly." [46] Both Bad Woman and Good Woman "chimerically seek freedom from masculine dominance and, at the same time,... union with the male which implies such dominance." [47] For Chaucer, the Good Woman is Good only insofar as she seeks a sanctioned union in marriage; because she defies "auctoritee" and seeks experience outside of that expected of women in her society, she must die (often by her own hand). Criseyde evades violent death, but destroys her reputation because she lacks "manly spirit" and "remarkable fortitude"—unlike the Good Woman, the Bad Woman is "slydynge of corage" (V, 825). Only in the Wife of Bath, who combines "experience" unavailable to most medieval women with (despite her disclaimer) "auctoritee," and marriage with "oother compaignye in youthe" (GP, 461); whose virtues are "curious parodies of those enjoined by the Church";[48] and whose stout "corage" has evaded such easy, popular categorizations as Good or Bad, does Chaucer produce a truly practicing feminist.[49]

Chaucer's Women and Women's Chaucer

ARLYN DIAMOND

"For he was evir (God wait) all wommanis frend," Gavin Douglas wrote of Chaucer in 1513,[1] but as twentieth-century readers we might ask what sort of friendship he offers. Can male and female readers, and characters, share the same moral universe in his works? Are women for him fully human in the same ways men are, or are they something different in nature, driven by different needs, seen always as complementary to some masculine strength or weakness? The question is worth asking, in part because Chaucer means so much to his readers. "No man ever wished it longer," was Dr. Johnson's final judgment on *Paradise Lost*, but we all, men and women, wish that the Canterbury pilgrimage had not ended so soon. Sometimes we hesitate to bring contemporary concerns to bear on literature we love from other periods lest we prove either that our approach is critically useless or that our affection is misplaced, but I hope to show here that both fears are unnecessary. I think that by our questions we can try to arrive at a sympathetic understanding of Chaucer that will allow his works to live for those of us who do not feel as betrayed by Criseyde as Troilus does, or who do not see in the Wife of Bath the personification of all their worst suspicions about what women really want.[2]

An examination of Chaucer inspired by feminist concerns is not an historical perversity to be equated with wondering what he thought about the Copernican system, but a very natural way of approaching him, given the lively, even obsessive interest the later Middle Ages took in the problem of female nature. Christine de Pisan, "the first of her sex to protest in writing against the scurrilous attacks that had been made upon it," [3] set a neglected precedent for modern critics when in 1399 she wrote an "Epistle to the God of Love," objecting to the treatment of women in that most popular of medieval works, Jean de Meun's *Roman de la Rose*. It would be easy to cite dozens of medieval poems, sermons, plays, educational treatises, etc. whose discussion of how women ought to be regarded justify sharing Christine's concern with images of her sex in literature, if not her methods.[4]

At the end of the Middle Ages, as in many periods, historical reality and the contemporary versions of that reality as presented in imaginative literature did not necessarily coincide. We need to examine the assumptions which underlie the fictions, and law courts and ledgers will tell us more about the "real" medieval woman than Andreas Capellanus ever can. What we see if we look back at actual social practices and laws governing property ownership, inheritance, marriage, feudal obligations, guild membership, religious institutions and so on, is a society in which women had little officially granted control over their own lives.[5] Few people would now argue with the assertion that a woman who has no right to choose her own husband (or to choose not to marry), to object to whatever living conditions or even physical violence her husband or father might inflict on her, or to take charge of her own property (unless widowed, and widowhood must have seemed in some ways a highly attractive state for strong-minded women), is in an unenviable position.[6] On the other hand, if we look at history as the record of individual lives, we find women who were admirably competent and independent. From the lady who was expected to run a large household which had more in common with a small village than with a suburban split-level, to the petty merchant who shared in her husband's business, to the peasant who hired herself out as a farm laborer, medieval women had a much wider sphere of action than we might realize if we focus too exclusively on religious lyrics and courtly romances. Margaret Paston's letters to her husband in London ask for crossbows for defense as well as material for dresses.[7] "How the Good Wiif Tauȝte hir Douȝter" [8] assumes a world in which women go to markets to sell goods of their own production, and can be

tempted by the conviviality of the tavern. (The Victorian editor
of this treatise felt constrained to note that "it bears trace of the
greater freedom of action allowed to women in early times than
now.")[9] Particularly in the middle and lower classes, where
women in some respects fared better than in the aristocracy in
relation to men and the law, wives shared much of their husbands'
lives and work.[10]

We can suspect that the contrast we feel between the inferior
legal status women were assigned and the abilities and will to self-
assertion they often demonstrated was not one lost on women
themselves. Unfortunately, students of a literature primarily written by men, transmitted to us in aristocratic and bourgeois forms,
can too easily forget that there were large groups of people for
whom the authors we normally read do not speak, and for whom
the great medieval structures were not comforting but oppressive.
Christine de Pisan's sense of belonging to a maligned sex may seem
so unusual because few women had her opportunities to put in
writing what they felt about themselves. Similarly, how many
Middle English works commonly read express the feelings which
found expression in the Peasants' Revolt of 1381?

The direct voices of women or peasants may be lost to us, although more and more scholars are beginning to suspect that they
exist to some extent and might be found, but indirectly they may
resonate in what literature and history we do have, if we choose
to listen. R. W. Southern, for example, finds "inarticulate discontent which—though often misguided—expressed the desire for
greater liberty" in those people who flocked to hear the teachings
of Meister Eckhart.[11] His female admirers, responding to sermons
that among other things preached the equality of men and women,
are perhaps not so different from other, more modern women,
whose desires and discontents ring louder and clearer to us than
theirs now can.

Women's humanity, their drive for autonomy, is reflected in
strange form even in medieval anti-feminism, which expresses not
the contempt for women's inadequacies we might expect, but fear
of their power. "How the Good Wiif Tauȝte hir Douȝtir" is
representative of all those works which preach with such a desperate insistence the need for women to submit that one is led to
conjure up the monstrous figure lurking behind them, that of the

disobedient female who would like to do to men what society allows them to do to her. The phenomenon is not unusual—think of the slave-owners terrifying themselves with thoughts of an insurrection by savages whose natures the owners themselves had defined. What better way to justify their own brutality than by that self-created specter? In the Middle Ages, influential Church teachers and Fathers, godfathers of anti-feminism like Ambrose and Jerome, taught that sex was evil, and then projected their fear and loathing of sex onto woman, the temptress of man. Again, not an unusual phenomenon.

Thomas Hoccleve, who translated Christine's "Epistle" in 1402, provides a compendium of medieval anti-feminism:

> Al-be-hyt that man fynde / o woman nyce,
> In-constant, recheles / or varriable,
> Deynouse, or proude / fulfilled of malice,
> Wythouten feyth or love / and deceyvable,
> Sly, queynt, and fals / in al Vnthrift coupable,
> Wikked, and feers / and ful of cruelte, . . .[12]

The passage is useful just because the qualities it jumbles together are so ill-assorted, dominated primarily by the feeling that it is in their willingness to betray men, or to despise them, that women are most hateful. Rather than claiming that women are bad because they are intellectually inferior, the fourteenth-century anti-feminist asserts that it is their perverse refusal to be good—obedient, faithful, loving, quiet—which makes them terrible. The good and the bad are embodied in Mary and Eve. The one is God's handmaiden, all willingness to serve, a Virgin and hence sexless Mother. She is chosen; she never chooses except to acquiesce. Eve not only chooses, she chooses to disobey, and by so doing betrays all mankind. Those who wished to defend women could point to Mary, who is in essence a second Eve, an inverse image. Mary's secular counterpart, the courtly mistress, is often equally passive, since her primary role is to be worthy of adoration. Eve's counterpart, the comic but amoral heroine of the fabliaux, marshalls her energies and intelligence for her own ends, and implicit in her stance is the cry, "Non serviam." In theory, as Eileen Power has said, "women found themselves perpetually oscillating between a pit and a pedestal," [13] neither location a comfortable one for human beings. In practice, women were continually testing the limits inflicted on them by theory, thanks to their own abilities and social and economic necessity.

For Chaucer it is not the reality which is most present—the responsibilities and daily preoccupations of women's lives—but the theory itself in all its manifestations. Nowhere in Chaucer, for example, can we find a passage comparable to this from one of his great contemporaries:

That thei with spynnynge may spare spenen hit in hous-hyre,
Bothe in mylk and in mele to make with papelotes,
To a-glotye with here gurles that greden after fode.
Al-so hem-selue suffren muche hunger,
And wo in winter-tyme with wakynge a nyghtes
To ryse to the ruel to rocke the cradel,
Bothe to karde and to kembe to clouten and to wasche,
To rubbe and to rely russhes to pilie,
That reuthe is to rede othere in ryme shewe
The wo of these women that wonyeth in cotes.[14]

Instead, what we find is something complicated, perhaps not fully resolved, an attention to the 'problem' of women which pervades in one form or another almost everything he writes.

"Lenvoy de Chaucer a Bukton" is typical of one stance, and clear enough in its jocular masculine cynicism:[15]

But thow shal have sorwe on thy flessh, thy lyf,
And ben thy wives thral, as seyn these wise;
And yf that hooly writ may nat suffyse,
Experience shal the teche, so may happe,
That the were lever to be take in Frise
Than eft to falle of weddynge in the trappe.
(19-24)

Clear too is the import of these lines from the *House of Fame* expressing the pity for women which so struck Gavin Douglas:

For this shal every woman fynde,
That som man, of his pure kynde,
Wol shewen outward the fayreste,
Tyl he have caught that what him leste;
And thanne wol he causes fynde,

And swere how that she ys unkynde,
Or fals, or privy, or double was.
(279–285)

The problem is: what sum is arrived at when we add all such passages together? It is no help to look at the *Legend of Good Women*, the tone of which is so subtle that critics still can't decide whether the poet is making fun, or saints, of all those women, nor does it help to look at the defensive lines from the end of *Troilus and Criseyde:*

Bysechyng every lady bright of hewe,
And every gentil womman, what she be,
That al be that Criseyde was untrewe,
That for that gilt she be nat wroth with me.
Ye may hire giltes in other bokes se;
And gladlier I wol write, yif yow leste,
Penelopeës trouthe and good Alceste.

N'y sey nat this al oonly for thise men,
But moost for wommen that bitraised be
Thorugh false folk; God yeve hem sorwe, amen!
(V, 1772–81)

His equivocal nature, his tendency to create increasing complexity where other authors might seek resolutions, his preference for the dramatic as opposed to the lyric, all make him one of the most elusive friends women have ever had.

"He has a passion for relationships," one of his most perceptive critics tells us,[16] and it seems logical to search for him in the relationships he creates, since when he seems to be speaking most openly and directly about himself, as wide-eyed Canterbury pilgrim, or love-dazed dreamer, he is least to be trusted. The *Canterbury Tales*, his best-known work, embraces an intricate web of connections and comparisons relevant to our subject, although almost all of his writing would merit feminist analysis. Most of the stories recited by the Pilgrims are concerned with the subject of men and women in one way or another, and it would be more just to talk about an entire compilation, one of whose major themes is possible relationships between the sexes, rather than simply about a "Marriage Group," as is commonly done. The way men and women regard one another is certainly an issue in the tales told by the Knight, the Miller, the Reeve, the Man of Law, the Physician, and others. Still, to begin considering a problem well worth a book, I would like to focus on the so-called "Marriage Group," and, not surprisingly, on the Wife of Bath in particular, that personification of "rampant 'femininity' or carnality," [17] and "militant feminism," [18] as we are told. Within this family of tales Chaucer examines the varied ways in which humans use and respond to sexual differences and conventional ideas about sexual roles, thus providing a convenient if artificially limited way for us to look at his ideas.[19]

According to the best evidence we now have, the tales which particularly concern us occur in the following sequence: *The Tale of Melibee, Nun's Priest's Tale, Wife of Bath's Tale, Clerk's Tale, Merchant's Tale, Franklin's Tale*.[20] If *Melibee* provides any introduction to the subject at all it does so by presenting in debate form all the commonplaces of the anti-feminist argument and then refuting them in the person and words of Dame Prudence. Her femininity can be seen as working to reinforce the tale's meaning, because she has to overcome the handicap of her inferior status *vis-à-vis* her husband, Melibee, who is unwilling to listen to any wisdom coming from a woman. Their relationship is a paradigm for any relationship with assigned social status, and the tale says that virtue and social position, or virtue and masculinity are not necessarily identical. Nonetheless, we can hardly talk of character in any real sense in this work, and Prudence is female more by an accident of Latin grammar than because of her intrinsic nature.

It is in the *Nun's Priest's Tale* that the saws about virtuous and wicked women Melibee quotes to his wife begin to take on flesh, albeit chicken's flesh. Discussion of the impetus of the tale almost always centers on the Nun's Priest's revenge on the Prioress.[21] The unexamined assumption behind this imputation of motive is that a man, especially one as virile as the Priest seems to be ("a trede-foul aright," the Host calls him),[22] would naturally resent having to serve a woman. Nor do the critics seem wrong in this instance. The Priest interrupts his story more than once to deliver an unflattering comment about women. Despite his denials, we can almost see his wink when he says:

"Wommennes conseils been ful ofte colde;
Wommannes conseil broghte us first to wo,

And made Adam fro Paradys to go,
Ther as he was ful myrie and wel at ese.
But for I noot to whom it myght displese,
If I conseil of wommen wolde blame,
Passe over, for I seyde it in my game.
Rede auctours, where they trete of swich mateere,
And what they seyn of wommen ye may heere.
Thise been the cokkes wordes, and nat myne;
I kan noon harm of no womman divyne."
(3256–66)

Still, this is a tale which juggles the possibilities of multiple levels of reality, belonging to a genre, the beast-fable, which forces us to think about the contrast between forms and substance. There is much more going on here than the story of a rooster who has a prophetic dream and an unbelieving wife, as told by a narrator who chafes at taking orders from a female. The action is framed by the description of the poor widow, who is a model of Christian poverty, in contrast to her courtly poultry and the worldly Prioress, all of whom put themselves in danger by caring too much about the images they wish to present to the world. When we first meet Chauntecleer and Pertelote they are playing at the comedy of courtly love. Chaucer allows us to forget that they are only chickens for dozens of lines at a time, so that when he abruptly reminds us he underscores the whole concept of sexual role-playing and sexual self-images. If chickens can be lovers too, then courtly love on one level is merely a mode of behavior, a series of predetermined actions and attitudes constraining men and women to respond to each other in certain ways. Pertelote, as courtly mistress, "kan nat love a coward, by my feith!" (2911). As mistress she ennobles Chauntecleer. As wife she depresses his pretensions with her laxatives and unsympathetic practicality. Humiliated by her refusal to reflect him as he wishes to be reflected, he overwhelms his wife/sister with a torrent of words about dreamlore and with the superior learning which is a prerogative of his sex. Two hundred lines of erudition can be viewed as his attempt to restore his wounded ego at her expense:

"By God! I hadde levere than my sherte
That ye hadde rad his legende, as have I."
(3120–21)

> *"Mulier est hominis confusio,—*
> Madame, the sentence of this Latyn is,
> 'Womman is mannes joy and al his blis.' "
> (3164–66)

Unfortunately, he cannot allow himself to trust in the superiority he is sure he possesses, and thus appear a coward in her eyes
by heeding his own dream. Ironically, the fact that he was right
does not matter, and what he finally falls prey to is the flattery
she refuses to give him. But, after all, he is just a chicken, and we,
the tale implies, with all our pretensions, are only human. Fine
language and elegant postures can't control the necessities of the
barnyard. Finally, if the poem is about, in one aspect, the work-
ings of the male ego and its need for feminine approval, then it
is more than the Nun's Priest's joke on the Prioress; it is also
Chaucer's joke on the Priest's delighted male audience.

A graceful transition from the *Nun's Priest's Tale* to the *Wife
of Bath's Prologue* and *Tale* is harder to find than one might suppose, because now the jokes are getting very serious indeed, and
the laughter the Wife is meant to evoke is nervous laughter, at
whose roots fear and ignorance lie buried. Embodied in the figure
of the vigorous, prosperous cloth-maker from Bath, are fundamental contradictions between what women are or might be and
what they are thought to be. "Experience, though noon auctori-
tee/Were in this world," Alisoun tells us to justify her views, and
a feminist critic can fully appreciate her defensive posture. "Experience" is female, "auctoritee" male. "Auctoritee" tells us that
Chaucer's portrait of the Wife of Bath is a masterpiece of insight
into the female character. Yet the general critical consensus on
this point, which is familiar to anyone who has read Chaucerian
scholarship, does not convince me. My disbelief is based on my
inability to recognize myself, or the women I know, or have
known in history, in this figure compounded of masculine inse-
curities and female vices as seen by misogynists.[23]

Beginning with the "General Prologue" we can see how Chaucer, in enriching Alisoun's description, made her both realistic and
ultimately unmanageable for his satiric purposes. Chaucer's use
of Jean de Meun's compulsively confessional hag as a source has
long been recognized. It is his modification of his source which
interests us here. Jean's old woman is fairly simple—in her youth

she was beautiful and used men; now that she is old and ugly they use her. She is the expression of a cliché about lecherous and unfaithful women, and Jean's scorn for her is obvious. By providing her with a specific background Chaucer begins to turn her into a three-dimensional figure. We learn about her clothes, her complexion, how she rides (astride, of course), her travels, and her skill as a cloth-maker. People have written about whether or not Bath cloth was of good quality, and whether or not she is unfashionably dressed, and what Chaucer's use of astrology and physiognomy reveals about her personality. I would like to write about a detail that is not much discussed, and does not at first seem integral to her character as it is developed—her profession.[24] Cloth-making was a common way for women to earn their own livings in the fourteenth century,[25] and Chaucer is giving her the equivalent of Virginia Woolf's five-hundred pounds a year and a room of her own—the financial independence which is the necessary basis for any psychic independence. But when we talk about a woman with a trade, who, unlike La Vieille has saved her money, a woman whose strength of personality enables her to be autonomous in a society where laws and beliefs militate against her acting as a free agent, we are not talking about Chaucer's character but about what she might have been in reality (and was not to be in literature for over four centuries). Intelligence, energy, and drive are all words appropriate to her, and they ought to be attractive, but when they are attached to a female they become threatening, hence Chaucer has transmuted her potential for genuine female strength into a constellation of fantasies and attributes which have been defined as the "aggressive female."

Because society still confuses the stereotypes of women with women themselves it is very easy to talk about the Wife's *Prologue* in terms of how human she is, but looking at it with an innate mistrust of the stereotypes, we can see how much Alisoun is the butt of Chaucer's jokes on domineering women. Even aside from her false doctrine on marriage and sex, which we can assume the medieval audience would have recognized as such, she personifies other equally recognizable "errors." She is not merely sensual like the Alisoun of the *Miller's Tale* when she says:

"An housbonde I wol have, I wol nat lette,
Which shal be bothe my dettour and my thral,

And have his tribulacion withal
Upon his flessh, whil that I am his wyf."
(154-157)

What we are presented with as the alternative to chastity and
secluded widowhood is female lust run rampant, demanding and
insatiable. It is instructive and entertaining to match what she
boasts of doing to her husbands with what she accuses her husbands (no doubt quite truthfully) of wishing they could say to
her, and with what Jankyn's book says about wicked wives. The
virtues she has are amoral, so that one might well admire her
cleverness while considering her reprehensible as a person; but
to admire her as a person while admitting her immorality, as
critics have done, is to say that women and men are to be judged
by separate standards.

In her opening remarks—

"Of tribulacion in mariage
Of which I am expert in al myn age,
This is to seyn, myself have been the whippe,"—
(173-175)

we recognize the device of the trickster's confession. This is not
the compulsive unmasking of the Pardoner, a felt tremor in the
psyche, but a way of allowing the Wife to condemn herself for
our enjoyment. She makes no claims to goodness; instead, she is
a mouthpiece for a whole series of accusations against her own
sex:

"For half so boldely kan ther no man
Swer and lyen, as a womman kan."
(227-228)

"We wommen han, if that I shal nat lye,
In this matere a queynte fantasye;
Wayte what thyng we may nat lightly have,
Therafter wol we crie al day and crave."
(515-518)

So far, I can find nothing of the feminist in her, unless one chooses
to define a feminist as a tricky combatant who loves to persecute
men. She is a nightmare born of guilt and fear, the woman who
refuses to "know her place."

Nonetheless Chaucer is not entirely a caricaturist, although I
have been describing a caricature. The Wife of Bath is also a
character whose self-awareness and courage are genuinely moving:

> "But, Lord Crist! whan that it remembreth me
> Upon my yowthe, and on my jolitee,
> It tikleth me aboute myn herte roote.
> Unto this day it dooth myn herte boote
> That I have had my world as in my tyme.
> But age, allas! that al wole envenyme,
> Hath me biraft my beautee and my pith.
> Lat go, farewel! the devel go therwirth!
> The flour is goon, ther is namoore to telle;
> The bren, as I best kan, now moste I selle;
> But yet to be right myrie wol I fonde."
> (469–479)

In her description of her life with Jankyn, the Oxford scholar,
can be seen the 'real' Wife of Bath painfully encountering the
same distorted image of herself in his books that we have been
given in the first two-thirds of her *Prologue*. Everything she has
she gives to him, but "He nolde suffre nothyng of my list" (633).
Because she has not made a special pre-marital financial agreement with him, whatever she has gotten before is now his to do
with as he likes, which is why marrying rich widows was a recognized path to success for a young man. Her humiliation and distress are genuine and well-motivated, but the problem is how we
can legitimately share her pain after Chaucer has had her prove in
her own person the "correctness" of everything in Jankyn's book.
There is a fundamental disparity between the manipulation of her
to exorcise the image of the overpowering female through comedy, and the creation of a sympathetically perceived woman suffering the loss of youth and affection. Were Chaucer not such a
genius in his use of the monologue and his control of tone, and
if we did not accept the premise that strong women are necessarily like this, we would feel the disparity rather than overlook
it.

Frequently her tale is regarded as admirably suited to her, a
private fantasy in which she can transform herself from an aging

crone to a young and beautiful wife with a young and adoring husband.[26] As an extension of her *Prologue,* however, it can be just as easily considered a male fantasy. The protagonist is male. He is a rapist, and yet it is the ladies of the court who save him from paying the penalty for his crime. In spite of the astringent comment on his unhappiness when beginning his quest to discover what women really want, "But what! he may nat do al as hym liketh" (914), the narrative point of view is such that we see events through his eyes and thus inevitably sympathize with him. In the course of his search the ostensible story-teller, the Wife, even digresses to make additional anti-feminist remarks hardly relevant to the story.

What women really want, we learn, is sovereignty, an answer we could have found in any misogynist text. The Knight has fulfilled his task, but he does not totally escape the consequences of his rape. Just as he forces the maiden into a physical intimacy she has not chosen, so the old hag forces him, or tries to force him. The first victim's feelings do not come into the narrative, but of the Knight we learn:

> Greet was the wo the knyght hadde in his thoght,
> Whan he was with his wyf abedde ybroght;
> He walweth and he turneth to and fro.
> His olde wyf lay smylynge everemo.
> (1083–86)

It would be awful were it not so funny. Fortunately for him, his problems are only temporary, because this is not a tale about women's fear of masculine violence and their consequent desire for dominance as a protection against and revenge on men. Potential parallels between maiden and knight as sacrifices to a more powerful will remain potential. The parallel we have is left as a comic detail. By a simple gesture of submission, the Knight ends by gaining from his crime the perfect wife, "trewe" and "humble," one who will never act against his wishes, and who will always be beautiful for him. This is more than he is offered in the analogues, where the choice is to have her fair by day and foul by night or vice-versa. The hag, with all her powers of *faery,* willingly reduces herself to the status of a creature lacking any will of her own:

> And she obeyed hym in every thyng
> That myghte doon hym plesance or likyng.
> (1255–56)

We well might wonder whose fantasy this really is.
The Wife's conclusion,

> "... and Jhesu Crist us sende
> Housbondes meeke, yonge, and fressh abedde,
> And grace t'overbyde hem that we wedde,"
> (1258–60)

is vitiated by the message of the tale itself. The most aggressively
virile males need not be afraid—even witches will capitulate to
their need of masculinity, if they are given some token respect.
The knight and his bride, like Jankyn and Alisoun, achieve absolute happiness because the woman, assured of sovereignty, really
only wants to make her man happy.

The first person to discuss the *Clerk's Tale* as a reply to the
Wife of Bath is the Clerk himself, when he denies that his purpose
is to refute her:

> This storie is seyd, nat for that wyves sholde
> Folwen Grisilde as in humylitee,
> For it were inportable, though they wolde;
> But for that every wight, in his degree,
> Sholde be constant in adversitee.
> (1142–46)

Nevertheless, to ignore the plot of the tale with its sovereign husband and submissive wife is impossible, and the Clerk knows it.
Nor can we ignore the fact that Griselde is presented to us as a
model of feminine virtue:

> But for to speke of vertuous beautee,
> Thanne was she oon the faireste under sonne;
>
> .   .   .   .
>
> But thogh this mayde tendre were of age,
> Yet in the brest of hire virginitee
> Ther was enclosed rype and sad corage;
> And in greet reverence and charitee
> Hir olde povre fader fostred shee.
> (211–222)

After her marriage she is described in terms appropriate to a courtly heroine. Her qualities are, it should be noted, totally unlike the Wife of Bath's. She is a conciliator, a nurturer, and above all, an obedient "flour of wyfly pacience" (919), for:

> Though clerkes preise wommen but a lite,
> Ther kan no man in humblesse hym acquite
> As womman kan, ne kan been half so trewe.
> (935–937)

Her submissiveness is not only Chaucer's way of acknowledging women's vulnerability to the power of fathers and husbands but also the reason she can be loved and pitied. We are left with a paradox: women have no choice but to suffer, and therefore their greatest virtue lies in suffering well.

Unfortunately it is not enough to admire her patience, because the plot which embodies the Christian lesson of her suffering has meanings of its own. Griselde's assurances to Walter are certainly meant to be examples of perfect love:

> "Ther may no thyng, God so my soule save,
> Liken to yow that may displese me;
> Ne I desire no thyng for to have,
> Ne drede for to leese, save oonly yee.
> This wyl is in myn herte, and ay shal be."
> (505–509)

In post-Romantic terms, the object of such a love is immaterial. Alternatively, the more unworthy the object the more perfect the love, and here we are in the murky realm of *The Story of O*, where the best way for a woman to attain absolute purity of emotion is through self-denial and the embrace of degradation. For Chaucer's audience the correct object is clear—it is God—and when we look at the events of the story and Griselde's statement on the level of human beings' proper relationship to the Deity we understand it perfectly. It is when we try to understand it on the literal level that we become uncomfortable. Nor can the literal level be disregarded, either, and this I think accounts for the critical difficulties with the work. Even though it has been pointed out how important the concept of lordship is in the poem[27] we cannot easily accept Walter's role. As husband and marquis he exercises absolute power over his wife, and she refers to him almost as if he were God. Not being God, Walter can be condemned for his treatment of Griselde, but not by her. She cannot reject him because she is his wife; she can only hope and submit virtuously.

Chaucer was not unaware of the problems inherent in the poem's literal meaning, and the characters of Walter and Griselde, but he can see no way around them. They are incorporated in the response of the Host, the first in a whole line of critics to see Griselde as a model for women. In accepting her as an ideal wife, Harry Bailey and others are implicitly endorsing Walter's power. The comments on Walter's abuse of his position are evidence that Chaucer objects to what he does, but the only real alternative is a change in the hierarchies which give men power over women, and this is too radical for him. For the orthodox medieval thinker the solution to injustice was not revolution but Christian forbearance, a welcoming of God's loving blows.

Chaucer's inability to confront the sexual dilemma woven into the very fabric of his tale may account for the confusing final stanzas, which have been the occasion for much critical ingenuity.[28] The tale could well end with the Clerk's "Let us thanne lyve in vertuous suffraunce" (1162), and in some manuscripts it does. Such an ending would retain the purity of tone sustained throughout but would leave unanswered the questioning of Walter and Griselde's marital relationship, a questioning made inevitable by the *Wife of Bath's Tale*. The Clerk's response (or Chaucer's—the two are indistinguishable at this point) is a savagely ironic attack on women who might reject his heroine as a model:

> O noble wyves, ful of heigh prudence
> Lat noon humylitee youre tonge naille,
> Ne lat no clerk have cause or diligence
> To write of yow a storie of swich mervaille
> As of Grisildis pacient and kynde.
>
> . . . .
>
> Beth egre as is a tygre yond in Ynde;
> Ay clappeth as a mille, I yow consaille.
>
> . . . .
>
> For though thyn housbonde armed be in maille,
> The arwes of thy crabbed eloquence

Shal perce his brest, and eek his aventaille.
(1183–1204)

The violent language is unexpected from the reserved Clerk, who does not seem suited to such hostile defensiveness. Whether we classify it as a failure in tone, or merely an abrupt shift, it might well be the sign of Chaucer's suppressed reservations about his tale's implications for real men and women.

The Merchant's reaction to the story of Patient Griselde is a spontaneous explosion of outraged misery. The perfection of her character as a wife is what appeals to him, and, ignoring the Clerk's religious purpose, he bewails his marriage and his own wife's shrewishness. The tale he tells, about an old man and his unfaithful young wife, seems to connect not only with his own situation but also, on the surface at least, with the *Miller's Tale*. Comparing the two narratives about cuckoldry is useful as a way of seeing how far from the basically cheerful fabliau tone the Merchant has come, and how close to one of the key dilemmas of the *Clerk's Tale*. In the *Miller's Tale* the relationship between John and Alisoun is left unexamined. Her betrayal of him is almost unmotivated—the result merely of animal good spirits and the demands of the fabliau genre. It is perfectly natural for young wives to behave so, as Justinus warns January:

> "Avyseth yow—ye been a man of age—
> How that ye entren into mariage,
> And namely with a yong wyf and a fair.
> By hym that made water, erthe, and air,
> The yongeste man that is in al this route
> Is bisy ynough to bryngen it aboute
> To han his wyf allone."
> (1555–61)

The dynamics of the relationship between January and May, on the other hand, are a major part of the *Merchant's Tale*. Even understanding that the triangle of May, Damian, and January is inevitable, one is still forced to examine what produces it. The grotesque and unlovable figure of January on his wedding night might seem sufficient to vindicate any infidelity, but the tale goes beyond mere physical disgust: January is not simply a dirty old man; he is also the spokesman for a naive and egocentric view of marriage. Like his creator, the Merchant, whom we meet in the *General Prologue* "Sownynge alwey th'encrees of his wynnyng," he habitually thinks in terms of ownership and possession. A wife for him is an object designed solely for a man's personal gratification. "His paradys terrestre, and his disport" (1332). A man's wife and his knife are both incapable of doing him harm, he illogically concludes, because they belong to him. But people can not be owned, knives if mishandled do not care whose blood is drawn, and women may have their own ideas and wishes in marriage.

Opposed to January's view of the "blisful ordre of wedlok precious" is the predictable cynicism of Justinus. He is the good counselor in this poem, but his anti-feminism need not be taken as final, after all, because it could be confuted by that other good counselor, Dame Prudence. We have to look at the specific pairing and the nature of the two participants in it for any real understanding of what the poet is suggesting about marriage.

May is at first presented as a doll, the faceless occasion of January's sexual fantasies. Her passivity lasts through the wedding (to which her assent is clearly a mere formality) and the travesty of a wedding night, and as long as she is submissive she retains a strong claim to our sympathy. In his emphasis on January's domineering lust the poet assures that we will see her as a victim:

> Adoun by olde Januarie she lay,
> That sleep til that the coughe hath hym awaked,
> Anon he preyde hire strepen hire al naked;
> He wolde of hire, he seyde, han some pleasaunce,
> And seyde hir clothes dide hym encombraunce,
> And she obeyeth, be hire lief or looth.
> (1956–61)

But when she chooses to assert herself, although "God above . . . knoweth that noon act is causeless," she must necessarily be condemned. "Lo, pitee renneth soone in gentil herte" is the narrator's ironic comment on her decision to find satisfaction in Damian, before comparing her with faithful wives.

By the time we are well into the story the narrative technique has served to alienate us from each of the three protagonists. January's blindness and his consequent "outrageous" jealousy create no immediate change in our perception of him, for he has been blind all along. His behavior to May only fuels her love for Damian and his repression of her acts to precipitate the final crisis:

> ... neither in halle, n'yn noon oother hous,
> Ne in noon oother place, neverthemo,
> He nolde suffre hire for to ryde or go,
> But if that he had hond on hire alway.
> (2088–91)

Lest we feel too much concern for a May almost literally manacled to a man whose waning potency sets no limits on his sensuality, and thus run the danger of condoning her adultery, the poet shifts the balance of sympathy at this point. Her husband's speeches become more pathetic and he shows a genuine (though necessarily limited) love for her. Her blatant lies to him, her willingness to use his back as a stepping-stone into the pear-tree after he has offered to help her "with myn herte blood," and the brutishness of her intercourse with Damian combine to make us lose whatever friendly feelings we might have had for someone in her position. She has repaid January in his own coin and at the end she is as monstrously egocentric as he is.

Chaucer's examination of selfishness in marriage through the eyes of the Merchant seems to leave no way out. According to the *Canterbury Tales* as we now have them, if Griselde were to protest her treatment by Walter she would have to become either a shrew like the Wife of Bath or an unfaithful bitch like May. No matter how degrading a woman's situation, and May's marriage is made to seem no better than a form of prostitution, she has no acceptable escape. By making Griselde a saint and removing her struggles from the human plane, and by making May totally unlikable, Chaucer has avoided having to face the implications of his morality. To portray a virtuous woman delivered over to January, without a father willing to kill her for her own good as in the *Physician's Tale*, would make the possible consequences of being dutiful too painfully apparent, or so we might speculate, for Chaucer has given us no such tale.

The *Franklin's Tale* has often been called the poet's last word on the ideal relationship between men and women, the answer to all the dilemmas posed in the "Marriage Group," a surprising judgment in view of the description of the Franklin in the *Prologue:*

> For he was Epicurus owene sone,
> That heeld opinioun that pleyn delit
> Was verray felicitee parfit.
> (336–338)

We ought not to expect any great moral insights from him, and his story is one whose meaning is far more problematic than he realizes. Through him Chaucer enables us to discern that the kinds of attractively simple formulations offered by characters as involved with the surface of life as the Franklin is, are ultimately not real solutions at all.

Perhaps in describing Dorigen's and Arveragus' seemingly unusual relationship, the Franklin is attempting to combine the pragmatic equality between man and wife, more typical of his own class, with the aristocratic ideals of "gentilesse" to which he aspires:

> But atte laste she, for his worthynesse,
> And namely for his meke obeysaunce,
> Hath swich a pitee caught of his penaunce
> That pryvely she fil of his accord
> To take hym for hir housbonde and hir lord,
> Of swich lordshipe as men han over hir wyves.
> And for to lede the moore in blisse hir lyves,
> Of his free wyl he swoor hire as a knyght
> That nevere in al his lyf he, day ne nyght,
> Ne sholde upon hym take no maistrie
> Agayn hir wyl, ne kithe hire jalousie
> But hire obeye, and folwe hir wyl in al,
> As any lovere to his lady shal,
> Save that the name of soveraynetee,
> That wolde he have for shame of his degree.
> She thanked hym, and with ful greet humblesse
> She seyde, "Sire, sith of youre gentilesse
> Ye profre me to have so large a reyne,
> Ne wolde nevere God bitwixe us tweyne,
> As in my gilt, were outher werre or stryf.

Sire, I wol be youre humble trewe wyf."
(738–759)

"Humility," "will," "sovereignty," "lordship," "mastery," all the
terms we have learned to question in the other tales switch from
speaker to speaker with suspicious facility. For the Franklin their
bargain, in reality a contradiction in terms, is a noble one:

> "For o thyng, sires, saufly dar I seye,
> That freendes everych oother moot obeye,
> If they wol longe holden compaignye.
> Love wol nat been constreyned by maistrye.
> Whan maistrie comth, the God of Love anon
> Beteth his wynges, and farewel, he is gon!
> Love is a thyng as any spirit free.
> Wommen, of kynde, desiren libertee,
> And nat to been constreyned as a thral;
> And so doon men, if I sooth seyen shal."
> (761–770)

Appealing as his opinions about love and women's need for free
will are to a modern audience, however, the narrative does not
truly validate them, as we realize when we examine the tale's language and plot more closely. Courtly love requires the man's perfect obedience, marriage the woman's, and these two opposed
systems are reconciled here only by a kind of sleight-of-hand.
Dorigen and Arveragus can not create a genuinely new and equal
way of living together, because they still accept the necessity of
preserving a conventional front. Arveragus is not willing to give
up the appearance of mastery, and therefore when a crisis comes
he is not ready to give it up in fact.

The narrator does not see the paradox created by their supposedly perfect love and Arveragus' departure:

> To seke in armes worshipe and honour;
> For al his lust he sette in swich labour.
> (811–812)

The essential conflict between the roles of lover and knight, familiar to medieval audiences in works like Chrétien's *Yvain* and *Erec*,
is glossed over. Dorigen is left as lonely as any lady whose hus-

band never felt the need to pay lip-service to the principles of marital equality.

Her sufferings and her hatred of the rocks which threaten the coast have seemed excessive to some critics, who think she ought to be more patient, which is to say more like Griselde, perfectly indifferent to her own feelings,[29] but emotions such as loneliness and anxiety are legitimate considerations in a tale about human love. Dorigen's denunciations of the rocks are worth taking seriously as a clue to her state of mind as opposed to her moral state. She never complains about having to stay behind while her husband pursues his other love; such a complaint would be unthinkable for the Franklin's courtly heroine. Instead, all her passionate unhappiness at her situation is focused on the rocks, neutral objects for her hostility. Thus, she (and the narrator) can avoid having to face the real cause of her grief.

Dorigen, who when we first meet her seems to have everything —youth, beauty, high birth—is reduced by marriage to a condition of quasi-widowhood. Her attempts to cope with her grief sensibly turn her into seemingly legitimate prey for other men. Aurelius is "right vertuous, and riche, and wys," and loves her "best of any creature" we are told, but he does not hesitate to use emotional blackmail to force her into becoming his mistress. She is compelled, as she and a convention not even now outmoded see it, to choose between death and dishonor.[30] One can well comprehend her instinctive reluctance to die because of a deliberately fantastic promise which is simply a way of avoiding an embarrassing social situation. The rash promise is a familiar motif in literature, but here the promise itself is almost subordinated to the victim's response to her situation.

Before we can feel her predicament too strongly, and start wondering why she ought to kill herself instead of refusing to be coerced by a love totally without consideration for her feelings (and the *Parliament of Foules* exists to tell us that such heresy is not unthinkable), or why for women the only possible response to aggressive masculine desire is self-destruction, the Franklin assures us that things will all work out. Arveragus respects her enough to think her honor consists of more than her chastity, but he does not respect her enough to allow her to make her own decisions. Without consulting her and forbidding her to speak about what is to happen he sends her to Aurelius, who has been unmoved by her misery but is sufficiently impressed by the magnanimity of her husband's gesture to send her right back. Both men, and Dorigen herself, automatically assume that her husband has the right to determine her fate. The Franklin, having apparently forgotten that love cannot be constrained, winds up his tale in naive admiration for the largesse of the male characters. He never realizes that the ideals he professes have never been genuinely tested, and that his tale speaks as much about selfishness in love as about generosity. His ending leaves unresolved the real issues that might have been raised.

The very simplicity of the narrative's values, coming as they do from the author of *Troilus and Criseyde* with its complex examination of human life, should warn us that Chaucer did not mean to rest here. The *Canterbury Tales* are incomplete and we are unable to say therefore what else he might have written, but certainly in what he left there is nothing comparable to the *Knight's Tale* in complexity or seriousness on the subject of marriage or the nature of real women. Perhaps the *Squire's Tale*, with its active and intelligent heroine, might have provided us with what we seek. One would like to know what he meant to have Canacee do and be, but he never finished her story.

We can say that in the list of Pilgrims, which is complete, we find no woman who is the moral equivalent of the Knight or the Clerk. Chaucer seems no more able to portray a female who is both virtuous and three-dimensional than he is able to portray a cleric who is both good and human. If admirable, his women are bloodless abstractions; if vivid personalities, they are limited like Dorigen or seriously flawed like the Prioress and the Wife of Bath. He can pity women, he can see some way into them, and make us see how often distorting the conventional sexual roles are, but we want more from him, perhaps because he has already given us so much. In the end, no matter how real his sympathy is, it is limited by his fundamental conservatism, a conservatism which has been noted by other readers on other grounds. Unwilling to abandon the values and hierarchies he inherits, unable to reconcile them with what he has observed of human emotion and social realities, he accepts uneasily the medieval view of women as either better or worse than man, but never quite the same. He cannot go further than Griselde or Dame Alisoun. The latter is a figure with enormous potential as we see her now, and Chaucer was fascinated with her, reworking her prologue, the longest allotted to any pilgrim, over a long period of time.[31] He is both attracted and repelled by the idea of a vigor and independence stretching beyond the narrow range of categories open to him, and in her figure, and in his lifelong mining of the subject of women and love we sense his own discomfort with the categories. It is as if his great psychological perception and concern for all the facets of human life, for which we value him, are straining the bounds imposed by his culture. He means to be women's friend, insofar as he can be, and it is this painfully honest effort, this unwillingness to be satisfied with the formulas of his age, which we as feminists can honor in him.

The Taming of the Shrew:
Shakespeare's Mirror of Marriage

COPPÉLIA KAHN

The true focus of interest in *The Taming of the Shrew* is not
Kate the shrew but Petruchio the tamer. Both characters and the
taming action in which they participate are creations of that social
habit called male dominance, but there is a crucial difference between Kate and Petruchio. He is a stereotype, animated like a
puppet by the *idée fixe* of male dominance, while she is realistically and sympathetically portrayed as a woman trapped in the
self-destructive role of shrew by her male guardians. Her form of
violence is a desperate response to the prevailing system of female
subjection; his represents the system itself, its basic mechanisms
displayed in exaggerated form.

Shakespeare lived in an age devoted to the maintenance of order
through hierarchy, an age in which the creation of Eve from
Adam's rib was both historical fact and article of faith. But he is
never an advocate of order for order's sake; he never fails to question the moral grounds and practical effect of hierarchy. While
endorsing the principle, he is skeptical of the practice: if Richard
II is the only true anointed king, he is also, as king, a failure. If
Petruchio must command and Kate submit so that harmony (or
at least decorum) may be maintained, the division of power and

This article appeared originally in *Modern Language Studies*, vol. 5,
no. 1, Spring 1975, and is reprinted here by permission of the editors,
Edna L. Steeves, English Department, and Armand B. Chartier, Language Department, University of Rhode Island, Kingston, R.I.

status according to sex alone is, he shows, irrational and ultimately illusory.

As Robert Heilman demonstrates, the taming is best viewed as a farce which "carries out our desire to simplify life by a selective anesthetizing of the whole person; man retains all his energy yet never really gets hurt." [1] Farce, according to Heilman, deals with people as though they lack normal physical, emotional, and moral sensitivity, and are capable only of mechanical responses. In making Kate react almost automatically to the contradictory kinds of treatment Petruchio administers (flattery before the wedding, and force afterwards), Shakespeare molds her to the needs of the farce. In the first three acts, before the taming begins in earnest, she is portrayed in terms of her resistance to male efforts to dispose of her in marriage. Our strongest impression of her is that she fights back. But though she declares she'll see Petruchio hanged before she marries him, marry him she does, and though she flatly refuses to obey his first command to her as a wife, she exits mutely with him at the end of Act III. Contrary to our expectations, she doesn't retaliate with all the shrewish weaponry said to be at her disposal. In the end, as I shall show, she subverts her husband's power without attempting to challenge it, and she does so in a gamesome spirit, without hostility or bitterness. Thus Shakespeare allows the male to indulge his dream of total mastery over the female without the real-life penalties of her resentment or his guilt.

But the farce has another purpose which Heilman and other critics fail to see. It exaggerates ludicrously the reach and force of male dominance and thus pushes us to see this wish for dominance as a childish dream of omnipotence. In short, the farce portrays Petruchio's manliness as infantile. A 1904 editor of the play roundly declared, "It will be many a day . . . ere men cease to need or women to admire, the example of Petruchio." [2] How pitiable that we should still need and admire it, almost seventy years later. That we do is revealed by the prevailing tendency of criticism to justify Petruchio's methods in Petruchio's terms, endorsing that version of masculinity which the farce undercuts as well as indulges. Though it has long been recognized that Shakespeare gives Kate's "shrewishness" a psychological and moral validity lacking in all literary predecessors, critics still argue that Petruchio's heavy-handed behavior is merely a role briefly assumed for a benign purpose. They claim that he is Kate's savior, the wise man who guides her to a better and truer self, or a clever doctor following homeopathic medicine.[3] They have missed the greatest irony of the play. Unlike other misogynistic shrew literature, this play satirizes not woman herself in the person of the shrew, but *male attitudes toward women*. My purpose is to reveal the ways in which Shakespeare puts these attitudes before us.

I

Long before Petruchio enters, we are encouraged to doubt the validity of male supremacy. First of all, the transformation of Christopher Sly from drunken lout to noble lord, a transformation only temporary and skin-deep, suggests that Kate's switch from independence to subjection may also be deceptive, and prepares us for the irony of the dénouement. More pointedly, one of the most alluring perquisites of Sly's new identity is a wife, and his right to domineer over her. As Scene 1 of the Induction begins, Sly suffers public humiliation at the hands of a woman when the Hostess throws him out of her alehouse for disorderly conduct. After he awakens from his sleep in the second scene, it is the tale of his supposed wife's beauty and Penelope-like devotion and patience that finally tips the balance, convincing him that he really is the aristocrat of the servants' descriptions:

> Am I a lord, and have I such a lady?
> Or do I dream? Or have I dreamed till now?
> I do not sleep: I see, I hear, I speak,
> I smell sweet savors and I feel soft things.
> Upon my life, I am a lord indeed
> And not a tinker nor Christopher Sly.
> Well, bring our lady hither to our sight,
> And once again a pot o' th' smallest ale.[4]
> (Ind. 2. 68–75)

He then glories in demanding and getting his "wife's" obsequious obedience:

SLY. . . . .
        Where is my wife?
PAGE. Here, noble lord. What is thy will with her?

SLY. Are you my wife and will not call me husband?
My men should call me "lord"; I am your goodman.
PAGE. My husband and my lord, my lord and husband,
I am your wife in all obedience.
(Ind. 2. 102–107)

The humor lies in the fact that Sly's pretensions to authority and grandeur, which he claims only on the basis of sex, not merit, and indulges specifically with women, are contradicted in his real identity, in which he is a woman's inferior. Similarly, as I shall argue later, Petruchio seems to find in Kate the reflection of his own superiority, while we know that he is fooled by a role she has assumed.

In the main play, the realistic bourgeois ambiance in which Kate is placed leads us to question the definition of shrewishness which the characters take for granted. In medieval mystery plays and Tudor interludes, shrews were already married to their pusillanimous husbands and were shown as domestic tyrants. Male fears of female freedom were projected onto the wife, who was truly a threatening figure because she treated her husband as he normally would have treated her. When the husband attempted rebellion he usually lost.[5] Shakespeare departs from this literary tradition in order to sketch Kate as a victim of the marriage market, making her "the first shrew to be given a father, to be shown as maid and bride." [6] At her entrance, she is already, for her father's purpose, that piece of goods which Petruchio declares her to be after the wedding. Baptista is determined not to marry the sought-after Bianca until he gets an offer for the unpopular Kate, not for the sake of conforming to the hierarchy of age as his opening words imply, but out of a merchant's desire to sell all the goods in his warehouse. His marketing technique is clever: make the sale of the less popular item the prerequisite of purchasing the desirable one. As Tranio sympathetically remarks after Kate's marriage is arranged, "'Twas a commodity that lay fretting by you" (II. 1. 321). Knowing that Gremio and Hortensio are interested only in Bianca, Baptista tactlessly invites them to court Kate, and does so in her presence. The two suitors then begin to insult her. Gremio refers to her as a prostitute by offering to "cart" her through the streets, a punishment for prostitutes, instead of to court her. When she indignantly asks her father, "Is it your will, sir, to

make a stale of me amongst these mates?" (I. 1. 57–58), she is
only reacting to the insult and aptly characterizing her situation
as that of a whore being loosed to anyone who'll have her for the
best price.

That money, not his daughter's happiness, is Baptista's real concern in matchmaking becomes evident when Petruchio brusquely
makes his bid for Kate. Previously, Petruchio's desire to marry
solely for money, even though he had inherited his father's fortune, was comically exaggerated. The rhetorical expansiveness of
his speech made humorous the profit motive which Baptista takes
seriously:

> ... if thou know
> One rich enough to be Petruchio's wife—
> As wealth is burden of my wooing dance—
> Be she as foul as was Florentius' love,
> As old as Sibyl, and as curst and shrewd
> As Socrates' Xanthippe or a worse,
> She moves me not, or not removes, at least,
> Affection's edge in me, were she as rough
> As are the swelling Adriatic seas.
> I come to wive it wealthily in Padua;
> If wealthily, then happily in Padua.
> (I. 2. 65–75)

Both Petruchio and Baptista pretend to make Kate's love the ultimate condition of the marriage, but then Petruchio simply lies
in asserting that she has fallen in love with him at first sight. Her
father, though he doubts this far-fetched claim ("I know not
what to say") claps up the match anyhow, for on it depends
Bianca's match as well. Both marriages provide insurance against
having to support his daughters in widowhood, promise grandsons
to whom he may pass on the management and possession of his
property, and impart to his household the prestige of "marrying
well," for the wealth of the grooms advertises Baptista's own
financial status. Petruchio's and Tranio/Lucentio's frequent references to their respective fathers' wealth and reputations remind
us that wealth and reputation pass from father to son, with woman
as mere accessory to the passing. As Simone de Beauvoir states in
The Second Sex, "The interests of property require among nobil-

ity and bourgeoisie that a single administrator take charge. This could be a single woman; her abilities were admitted; but from feudal times to our days the married woman has been deliberately sacrificed to private property. The richer the husband, the greater the dependence of the wife; the more powerful he feels socially and economically, the more authoritatively he plays the *paterfamilias*." [7]

As the wedding party waits anxiously for the tardy groom (Act III, scene 1), Baptista alludes to "this shame of ours" and Kate corrects him: "No shame but mine." Baptista's first person plural reveals that he thinks in terms of his reputation as *paterfamilias;* Kate's insistence that the shame resides with her, the woman conned into marrying a man she doesn't love and then deserted by him at the church door, doesn't penetrate her father's consciousness. His next lines shock us because they apply the stereotype of the shrew to Kate when we have been seeing her as a particular woman wronged by the socio-economic system of marriage:

> Go, girl, I cannot blame thee now to weep.
> For such an injury would vex a very saint,
> Much more a shrew of thy impatient humor.
> (III. 2. 27–29)

Even the Bianca plot emphasizes heavily the venal aspects of marriage, though it is usually characterized as romantic, in contrast to the realism and farce of the taming. In Act II, scene 1, Baptista awards Bianca to Tranio/Lucentio solely because he offers more cash and property as "widowhood" (that is, claims to have more total wealth) than Gremio does. As George Hibbard has shown, the scene satirizes the hard-headed commercial nature of marital arrangements.[8] Baptista's chivalric " 'Tis deeds must win a prize" puns on title deeds to property, and the length and specificity of each suitor's inventory of wealth calls inordinate attention to the fact that dutiful, submissive Bianca, courted in high-flown style by the ardent Lucentio, is still a piece of property, to be relinquished only with the guarantee that Baptista will profit if the groom expires. Always the clever businessman, Baptista accepts Lucentio's bid pending his father's assurance of his fortune, but keeps Gremio in reserve should the deal fall through.

II

It is time to turn with Kate from the father to the husband. From the moment Petruchio commands his servant "Knock, I say," he evokes and creates noise and violence. A hubbub of loud speech, beatings, and quarrelsomeness surrounds him. "The swelling Adriatic seas" and "thunder when the clouds in autumn crack" are a familiar part of his experience, which he easily masters with his own force of will or physical strength. Like Adam, he is lord over nature, and his own violence has been well legitimized by society, unlike Kate's, which has marked her as unnatural and abhorrent. But let us examine the nature of Petruchio's violence compared to Kate's.

The hallmark of a shrew is her scolding tongue and loud raucous voice—a verbal violence befitting woman, since her limbs are traditionally weak. It is interesting that Kate is given just twelve lines in her entrance scene, only five of which allude to physical violence:

> I'faith, sir, you shall never need to fear:
> Iwis it [marriage] is not halfway to her heart.
> But if it were, doubt not her care should be
> To comb your noddle with a three-legged stool
> And paint your face and use you like a fool.
> (I. i. 61–65)

Here she threatens Hortensio in response to his greater threat, that no man will marry her. These lines have a distinctly defensive cast; Kate refers to herself in the third person, and denies any interest in a mate because two prospective mates (Hortensio and Gremio) have just made it clear that they have no interest in her. Kate's vision of breaking furniture over a husband's head is hypothetically couched in the subjunctive. Yet later Tranio describes her speech in this scene as "such a storm that mortal ears might hardly endure the din" (I. i. 172–173). Throughout the play, this kind of disparity between the extent and nature of Kate's "shrewish" behavior and the male characters' perceptions of it focuses our attention on masculine behavior and attitudes which stereotype women as either submissive and desirable or rebellious and shrewish. Kate is called devil, hell, curst, shrewd (shrewish), and wildcat, and referred to in other insulting ways because, powerless to change her situation, she *talks* about it. That her speech is defensive rather than offensive in origin, and psychologically necessary for her survival, is eloquently conveyed by her own lines:

> My tongue will tell the anger of my heart,
> Or else my heart, concealing it, will break,
> And rather than it shall I will be free
> Even to the uttermost, as I please, in words.
> (IV. 3. 77–80)

Though she commits four acts of physical violence onstage (binding and striking Bianca, breaking a lute over Hortensio's head, hitting Petruchio and then Grumio), in each instance the dramatic context suggests that she strikes out because of provocation or intimidation resulting from her status as a woman.[9] For example, the language in which her music lesson with Hortensio is described conveys the idea that it is but another masculine attempt to subjugate woman. "Why, then thou canst not break her to the lute?," asks Baptista. "I did but tell her she mistook her frets/ And bowed her hand to teach her fingering," replies Hortensio (II. 1. 147, 149–150). Later Petruchio explicitly attempts to "break" Kate to his will, and throughout the play men tell her that she "mistakes her frets"—that her anger is unjustified.

On the other hand, Petruchio's confident references to "great ordnance in the field" and the "Loud 'larums, neighing steeds, trumpets' clang" of battle bespeak a lifelong acquaintance with organized violence as a masculine vocation. The loud oaths with which he orders his servants about and startles the priest in the wedding service are thus farcical exaggerations of normal masculine behavior. In its volume and vigor, his speech suggests a robust manliness which would make him attractive to the woman who desires a master (or who wants to identify with power in its most accessible form). Grumio characterizes his master in terms of his speech, in lines which recall the kind of speech attributed to Kate: "A my word, and she knew him as well as I do, she would think scolding would do little good upon him. She may perhaps call him half a score of knaves or so—why, that's nothing. And he begin once, he'll rail in his rope-tricks. I'll tell what, sir, and she stand him but a little, he will throw a figure in her face and so disfigure her with it that she shall have no more eyes to see withal than a cat. You know him not, sir" (I. 2. 107–115).

If Petruchio were female, he would be known as a shrew and shunned accordingly by men. Behavior desirable in a male automatically prohibits similar behavior in a female, for woman must mold herself to be complementary to man, not competitive with him. Indeed, if manhood is defined and proven by the ability to dominate, either in battle or in the household, then a situation which does not allow a man to dominate is existentially threatening. When Petruchio declares, "I am as peremptory as she proud-minded," he seems to state that he and his bride-to-be are two of a kind. But that "kind"—bold, independent, self-assertive—must only be male. Thus his image of himself and Kate as "two raging fires" ends on a predictable note:

> And where two raging fires meet together
> They do consume the thing that feeds their fury.
> Though little fire grows great with little wind,
> Yet extreme gusts will blow out fire and all.
> So I to her, *and so she yields to me,*
> For I am rough and woo not like a babe.
> (II. 1. 132–137; emphasis mine)

His force must necessarily triumph over Kate's because he is male and she is not. Those critics who maintain that his is acceptable because it has only the limited, immediate purpose of making Kate reject an "unbecoming" mode of behavior miss the real point of the taming. The overt force Petruchio wields over Kate by marrying her against her will in the first place, and then by denying her every wish and comfort, stamping, shouting, reducing her to exhaustion, etc., is but a farcical representation of the psychological realities of marriage in Elizabethan England, in which the husband's will constantly, silently, and invisibly, through custom and conformity, suppressed the wife's.

At the wedding in Act III, scene 1, Petruchio's behavior travesties the decorum, ceremony and piety which all those present feel ought to accompany a marriage. It is calculated to deprive Kate of the opportunity to enjoy the bride's sense of triumph, of being the center of admiration and interest; to humiliate her in public; to throw her off guard by convincing her he is mad; and to show her that now nothing can happen unless and until her husband pleases. The final effect of the wedding scene, however, is less comical than the rhetorically delightful accounts of Petruchio's off-stage antics. When all the trappings are stripped away (and they are, by his design), the groom is simply completing the legal arrangements whereby he acquires Kate as he would acquire a piece of property. When he declares he'll "seal the title with a lovely kiss," he refers not just to Kate's new title as his wife, but also to the title-deed which, sealed with wax, passed to the purchaser in a property transaction. (The pun recalls Baptista's "deeds," a similar play on words discussed above.) Tranio remarks of Petruchio, "He hath some meaning in his mad attire," and he is right. When Petruchio says "To me she's married, not unto my clothes," he assumes a lofty morality, implying that he offers Kate real love, not just its worldly show. This moralistic pose becomes an important part of his strategy in Act IV when he claims to do nothing that isn't for Kate's "good." But in the brutally plain statement he delivers at the conclusion of the wedding scene, he momentarily drops this pose:

> She is my goods, my chattles; she is my house,
> My household stuff, my field, my barn,
> My horse, my ox, my ass, my anything.
> (III. 2. 230–232)

His role as property-owner is the model for his role as husband; Kate, for him, is a thing. Or at least she will become a thing when he has wrenched unquestioning obedience from her, when she no longer has mind or will of her own. It is impossible that Shakespeare meant us to accept Petruchio's speech uncritically: it is the most shamelessly blunt statement of the relationship among men, women, and property to be found in the literature of this period. After the simple declarative statements of possession, quoted above, which deny humanity to Kate, the speech shifts to chivalric challenges of imaginary "thieves" who would snatch her away. Is she goods, in the following lines, or a medieval damsel?

> .... Touch her whoever dare,
> I'll bring mine action on the proudest he
> That stops my way in Padua. Grumio,
> Draw forth thy weapon, we are beset with thieves.

Rescue thy mistress, if thou be a man.
(III. 2. 233–237)

The point is that Petruchio wants to think of her on both kinds
of terms. The speech concludes grandly with the metamorphosis
of Petruchio into a knight-errant:

Fear not, sweet wench; they shall not touch thee, Kate.
I'll buckler thee against a million.
(III. 2. 238–239)

The modulation of simple ownership into spurious chivalry reveals the speaker's buried awareness that he cheapens himself by
being merely Kate's proprietor; he must transform the role into
something nobler.

Petruchio's thundering oaths and physical brutality reach a
crescendo at his country house in Act IV, when he beats his
servants, throws food and dishes on the floor, stomps, roars and
bullies. These actions are directed not against his bride but at his
servants, again in the name of chivalry, out of a fastidious devotion to his bride's supposed comfort. But his stance is rooted realistically in his status as lord of a manor and master of a household
which is not Kate's but his. He ordered her wedding clothes,
chose their style and paid for them. Kate wears them not at her
pleasure but at his, as Grumio's jest succinctly indicates:

PETRUCHIO. Well, sir, in brief, the gown is not for me.
GRUMIO. You are i' th' right, sir; 'tis for my mistress.
(IV. 3. 153–154)

In the famous soliloquy which opens "Thus have I politicly begun my reign" (IV. 1. 182–205), Petruchio reduces Kate to an
animal capable of learning only through deprivation of food and
rest, devoid of all sensitivity save the physical. The animal metaphor shocks us and I would suggest was meant to shock Shakespeare's audience, despite their respect for falconry as an art and
that reverence for the great chain of being emphasized by E.M.W.
Tillyard. I suppose Kate is actually being elevated in this speech,
in view of previous references to her as her husband's horse, ox,
and ass, for a falcon was the appurtenance of a nobleman, and a
valued animal. But the blandness of Petruchio's confidential tone,
the sweep of his easy assumption that Kate is not merely an animal, but *his* animal, who lives or dies at his command—has a

dramatic irony similar to that of his exit speech in the wedding scene. Both utterances unashamedly present the status of woman in marriage as degrading in the extreme, plainly declaring her a sub-human being who exists solely for the purposes of her husband. Yet both offer this vision of the wife as chattel or animal in a lordly, self-confident tone. Urbanity is superimposed on outrage, for our critical scrutiny.

III

Shakespeare does not rest with showing that male supremacy in marriage denies woman's humanity. In the most brilliant comic scene of the play (IV. 5), he goes on to demonstrate how it defies reason. Petruchio demands that Kate agree that the sun is the moon in order to force a final showdown. Having exhausted and humiliated her to the limit of his invention, he now wants her to know that he would go to any extreme to get the obedience he craves. Shakespeare implies here that male supremacy is ultimately based on such absurdities, for it insists that whatever a man says is right because he is a man, even if he happens to be wrong. In a male-supremacist utopia, masculinity might be identical with absolute truth, but in life the two coincide only intermittently.

Why does Kate submit to her husband's unreason? Or why does she *appear* to do so, and on what terms? On the most pragmatic level, she follows Hortensio's advice to "Say as he says or we shall never go" only in order to achieve her immediate and most pressing needs: a bed, a dinner, some peace and quiet. Shakespeare never lets us think that she believes it right, either morally or logically, to submit her judgment and the evidence of her senses to Petruchio's rule. In fact, the language of her capitulation makes it clear that she thinks him mad:

> Forward, I pray, since we have come so far,
> And be it moon or sun or what you please.
> *And if you please to call it a rush-candle,*
> Henceforth I vow it shall be so for me.
>
> .   .   .
>
> But sun it is not when you say it is not,
> *And the moon changes even as your mind.*
> (IV. 5. 12–15, 19–20; emphasis mine)

At this point, Hortensio concedes Petruchio's victory and applauds it; Petruchio henceforth behaves and speaks as though he has indeed tamed Kate. However, we must assume that since he previously donned the mask of the ardent lover, professing rapture at Kate's rudeness, he can see that she is doing the same thing here. At their first meeting he turned the tables on her, praising her for mildness and modesty after she gave insults and even injury. Now she pays him back, suddenly overturning his expectations and moreover mocking them at the same time. But he is not fooled, and can take that mockery as the cue for compromise. It reassures him that she will give him obedience if that is what he must have, but it also warns him that she, in turn, must retain her intellectual freedom.

The scene then proceeds on this basis, each character accepting the other's assumed role. Kate responds to Petruchio's outrageous claim that the wrinkled Vincentio is a fair young maiden by pretending so wholeheartedly to accept it that we know she can't be in earnest. She embroiders the fantasy in an exuberant declamatory style more appropriate to tragedy than comedy:

> Young budding virgin, fair and fresh and sweet,
> Whither away, or where is thy abode?
> Happy the parents of so fair a child!
> Happier the man whom favorable stars
> Allots thee for his lovely bedfellow!
> (IV. 5. 36–41)

Her rhetoric expresses her realization that the power struggle she had entered into on Petruchio's terms is absurd. It also signals her emancipation from that struggle, in the terms she declared earlier: "... I will be free/ Even to the uttermost, as I please, in words."

Of course, a freedom that exists only in words is ultimately as limited as Petruchio's mastery. Though Kate is clever enough to use his verbal strategies against him, she is trapped in her own cleverness. Her only way of maintaining her inner freedom is by outwardly denying it, which thrusts her into a schizoid existence. One might almost prefer that she simply give in rather than continue to fight from such a psychologically perilous position. Furthermore, to hold that she maintains her freedom in words is to posit a distinction without a difference, for whether she remains spiritually independent of Petruchio or sincerely be-

lieves in his superiority, her outward behavior must be the same—
that of the perfect Griselda, a model for all women. What complicates the situation even more is that Kate quite possibly has
fallen in love with her tamer, whose vitality and bravado make
him attractive, despite his professed aims. Her failure to pursue
her rebellion after the wedding or in the country house supports
this hypothesis as does the tone of her mockery in Act IV, Scene
5, and thereafter, which is playful and joyous rather than bitter
and angry as it was in the first three acts.

Finally, we must remember that Shakespearean comedy cele-
brates love; love by means of any contrivance of plot or character. Here Shakespeare parts company with sterner moralists such
as Jonson, or more relentless social critics such as Ibsen. As
Northrop Frye states, "In comedy and in romance, the story
seeks its own end instead of holding the mirror up to nature." [10]
Though Shakespeare quite astutely mirrors aspects of the human
condition in the comedies, that is not his main purpose. In this
play as in the other early and middle comedies, he aims to present an idealized vision of life as the triumph of love in marriage.
The match between Kate and Petruchio bespeaks a comic renewal
of society, the materialism and egotism of the old order transformed or at least softened by the ardor and mutual tolerance of
the young lovers. Shakespeare wants to make us feel that Kate
has not been bought or sold, but has given herself out of love.
Thus he makes her walk a tightrope of affirming her husband's
superiority through outward conformity while questioning it
ironically through words. Portia, Beatrice, Viola and Rosalind
perform similar athletic feats on their way to the altar, but their
wittiness, unlike Kate's, ends with the wedding.

Words, as an instrument of command and an assertion of individuality, have been important throughout the play. In the first
scene, the mere fact that Kate protested her father's plan for dis-
posing of her, instead of submitting wordlessly, marked her for
the male audience as a shrew, while Bianca's demure silence defined her as the epitome of desirability. Petruchio shrugged off
the challenge of taming Kate by comparing her scolds to the
noise of thunder, lions, and cannon, and mustered a volume of
abuse far greater than hers when dealing with his servants. Kate
whetted his desire by matching him taunt for taunt at their first
meeting, and he lectured her to dumb amazement during their

honeymoon on diet, continency, and fashions in dress. On the way back to Padua, she finds in words a way out of subjection, creatively evolving a rhetoric of satirical exaggeration. This rhetoric and the ironies it produces are Shakespeare's way out of the difficulty he encountered in writing a critique of marriage in the form of a comedy which must, somehow, celebrate marriage.

In the last scene, Shakespeare finally allows Petruchio that lordship over Kate, and superiority to other husbands, for which he has striven so mightily. He just makes it clear to us, through the contextual irony of Kate's last speech, that her husband is deluded. As a contest between males in which woman is the prize, the closing scene is analogous to the entire play. It was partly Petruchio's desire to show his peers that he was more of a man than they which spurred him to take on the shrew in the first place. Gremio refers to him as a Hercules and compares the subduing of Kate to a "labor ... more than Alcides' twelve" (I. 2. 256–257). Hortensio longs but fails to emulate his friend's supposed success in taming. Lucentio, winner in the other wooing context, fails in the final test of marital authority. Petruchio stands alone in the last scene, the center of male admiration.

As critics have noted, the wager scene is punctuated by reversals: quiet Bianca talks back and shrewish Kate seems to become an obedient wife. In a further reversal, however, she steals the scene from her husband, who has held the stage throughout the play, and reveals that he has failed to tame her in the sense he set out to. He has gained her outward compliance in the form of a public display, while her spirit remains mischievously free. Though she pretends to speak earnestly on behalf of her own inferiority, she actually treats us to a pompous, wordy, holier-than-thou sermon which delicately mocks the sermons her husband has delivered to her and about her. It is significant that Kate's speech is both her longest utterance and the longest in the play. Previously, Petruchio dominated the play verbally,[11] and his longest speech totalled twenty-four lines, while Kate's came to fifteen. Moreover, everything Kate said was a protest against her situation or those who put her in it, and as such was deemed unwomanly, or shrewish. Petruchio's impressive rhetoric, on the other hand, asserted his masculinity in the form of command over women and servants and of moral authority. Now Kate apes this verbal dominance and moralistic stance for satirical effect.

In content, the speech is thoroughly orthodox. Its sentiments can be found in a dozen treatises on marriage written in the sixteenth century.[12] The arguments that a woman's beauty is her greatest asset and depends on her amiability; that her obedience is a debt rendered in return for financial support; that the household is a hierarchy like the state, with husband as lord and wife as subject; that the female's physical delicacy fits her only for meekness—all were the platitudes of male dominance. Kate offers them with complete seriousness, straightforwardly except for a few verbal ironies, such as the reminder of her husband's rhetorical patterns in "thy lord, thy life, thy keeper,/ Thy head, thy sovereign," which echoes his "my goods, my chattels; . . . my house,/ My household stuff, my field, my barn,/ my horse, my ox, my ass, my anything." The grave moral tone of the speech, as I have noted, comes from Petruchio also, but its irony emanates primarily from the dramatic context. First, it follows upon and resembles Kate's rhetorical performance on the road back to Padua. It is a response to her husband's demand that she demonstrate her obedience before others, as she did then before Hortensio, and as such it exceeds expectations once more. It fairly shouts obedience, when a gentle murmur would suffice. Having heard her address Vincentio as "Young, budding virgin," we know what she is up to in this instance. Second, though the speech pleads subordination, as a speech—a lengthy, ambitious verbal performance before an audience—it allows the speaker to dominate that audience. Though Kate purports to speak as a woman to women, she assumes the role of a preacher whose authority and wisdom are, in the terms of the play, thoroughly masculine. Third, the speech sets the seal on a complete reversal of character, a push-button change from rebel to conformist which is, I have argued, part of the mechanism of farce. Here as elsewhere in the play, farce has two purposes: it completes the fantasy of male dominance, but also mocks it as mere fantasy. Kate's quick transformation perfectly fulfills Petruchio's wishes, but is transparently false to human nature. Towards the end of her lecture, Kate hints that she is dissembling in the line "That seeming to be most which we indeed least are." Though she seems to be the most vocal apologist for male dominance, she is indeed its ablest critic.[13]

On one level, the dénouement is the perfect climax of a masculine fantasy, for as Kate concludes she prepares to place her hand beneath her husband's foot, an emblem-book symbol of wifely obedience. On a deeper level, as I have tried to show, her words speak louder than her actions, and mock that fantasy. But on the deepest level, because the play depicts its heroine as outwardly compliant but inwardly independent, it represents possibly the most cherished male fantasy of all—that woman remains *un*tamed, even in her subjection. Does Petruchio know he's been taken? Quite probably, since he himself has played the game of saying-the-thing-which-is-not. Would he enjoy being married to a woman as dull and proper as the Kate who delivers that marriage sermon? From all indications, no. Then can we conclude that Petruchio no less than Kate knowingly plays a false role in this marriage, the role of victorious tamer and complacent master? I think we can, but what does this tell us about him and about men in general?

It is Kate's submission to him which makes Petruchio a man, finally and indisputably. This is the action toward which the whole plot drives, and if we consider its significance for Petruchio and his fellows we realize that the myth of feminine weakness, which prescribes that women ought to or must inevitably submit to man's superior authority, masks a contrary myth: that only a woman has the power to authenticate a man, by acknowledging him *her* master. Petruchio's mind may change even as the moon, but what is important is that Kate confirm those changes; moreover, that she do so willingly and consciously. Such voluntary surrender is, paradoxically, part of the myth of female power, which assigns to woman the crucial responsibility for creating a mature and socially respectable man. In *The Taming of the Shrew*, Shakespeare reveals the dependency which underlies mastery, the strength behind submission. Truly, Petruchio is wedded to his Kate.

Moll Flanders:
"A Woman on her own Account"
MIRIAM LERENBAUM

Ian Watt's *Rise of the Novel* has inspired many readers to
study *Moll Flanders* with new appreciation, and many critics to
engage in what amounts to a pamphlet war on a number of issues
Watt has raised. None, though, seems to have given serious consideration to his thoughts on Moll's femininity, or rather her *non*-
femininity. Watts writes: "The essence of her character and
actions is, to one reader at least, essentially masculine. . . . it is at
least certain that Moll accepts none of the disabilities of her sex,
and indeed one cannot but feel that Virginia Woolf's admiration
for her was largely due to admiration of a heroine who so fully
realized one of the ideals of feminism: freedom from any involuntary involvement in the feminine role." [1]

The purpose of this paper is to marshal evidence from the novel
itself, from social histories of the period, and from recent biological and psychological writings to suggest that, contrary to
Watt's impression, Defoe has given us in *Moll Flanders* an excep-
tionally accurate rendering of his heroine's "involuntary involvement in the feminine role." Or, as Virginia Woolf puts it, Defoe
"makes us understand that Moll Flanders was a woman on her
own account and not only material for a succession of adventures." [2]

Such a thesis about *Moll Flanders* would certainly not make
the book an anomaly in his writings. In such early short works as
the section advocating advanced education for women in *An Essay on Projects* (1697) and the verse-satire *Good Advice to the*

Ladies (1702) and in his close examinations of marriage both fictional (*Roxana*, 1724) and non-fictional (*Conjugal Lewdness*, 1727), Defoe shows that he is an acute observer of women and sympathetic to their plight. Similarly, in *Moll Flanders* he has contrived a narrative in which the major turning points of the heroine's life and her responses to them are in great part peculiarly feminine. Although there is no absolute line to be drawn between a voluntary and involuntary acceptance of the feminine role, there is a wealth of evidence to support the view that Moll's responses and attitudes are intimately tied to the social expectations for and restrictions upon women of her time and place and to the biological processes that continue to affect women of our time and place. Defoe has not fashioned Moll according to a moral model. He has created her out of everyday fact and human psychology, particularly as they relate to the actualities of feminine roles.

In *Moll Flanders*, Defoe takes cognizance of Moll's roles as young woman, wife, mother, thief, and pioneer, most especially by correlating the stages in her aging process with crises in her personal life. He concludes each stage and introduces the next with an episode in which Moll, confronted by a seeming impasse, falls psychosomatically ill, becomes inert and passive for a period of time, and then subsequently recovers to begin a wholly new career with energy and optimism. There are three major instances: the first precedes her matrimonial career; the second comes at its conclusion and introduces her thieving career; the third occurs in Newgate and marks the beginning of her "new life," reunited with her favorite husband and pioneering in the New World. Between the first and second of these major crises, there is an important minor episode of the same kind: she falls ill when she is pregnant and "between husbands." These episodes help to give shape to the narrative and provide a convenient way of organizing a consideration of the essentially feminine nature of Moll's behavior.[3]

MOLL AND HER PROSPECTS

The first of Moll's three major bouts of illness occurs in the midst of the well-known sequence of scenes describing her affair with the "elder brother" and her subsequent marriage to Robin, the "younger brother." Moll is here between seventeen and eighteen years old. Her report of her illness occupies three paragraphs, the major details of which I quote:

> The bare loss of him as a gallant was not so much my affliction as the loss of his person, whom indeed I lov'd to distraction; and the loss of all the expectations I had, and which I always built my hopes upon, of having him one day for my husband. These things oppress'd my mind so much that, in short, the agonies of my mind threw me into a high fever, and long it was that none in the family expected my life. . . . After the end of five weeks I grew better, but was so weak, so alter'd, and recover'd so slowly, that the physicians apprehended I should go into a consumption; and which vex'd me most, they gave their opinion that my mind was oppress'd, that something troubl'd me, and, in short, that I was in love.
> (P. 38)[4]

From this description we learn that Moll is psychosomatically ill with delirium and high fever, but that she and the doctor only partly concur in assigning this illness a cause. He calls it love, but she tells us that it was this and more—that she has also lost all her expectations of marrying well and marrying for love. Between her first rendezvous and her illness, Moll has moved from innocence to experience with traumatic consequences.[5]

A number of genuinely depressing truths have impressed themselves upon her mind during this interval. She learns that despite their mutual passion, the elder brother will not marry her; that he will not come into his inheritance for years; that his loyalty to his younger brother exceeds his devotion to her; that Robin is highly unlikely to gain his family's approval to marry her; and that willy-nilly she will be cast into the servitude she sees as a yawning abyss, has stubbornly sought to avoid, and had been misled into thinking she has completely, if narrowly, escaped. If we are willing to take Moll's plight seriously, we will see how brilliantly Defoe has depicted the crisis of a young woman whose whole future life has turned to ashes.

In making our judgment of Moll's own assessment, we must avoid romanticizing her prospects. Not only Moll, but everyone around her, thinks the younger brother mad to marry solely for love. Moll herself has no dowry, no social position, no special assets with which to gain a husband or earn a decent living. There was a time when English women of all classes had held important places in the working life of the community, but that time had passed.[6] One could not make a casual decision to enter those sectors of the work force that promised a decent wage in a respectable profession, for apprenticeship and licensing were required for most occupations, and both Moll's upbringing and society's active discouragement effectively closed such an alternative—to married women as well as to unmarried ones.

Remaining single is not in any event a real alternative for Moll. Although many men freely chose a single life, both the law and the practicalities of everyday life treated every woman of the period as married or about to be. Even such severe critics of marriage as Defoe himself never suggest that women might validly choose not to be married; their only advice is the kind Defoe proffers: that women choose their husbands with great care. At the outset of her marriage career, Moll is not able to make even this choice. If she has been nourishing a *Pamela*-like fantasy, her inquisition of the elder brother has decisively toppled it.

That Moll does not exaggerate her fears of unattractive and extended servitude if she cannot successfully extricate herself from her impasse is clear from Dorothy George's meticulous account of the fate of most parish children of the period: ". . . there can be no doubt that those [cases] which came into court represent an infinitesimal proportion of the little apprentices who were beaten, starved and neglected, still less of those who ran away to become beggars and vagrants. *Little girls especially were liable to be horribly ill-used.* . . . There were also trades so unprofitable or disagreeable that only parish children or the children of the very poor were apprenticed to them."[7] Although a combination of good luck and fearful stubbornness has so far relieved Moll of the worst possibilities of being a parish child, she is certainly entitled to feel terrified of her possible future fate. Her skill in needlework would only consign her to an even bleaker future than entry into domestic service.[8] Yet if Moll incurs the enmity of her protectors, only these prospects confront her. The elder brother represents Moll's introduction to male complacency as he slickly extricates himself from his vows, speaking of *his* possible "ruin" (p. 35) while appearing "surpriz'd at [Moll's] obstinacy" (p. 37). Moll does not choose her future career; it is thrust upon her by all the forces of society.

Society prepares her ill for the marital career it virtually demands of her. Although we hear few details of Moll's day-to-day married life, we know enough of her early life to draw some conclusions, and it seems clear that she is neither better nor worse than she should be. Pleading for a better education for women, William Law might almost be describing Moll's upbringing and its consequences: "The corruption of the world indulges them in great vanity and mankind seems to consider them in no other view than as so many painted idols, that are to allure and gratify their passions; so that if many women are vain, light gewgaw creatures, they have this to excuse themselves, that they are not only such as their education has made them, but such as the generality of the world allows them to be." [9] If Moll is self-indulgent and wilful, it is because she has been encouraged to be so by those around her. Her orphaned state serves only to sharpen her vulnerability to flattery and praise. The memoir form encourages her to be honest and outspoken about her aspirations, but her wishes and values are themselves neither unconventional nor unfeminine. She does not rebel against the feminine role: Moll assures us that for the duration of each of her marriages she was a good wife and mother, amiable and docile, and we have no reason to disbelieve her.[10] She displays initiative and independence only in picking up and starting again in the one career that is available to her.

In her succession of short-lived marriages Moll is also more representative than we might think. After recounting a number of reports of deaths by starvation in eighteenth-century London, Dorothy George writes: "It is significant that all the victims should have been women; there can be little doubt that the hardships of the age bore with especial weight upon them. Social conditions tended to produce a high proportion of widows, deserted wives, and unmarried mothers, while women's occupations were overstocked, ill-paid and irregular." [11] As if intent on illustrating this extract, Defoe has caused Moll to exemplify all those varieties of abandoned women at one stage or other of her marital career. If she anxiously tallies her assets at the close of each of her marriages, it is not because she is paranoid or obsessively greedy, or a symbol of the capitalist spirit, but because she has a clear and accurate picture of her possible fate. If she is never quite so poor or quite so close to disaster as she imagines, neither is she safe. We should not be surprised that much later in life she finds a beggar's dress (one of her temporary robbing costumes) "ominous and threatening" (p. 222). Moll's society does not grant her the luxury of making Alfred Doolittle's choice to be one of either the deserving or undeserving poor. In Shaw's *Pygmalion*, Doolittle claims that "my needs is as great as the most deserving widow's that ever got money out of six charities in one week for the death of the same husband." But England in Moll's lifetime did not yet boast such charitable societies, and even the indomitable Doolittle hasn't "the nerve for the workhouse."

Although all of Moll's marriages are shortlived, she moves from one to the next with increasing concern but without excessive anxiety. We hear of severe emotional distress only at the opening and close of her marital career. The first of these illnesses is as genuine as the last. More than merely extreme adolescent disappointment or particular vanity and egotism, it is an acknowledgement of the disillusionment experienced by the generality of women in Moll's condition and era. Before the age of twenty, all of Moll's romantic hopes are dashed and all of her options are foreclosed. Her severe illness in the face of this crisis is therefore a plausible and significant emblem of her involvement in the feminine role.

MOLL AS MOTHER

The second illness Moll reports is a minor one; it occurs while she is pregnant with a child whose father is Jemy, her highwayman-husband. Although it does not mark a turning-point in her life, it is significant in relation to the question of her femininity, and provides a useful starting point for an exploration of her role as a mother.

Moll describes this illness: "In the course of this affair I fell very ill, and my melancholly really encreas'd my distemper; my illness prov'd at length to be only an ague, but my apprehensions were really that I should miscarry; I should not say apprehensions, for indeed I would have been glad to miscarry, but I cou'd never entertain so much as a thought of taking any thing to make me miscarry, I abhorr'd, I say, so much as the thought of it" (pp. 139–

140). This episode is really one of a pair. At this point she is looking for a midwife; subsequently she searches for a way to disencumber herself of the newly-born child. It was, she says, an "inexpressible misfortune. . . . to have a child upon my hands" (p. 149), for it will interfere with her plan to marry the banker. Throughout this sequence, she reflects—to herself, her governess, and the reader—upon the difficulties and the responsibilities that child-bearing entails, and these reflections, together with her earlier cavalier attitudes towards her children and her later ecstatic reunion with her son in Virginia, have seemed to many readers the epitome of hypocrisy, immorality, inhumanity, and certainly un-femininity.[12]

It is certainly clear that Moll, presumably (or as Ian Watt would say, "suspiciously") like her creator, displays little interest in her children, even to the point of forgetting their existence once they have left her immediate care. Nor do we hear any thing of them while they remain in her care. However, we cannot on that account convict her of unnatural cruelty, for the weight of historical and psychological evidence suggests that in her ma-ternal role, as in other roles, Moll is at one with her female con-temporaries.

Although statistics about the facts of seventeenth- and eight-eenth-century motherhood are hard to come by, a number of useful clues to general attitudes and practices are available. Within *Moll Flanders* itself, the strictures against deliberately-induced abortion suggest that such a practice cannot have been rare or exotic. Numbers of pregnant women must have sought to avoid parenthood.[13] Some even resorted to infanticide: "If, in the worst years [1720–1750], according to the Bills [of Mortality], over 74 per cent of the children born in London died before they were five, parish children, that is, children in workhouses, or put out to nurse by the parish, died in still greater numbers. . . . The prob-lem of deserted children—children exposed in the streets, orphans, and the children of poor parents—had long been an urgent one in London. . . . The Foundling Hospital [granted a charter in 1739] aimed at stopping the exposure, desertion, and murder of infants." [14] The more morally abhorrent of these practices were clearly committed by mothers who were themselves desperately poor and abandoned by the infants' fathers. Few of Moll's moral protestations stand up to close examination, but child-murder and abandonment (along with committing incest and inducing abortion) seem genuinely shocking to her. Apparently, however, Moll's sociey did not see these acts as heinous crimes. In the eighteenth century it was not uncommon to see corpses of abandoned infants lying about on the streets, and in the rare instances that perpetrators were discovered and brought to court, they were usually let off with a light sentence. William Langer notes the implications of this phenomenon: "It seems reasonable in the light of this painful record to conclude that infanticide, covert or flagrant, was at least as important as celibacy in checking population growth from the middle of the 18th century to the middle of the 19th. *It is also evident that a marked change of attitude with respect to children, particularly the newborn, took place thereafter. What was then commonplace now seems intolerable cruelty.*" [15]

An attitude of relative indifference to the fate of young children in this period extends even to parents of considerable wealth and sensibility. Numerous instances up through the seventeenth century attest to the continuity of the practice of sending children away from home at an early age to be nursed, schooled, or trained in another household. Although, like many other traditions, this one was beginning to disintegrate during the period in which Moll was raising her children, the child-centered home we are used to had clearly not replaced it. Children were often sent away from the best of motives: their mothers were ill and could not nurse them, they were sent to the country because cities were the centers of plague, or they were sent away for educational advantages. John Evelyn, for instance, was first sent to a neighbouring tenant's wife to be nursed for over a year "(in reguard for my Mother's weaknesse, *or rather custome of persons of quality*)," then "sent by my Father to Lewes in Sussex, to be with my Grandfather, with whom I pass'd my Childhood." [16] Custom also decreed that even when children were raised at home, they were likely to be in the care of servants rather than their mothers. However affectionate or tenderhearted, mothers rarely absorbed themselves in personally raising their children. And when children died: "The carelessness of the nurses was often matched by an indifference on the part of parents, an attitude almost inevitably induced at a time when parents had so many children that they ceased to take an interest in them individually. 'Mrs. Thrale,' we are told, 'regarded the death of various daughters at school with great equanimity'; and Sir John Verney cheerfully remarked when two of his fifteen children died that he still had left a baker's dozen. On such occasions as parents were not merely indifferent, they were often fatalistic, seeing in the death of their little ones the mysterious ways of God." [17] Ignorance of obstetrical science and pediatrics as well as culpable neglect and cruelty created enormously high infant mortality rates. The probability that many children would not survive occasioned the indifference and fatalism of parents, but so too did a general psychological attitude. Children were not seen as having special and individual personalities, but as miniature adults, only duller and more burdensome.

It is in any case a gross distortion to list Moll's first five surviving children as "the two children discarded with her first husband's parents or the two children abandoned in Virginia or the boy left with her Bath gentleman." [18] The first two verbs are loaded with meanings they cannot bear. There is a world of difference between saying (which is certainly true) that Moll does not wish to be personally responsible for her children and saying (what is not true) that she does not care what happens to them. To consign her children to the care of rich, doting, and settled grandparents can readily be seen as a sign of responsibility rather than irresponsibility; neither Moll's words nor her actions in these cases prove her to be morally culpable. Nor are they inconsistent with her words about "unnatural mothers," whom she defines as those who try to induce abortion or turn their children over to custodians without seeing that they will be well-tended rather than neglected or destroyed. Moreover, Moll speaks of the need of children for "an assisting hand, whether of the mother, *or some body else*" (p. 150, my italics). Her phrasing is compatible with that of modern child psychologists, who speak of "mothers or mother-substitutes" and of "mother-figures" rather than exclusively of natural mothers. All the evidence provided by her own words, as well as those of her contemporaries and the scientists and historians of our own period, suggests that Moll is neither unnatural, culpable, nor unfeminine in her indifference to her children, certainly not by the standards of her own period, and probably not even by the standards of ours.

Investigation suggests that motherliness is not a purely innate trait, but a complex one, involving considerable admixtures of learning, experience, and accommodation to cultural expectations.[19] Many normal women do not experience maternal feelings before their children are born; love for their offspring may not develop until after birth, during the nursing process, or even later in their interaction with their infants.[20] Other scientists report that "many prospective parents take up the responsibilities of parenthood soberly, not necessarily with exhilaration," and note further that an eager desire to procreate may sometimes mask unhealthy and immature attitudes rather than express feminine maturity and tenderness.[21]

It is clear that there is a wide range of appropriate, "normal," female responses to the role of motherhood, or, in technical phraseology, research indicates a "large number of intrapsychic, interpersonal, and cultural variables that converge in the enterprise of being a parent." [22] For instance, in studies on the motherly traits of non-human primates—in whom one might expect to find maternal instinct in a purer form than in human mothers—it has been found that mothers who themselves have neither received mothering nor had an opportunity to observe or practice often prove to be totally inadequate mothers themselves, and are indifferent or abusive to their children.[23] Investigation of the behavior of human mothers supports this finding.[24] Moll is herself an example of a woman deprived of maternal care in infancy. Even without bringing this background information to bear, it seems clear that she does not forego her claim to femininity by bearing children mainly because her society expects her to while it provides her with no means of contraception and no other source of gratification.

Moll, however, sometimes exhibits considerable sentiment over parting with her children, thereby giving rise to charges of hypocrisy. She tells us that "it was death to me to part with the child" of her Bath lover (p. 109), and that only "with a heavy heart and many a tear" (p. 153) did she relinquish the son of Jemy, her Lancashire husband, to the care of a nurse in the country. But these protestations together with her later pleasure in meeting her son in Virginia have causes other than hypocritical ones, not the least of which is that Moll, like many people, mellows as she ages. When she is young she wishes to be carefree, and, believing that she will give birth many times in the future, displays no interest in her children. The children over whom she waxes sentimental are, in contrast, born to her in her late thirties and forties, and are

more precious to her partly because each may be her last. Moreover, the children of her later years are the offspring of men for
whom she cared far more than she did her earlier husbands. These
variables seem powerful reasons for considering her differing attitudes as humanly inconsistent but not as incredible or unforgiv-
able. Even her attitude towards her son in Virginia, assuredly
complicated though it is by her hearty interest in financial gain,
need not be reduced wholly to economic interest. Given the pre-
dispositions of the period to romanticize gallant young men if
not young children, it is surely understandable that Moll, seeing a
"handsome comely young gentleman in flourishing circumstances"
(p. 279), should be pleased with what "she hath wrought." To
want to take pride in and make herself known to a prosperous
independent adult is not inconsistent with seeing a dependent
infant as an unpleasant burden she is pleased to leave behind her.

In fact all Moll's attitudes towards her children are readily comprehensible in terms of her sex, her age, and her culture: she is
indifferent to them when both she and they are young, she is concerned about their welfare but uninterested in rearing them herself, and she responds to them when they are thriving or when
they are the children of men whom she cares for. One would
hardly want to claim that Moll is an exemplary mother; nonetheless, her attitudes and actions fall well within the range of normal,
feminine behavior.

MOLL'S CHANGE OF LIFE

Moll's most protracted illness occurs at the end of her marriage
career. Many readers find it and its startling conclusion—her entry
into her criminal career—improbable and ill-motivated, but the
text provides a number of clues to causes specifically related to her
femininity. Moll describes her illness in a passage whose style
recaptures the distraction she is recalling:

> But my case was indeed deplorable ... I saw nothing be-
> fore me but the utmost distress, and this represented it self so
> lively to my thoughts that it seem'd as if it was come before
> it was really very near. ...
> In this distress I had no assistant, no friend to comfort or
> advise me, I sat and cried and tormented myself night and

day; wringing my hands, and sometimes raving like a distracted woman; and indeed I have often wonder'd it had not affected my reason, for I had the vapours to such a degree that my understanding was sometimes quite lost in fancies and imagination.

I liv'd two years in this dismal condition, wasting that little I had, weeping continually over my dismal circumstances, and as it were only bleeding to death. (P. 165)

This passage follows another highly revealing one:

I foresaw the blow, and was extremely oppress'd in my mind, for I saw evidently that if he died I was undone.

I had had two children by him and no more, for it began to be time for me to leave bearing children, for I was now eight and forty, and I suppose if he had liv'd I should have had no more.

I was now left in a dismal and disconsolate case indeed, and in several things worse than ever. First, it was past the flourishing time with me when I might expect to be courted for a mistress; that agreeable part had declin'd some time, and the ruins only appear'd of what had been. (P. 164)

Taken together, these passages describe a constellation of female tribulations that makes Moll's anxiety perfectly comprehensible. At one and the same time she has lost her husband, her means of livelihood, her childbearing capacity, her sexual attractiveness. The loss of any one of these would be a major blow; the loss of all of them together represents the loss of every source of security and gratification she is entitled to expect. Although these losses are tightly intertwined, it is worthwhile attempting to separate out and comment on each in order to emphasize the import and the specifically feminine qualities of this crisis.

Ian Watt professes difficulty in understanding Moll's conflicting feelings during her marriage to her fifth husband: "Moll's life with him is treated as a brief and wholly self-contained episode whose emotional premise does not have to be reconciled with other features of her life and character." [25] Yet Moll's expressed satisfaction with this marriage and her grief upon the banker's death are surely not perplexing. The banker is "a quiet, sensible, sober man, virtuous, modest, sincere, and in his business diligent and just" (p. 164).

He has, moreover, courted her with persistence, and has fallen in love with her (*her* and not her money) when she is forty-three years old "and did not look the better for my age, nor for my rambles to Virginia and back again" (p. 111) and when "nothing offered" for a long time despite her anxious attention to her prospects. Moll has found to her dismay that success in her matrimonial career has become increasingly more difficult to achieve as she ages. Unlike her earlier manner of proceeding—when time was on her side—her search for her last two husbands is attended by an air of desperation. Her Bath interlude makes her several hundred pounds richer, but six years older. Her desperation overcomes her normal caution and accounts for her falling victim to Jemy's ruse, but at least she has prudentially kept the eager banker dangling lest her Lancashire adventure misfire. Given these circumstances, no wonder that despite her passion for Jemy, Moll responds eagerly to the banker's continuous opportunings and marries him with vast relief, thinking she is settled pleasurably and safely for life. And no wonder, then, that his death casts her into profound depression.

As we might expect, Moll dwells on her "dismal condition" primarily in financial terms. Yet the most convincing proof of the seriousness of her distress, marking it off from all the setbacks that have intervened since her first major illness, is what she does *not* say: she does *not* tally up her assets, a recurrent ritual here conspicuous by its absence. She alludes to this omission by confessing that her fears outstripped reality, that her actual capital exceeded her fancied perception of it, and that she only aggravated her financial condition by allowing her fears to paralyse her. But her exceptional misery *is* warranted: she ends this marriage with less capital than ever before and she has literally no prospect of maintaining or increasing it. She has come to the close of the only career society has allowed her.

Together with the loss of her financial dowry, Moll has lost her sexual endowments—her ability to bear children and her attractiveness. All her marketable assets have gone, and she naturally becomes extremely anxious about her future. However uninterested she is in her children as persons, her ability to create them has given her her main value in the eyes of society. The loss of this immensely significant role naturally causes an immense loss of self-esteem. The immediate strain she has suffered tending her husband in his decline has accelerated the natural process of aging, and she suffers not only a financial crisis, but a crisis of self-confidence. These biological processes affect many women in much the same way. For the underlying cause of Moll's depression is surely her inevitable involvement in the female condition: Moll is undergoing her climacterium.

There is considerable controversy in current psychosexual research concerning the extent to which climacteric depression is the result of physiological change or of cultural conditioning, and whether traditionally-oriented women or women discontented with their feminine role are likely to suffer more severely.[26] Whatever the balance of causes, there is general agreement that depression is unquestionably a normal fate of women during this stage in their aging process. According to Helene Deutsch, "almost every woman in the climacterium goes through a shorter or longer phase of depression." [27] Although some men may also suffer middle-age depression, they do not as a group experience the loss of biosexual function and attractiveness and the loss of cultural value so absolutely nor respond to it so acutely as the generality of women.[28]

The two writers of classic psychosexual studies of the climacterium, Helene Deutsch and Therese Benedek, agree upon two tendencies often accompanying responses to the climacterium that have special bearing upon Moll's experience. The first is that a woman's manner of reacting to her climacterium is likely to manifest itself as a more exaggerated version of a life-long pattern.[29] That is, women who have earlier responded to their female role with depression or psychosomatic illness will respond to the onset of their climacterium in a similar but more intense form. Moll's two-year period of intense distress is therefore grounded in psychological probability. It is not mere fictional license or a lazy way of transporting her to the age of fifty. The second relevant point of agreement is that women respond to the end of their climacteric experience with a sense of relief and release that often takes the form of a drastic and even incongruous change in their life styles, interests, and behavior.[30] This finding suggests an important reason for Moll's entry into her criminal career. Economic motives play a large role in spurring her on in this career, but as is evident from her own perplexity about why she continues to steal once her financial prosperity is assured, they do not wholly ex-

plain her behavior. Her criminal expertise provides her with intellectual and emotional satisfaction, a sense of achievement, and constant stimulation; she has found compensation for the loss of her
roles as wife and mother, roles now denied to her by society and
biology.[31]

The particular details of Moll's criminal career are not especially relevant to the question of her femininity. On the other
hand, none of her exploits or attitudes is inconsistent with her female role. She harbors no grudge against society, and accepts her
difficulties without bitterness. Ian Watt is correct in saying that
Moll rarely displays the characteristics of a criminal, for she sees
herself not as an outcast but as a successful career woman, finding
gratification in a new and challenging role. Her professionalism
is thoroughgoing: she passes through a nervous apprenticeship
period, then a period when she refines upon her teachers and
learns to specialize, and finally becomes a "mastercraftsman." Her
thieving career provides her with a truly absorbing activity and
a reliable protector, as her earlier years had not. Moll's change of
life commences with a shattering confluence of difficulties deeply
rooted in the female condition, to which she, in common with
many other women, responds first with paralysing depression, followed by relief, release, and the start of a new life.

THE BEST YEARS OF HER LIFE

Moll's criminal career comes to an abrupt close with her entry
into Newgate prison. Her torpor in Newgate is readily understandable. She has arrived at the most absolute of the seeming
impasses that had occasioned her earlier illnesses. On this occasion,
her crisis has a religious context; it appears to represent the hard-
ness of heart that precedes her confession, her experience of "secret
surprising joy," and her spiritual repentance. Yet she describes her
state "of the compleatest misery on earth" in terms very reminis-
cent of her earlier withdrawals into extreme passivity: "I degen-
erated into stone . . . a certain strange lethargy of soul possess'd
me; I had no trouble, no apprehensions, no sorrow about me, the
first surprise was gone. I was, I may well say, I know not how;
my senses, my reason, nay, my conscience, were all asleep" (pp.
242–243). This "strange lethargy of soul" must be seen as a significant part of a lifelong pattern.

This crisis is most interesting not for its symptoms but because of the manner of Moll's recovery. During the period when she is still unrepentant, a significant event rouses her from her lethargy —not a religious experience but the reappearance of Jemy, her highwayman-husband. Moll reiterates its effect four times: "In the middle of this harden'd part of my life, I had another sudden surprize, which call'd me back a little to that thing call'd sorrow, which, indeed, I began to be past the sense of before.... Nothing could express the amazement and surprize I was in, when the first man that came out I knew to be my Lancashire husband.... I was struck dumb at the sight.... The surprize of this thing only struck deeper in my thoughts, and gave me stronger reflections than all that had befallen me before" (pp. 244–245). This experience re-vivifies Moll: "in a word, I was perfectly chang'd, and became another body" (p. 245). In comparison with *this* "secret, sur-prizing joy," Moll's subsequent description of her religious pen-itence is secondary and pallid.

Moll ascribes her rebirth to her sense of having been the oc-casion of Jemy's criminal career and capture: "This gentleman's misfortunes I plac'd all to my own account" (p. 244); "I was overwhelm'd with grief for him; my own case gave me no dis-turbance compar'd to this, and I loaded myself with reproaches on his account" (p. 245). Moll's penitent love for Jemy is the foundation for her recovery. To notice this is to see the episode as an organic part of the narrative. Interpreted this way, it also makes the characterization of Moll at this point more convincing, and indeed more feminine. Receptivity to the softening effects of love is by no means exclusively a feminine trait. However, the de-tails Moll provides serve to remind us of her capacity for love and tenderness, and they remind us too of the passionate attachments she has had to her first seducer, to her Bath gentleman, and espe-cially to the younger Jemy. Coming at a crucial point in her life, this experience reawakens latent tendencies which her struggle to conform to the role society demanded of her required that she suppress.

Moll's experience of renewal brings with it her capacity for practical action, and the subsequent scenes show her rallying Jemy from *his* lethargy, making arrangements for their comfort-able passage to America, and providing the conditions for their successful experience as "new people in a new world" (p. 264).

Her final American experience is the crowning happiness of her life. She has found an exciting, socially desirable, and rewarding outlet for her energies, talents, and feelings. Her earlier matrimonial career was uncertain and restrictive, her criminal career morally distressing and dangerous; neither fully satisfied her. Not at all unaware of Jemy's weaknesses, she displays tenderness, trust, and generosity towards him. She is indeed positively uxorious. In her old age, Moll reaches the culmination of her fortunes. If this is a sentimental conclusion, it is also one that is psychologically credible and satisfying, both in relation to her past experiences and to her consistently feminine behavior.

Moll's improbably crowded and sensational career has tended to obscure the ways in which her behavior, aspirations, and responses are consonant with and explicable by attention to the nature and limitations of the conventional female role. No woman typically runs through five husbands, several colorful careers, and a miscellany of adventures that includes living with gypsies, committing incest, bearing innumerable children, and suffering many financial disasters, and yet manages to live happily ever after and tell her tale with great aplomb. Strict conformity to matters of fact and to notions of genteel propriety would have required that any one of these sets of experiences consign Moll to bitterness, genteel poverty, ruin, or death—and the result would have been a tragic story, or more probably none at all. Hindsight should allow us to see that Defoe has romanticized the details of Moll's life and the degree to which good fortune attended it, but has sympathetically and convincingly rendered the underlying actualities of women's role. As Virginia Woolf writes, "Whatever his ideas upon the position of women, they are an incidental result of his chief virtue, which is that he deals with the important and lasting side of things and not with the passing and trivial." [32] Moll's stubborn instinct for self-preservation manifests itself not in freedom from the requirements of the female role but in refusal to give way to the depressing consequences that too often surround it. She never willingly seeks adventures; all of them are thrust upon her by the necessities of her condition. Her ability to weather her crises with stamina, perseverance, and buoyancy is, in itself, a tribute to the very femininity—unglamorous but not inglorious—that modern readers deny her.

Richardson's Empathy with Women

KATHERINE ROGERS

I

Samuel Richardson has long been recognized as a writer sympathetic to women—expressing their feelings and point of view, defending their rights in a male-dominated society. He not only defended women in a general way, but systematically refuted the charges commonly made against them, such as that intellectual women show off and domineer—sometimes by direct argument, sometimes by attributing antifeminist opinions to fools or villains.

Genuinely convinced that women's minds were as worthy of development as men's, Richardson praised qualities that most of his contemporaries either could not see or did not value in women. Unique in his time, he represented women as autonomous beings rather than appendages to fathers, brothers, lovers, or husbands. His defense of women against exploitation appears indirectly in his penetrating exposure of male chauvinism, in the books in which he dissected not only obviously criminal oppression of women, but the oppression which was conventionally accepted in his society. His views began to emerge as he modified traditional romance in *Pamela* (though in Part I she *is* primarily a sex object), find full expression in *Clarissa*, and remain conspicuous even in the more conventional *Sir Charles Grandison*.

© 1976 by *Novel Corporation*. This article originally appeared under the title "Sensitive Feminism vs. Conventional Sympathy: Richardson and Fielding on Women," in *Novel*, vol. 9, no. 3, Spring 1976, pp. 256–270.

Richardson's radicalism can be most fully appreciated if we contrast him with Henry Fielding, whose loving presentation of romantic heroines is conditioned by the antifeminist prejudices of his time. Both writers, reflecting the increasingly middle-class sensibility of the eighteenth century, emphasized the sacredness of marriage and insisted that it be based upon love and mutual respect. Reacting against Restoration licentiousness, they condemned men who seduced or brutally exploited women and they repudiated the cruder reductions of women to sexual objects. Fielding condemned those who regarded a beautiful woman as prey or meat. They opposed the libertine view that men lose by marriage, and discountenanced the double standard, though Fielding was not very convincing on this point. They insisted that men should treat all women with consideration, and their wives as companions. They found fortitude, good sense, and generosity in women as well as men, and emphasized the importance of mental qualities over mere physical beauty.

On the other hand, both men accepted some of the limitations placed upon women by bourgeois marriage and family structure. They overemphasized women's chastity as a priceless possession which must be guarded at all costs and elaborately fenced in by "delicacy." Their insistence that women be considered had its traditional unfortunate corollary that women must be protected because they are weak; and accordingly, their heroines faint and totter too frequently for modern taste. Above all, both Fielding and Richardson accepted the hierarchical structure of the eighteenth-century family, which required women to obey parents and husbands. Fielding's Sophia and Amelia are quite as submissive as Richardson's Clarissa, though this is not so apparent because they do not talk about their feelings so much.

Nevertheless, while Richardson was a radical feminist, Fielding accepted the male chauvinism of his culture. Richardson responded to the new sensibility about women by probing traditional assumptions about male-female relationships: if a woman is not to be regarded as sexual prey, perhaps she exists as a human individual apart from her sexuality; if marriage is to be more than a mercenary contract for the propagation of lawful children, perhaps it should be a partnership between equals. Fielding, on the other hand, incorporated the new sensibility into the old system of male dominance, so that his views remained entirely conventional. Though his humane disposition made him unusually sympathetic to loose girls and errant wives, it did not prompt him to apply the same standards to men and women.

Richardson's rigid legalism and stricter attitude toward sexual indulgence might be expected to entail a more repressive attitude toward women than Fielding's generous exuberance, and it is true that Fielding's good women, like his good men, act from spontaneous good nature rather than obedience to law. But actually their good nature expresses itself in a love for their men which is not free but submissive. Fielding's heroines want to submit to husbands and fathers without question and without limit. Sophia Western's love for her father, selfish brute that he is, makes obedience to him "not only easy, but ... delightful" and almost disables her from refusing him anything. Clarissa and Harriet Byron also find it hard to resist the voice of authority, but both they and Richardson recognize this as a weakness resulting from the compliance trained into women.[1]

Richardson's heroines are obligated not by feeling but by moral law. Because their motive is conscious, it is subject to rational evaluation and, therefore, questioning. Thus Clarissa is free to suggest that the subordination of wife to husband might be derived from human self-interest as well as God's ordinance and/or the natural inferiority of women: "the men were the framers of the Matrimonial Office, and made *obedience* a part of the woman's vow" (I, 292). The more outspoken Anna Howe calls this "that little piddling part of the marriage-vow which some Prerogative-monger foisted into the office, to make That a *duty*, which he knew was not a *right*" (II, 150).

Thinking in terms of moral law rather than unmeasurable love, Richardson imposed definite limits on a wife's obedience, though these limits are of course much wider than modern ones. The total submissiveness of Clarissa's mother, especially in view of her superior sensitivity and judgment, is presented as a sign of weakness rather than virtue, and is shown to be self-defeating: instead of influencing through meek expostulations (as wives were exhorted to do), she fails to influence at all; and she does not even buy domestic peace. Her compliance is also immoral, for in obeying her husband she fails in her duty to her daughter. As Anna rightly exhorts Clarissa, "Justice is due to ourselves, as well as to every-body else" (II, 9).

Good marriages in Richardson are never as oppressive to the wife as the marriage of Fielding's Amelia is to her. Lord L. in *Sir Charles Grandison* does not exert his legal right to control the family property; instead, he and his wife pool and spend their money on a completely equal basis (III, 374). Sir Charles assures Harriet that he will take no important step without her advice and invites her to blame him if she thinks him wrong: "I shall doubt your Love, if you give me reason to question your freedom" (VI, 87, 140). Admittedly, the fact that he never is wrong lessens the significance of this concession.

Richardson recognized the stresses of marriage, even a good marriage between two virtuous people. As Anna says, "*Men*, no more than *women*, know how to make a moderate use of power. ...All the animals in the creation are more or less in a state of hostility with each other" (III, 230). It would be nice to think that love could dissolve this hostility, but it can do so only by suppressing the interests of one partner. Booth loves Amelia, but he also exploits and oppresses her. What Richardson suggests is a system of mutual concessions and obligations, anticipating the contracts coming into use between married people today. Anna suggests that a couple should agree on boundaries "beyond which neither should go: And each should hold the other to it; or there would probably be encroachments in both" (II, 149).

Let us contrast this balance of powers with Fielding's most detailed presentation of a good marriage: that of the Booths in *Amelia*. Booth does love Amelia dearly and admire her virtues, but that is the extent of his contribution to their relationship. While Booth diverts himself outdoors, Amelia stays home to prepare comforts for him with the inadequate means he provides. Though she is desolate at the thought of his departure on overseas duty, she soon reproaches herself for wanting him with her during her first childbirth: "I perceive clearly now that I was only wishing to support my own weakness with your strength, and to relieve my own pains at the price of yours" (I, 109).

While Amelia is denying tarts to her children and a glass of wine to herself in order to save sixpence, Booth is gambling away sixty-two pounds. Yet she begs him not to worry about "the trifle" he has lost, cheerfully pawns her clothes and the children's toys, and hands over the total proceeds to him. Despite his demonstrated incompetence, she "would not presume to advise him" on financial matters (III, 102–103, 158, 161). While Amelia constantly worries about preserving her chastity for Booth and finds the attention of any other man "highly disagreeable," he enjoys an affair with Miss Matthews. Yet when he indulges in jealous outbursts against her, she falls on her knees and pleads. Nevertheless, she is convinced that Booth has "made her the happiest of women" (III, 242).

Richardson would never have shown this one-sided relationship as ideal. Instead, he pointedly discredited such by attributing a similar conception of the ideal relationship between man and woman to an obviously sadistic oppressor of women, Lovelace. Richardson's detailed portrait of Lovelace focuses attention on what men do to women, and his convincing blend of overt sadism with conventionally accepted views brings out the hostility and contempt for women in the culture as a whole.

Lovelace shies away from marriage because he feels it gives a woman too many rights, but actually the "life of honor" he describes is unpleasantly like the romantic marriage idealized by Fielding. Lovelace would have his woman "governed in her behaviour to me by Love," not "by Generosity merely, or by blind Duty . . . I would have her look after me when I go out, as far as she can see me . . . and meet me at my return with rapture. I would be the subject of her dreams, as well as of her waking thoughts. I would have her think every moment lost, that is not passed with me. . . . When I should be inclined to Love, overwhelm me with it; when to be serious or solitary . . . retiring at a nod" (IV, 264). Only in the "life of honor" does Lovelace feel confident that a woman will defend herself in an argument solely with "expostulatory meekness, and gentle reasoning, mingled with sighs as gentle, and graced with bent knees, supplicating hands, and eyes lifted up to your imperial countenance." But this libertine cloaks his tyranny with the respectable patriarchal rationalization of his time: by dutifully submitting to her man, especially when he is wrong, a woman will come to deserve his "high opinion . . . of her prudence and obligingness—And so, by degrees, she will become her master's master" (IV, 235–236).

Only the phrasing makes this passage more sadistic than the sober advice on wifely conduct offered by such moral works as *The Ladies Calling*. Moreover, what Richardson presents as the wishful fantasy of a sadist is markedly similar to what Fielding presents as the behavior of the ideal wife. Amelia becomes "her master's master" in the way that Lovelace recommends, and she is as self-abnegating as Lovelace would like Clarissa to be; the only difference is that Booth enjoys these delights in marriage. She gives him the ultimate gratification of being totally dependent on him for her happiness, while making no demands on him.

Lovelace feels justified in making exorbitant demands on women because he assumes that the woman a man loves is his property, existing as the object of his erotic desire rather than as a human being like himself, and that her only fulfillment is marriage to him. He constantly uses expressions like "this prime Gift, WOMAN" and minimizes his guilt on the grounds that he has invaded no one's property in raping Clarissa: "Have not those who have a right in her, renounced that right? . . . is she not a *Single woman?*" (III, 241, IV, 377). Besides, he can always wipe out his crime by marrying her, since if she becomes his wife, "whom but myself shall I have injured?" (IV, 217). That a woman could be her own property or have her own honor, simply does not occur to him. Similarly, when he considers raping Anna, his only qualm is about the injury he would do to Hickman (V, 49). Though Lovelace states these views with unusual openness, they are implicit in his whole culture and evident in such apparently sympathetic writers as Fielding.

For example, Tom Jones refrains from courting Sophia not for her sake, but for her father's: it would be "robbing him of his whole fortune, and of his child into the bargain" (I, 161). The highest happiness Fielding can conceive is "the possession of such a woman as Sophia" (IV, 306). Adultery is, according to virtuous Dr. Harrison, "robbing" a man "of that property, which, if he is a good man, he values above all others" (*Amelia*, III, 75). Amelia values her chastity for the sake of *Booth's* honor (III, 107), and Mrs. Heartfree was "resolutely bent to preserve myself pure and entire for the best of husbands" (*Jonathan Wild*, 215).

It is easier to consider a woman a piece of property if one sees her primarily as a sex object, as Fielding, with all his professed admiration for women's minds, did tend to do. Not only are his heroines objects of interest because they are in love with some man, but it is implied that physical violation would ruin them completely, even (or especially?) in the eyes of the men who so passionately love them. When Fanny is abducted by a squire,

Joseph Andrews' anguish that the woman he prizes will be spoiled is at least as evident as his sympathy for her sufferings. Adams seems to agree that Fanny is permanently "lost," that physical violation would destroy her innocence and therefore her worth (II, 96–97). Similarly, if Lord Fellamar had succeeded in raping Sophia, this undeserved misfortune would have "for ever destroyed" "the peace of her mind" (IV, 73). Moreover, one is to assume that in this case she would have been forced to marry Fellamar because Tom would not have had her.

In refreshing contrast, Richardson proved in *Clarissa* that a woman's sexual condition does not define her moral status. Clarissa loses her virginity, but she retains her chastity; having preserved what counts, her mental integrity, she can die morally triumphant. She rejects with scorn the marriage to Lovelace that her society considered reparation for his wrong: she will not subject her mind to a man because he has had her body, merely to improve her social and legal status. By having Wyerly renew his proposal, Richardson makes clear that—contrary to conventional thought at the time—Clarissa remains an eligible bride. It is only a villain like Lovelace who can see nothing in a woman but her body, who believes that once a woman's body is violated she has no integrity left and will be "always subdued." The connection between devaluing women and regarding them as sex objects is explicitly drawn by Harriet Byron in *Grandison*: "what can give more importance" to men and less to women? To overestimate the importance of a woman's body reduces her to an object existing for man's gratification; to value her mind makes her a human being in her own right (I, 19–20).

Since Lovelace is so obsessed with Clarissa as a sexual object that he cannot see her as a human being like himself, he never does understand what he has done to her. Lacking respect for her mind, he cannot see that his violation of her will and self-respect was more significant than that of her body; therefore he cannot see why she will not accept a marriage which would cover up the physical violation while laying her under mental subjection for life. Unable to recognize her mental independence, he expects her to respond automatically to his "love." Because he assumes that women are not entitled to the rights of men, Lovelace cannot see that a woman has a *right* to be treated decently, and thus expects

Clarissa to be grateful if he should do her the poor justice of offering marriage (IV, 20).

Richardson indignantly demonstrated in *Clarissa* that Lovelace's society, despite its professed chivalry, tacitly supported his claim to take Clarissa, by marriage if not by rape, because he wanted her. The honorable Colonel Morden praises Lovelace's generosity in offering to marry Clarissa in exchange for having deceived, bullied, and (as he thinks) seduced her (VII, 355–357). Lovelace's whole society concurs in belittling wrongs done to women. Knowing that he has treated a worthy woman abominably, all the guests at a party still accept Lovelace; he is perfectly at ease while Anna, his victim's friend, is embarrassed. It is ironic that, but for the chance that Clarissa has a cousin who is a better swordsman, Lovelace would escape scot free after having ruined her life. It is even more ironic that everything he does to her—including imprisonment and rape—would be legally and, in conventional eyes, morally justified had she been his wife (VI, 68).

If women are considered the sexual property of men, the highest end of their existence must be marriage. Hence, regardless of Clarissa's superiority to him, regardless of the appalling way he has treated her and the selfishness he intends after marriage, Lovelace is convinced that he will be doing her a favor to propose—a conviction which Richardson made a point of attacking (VI, 408, 454–455, VIII, 307). Lovelace is equally convinced that he will be sacrificing his "liberty" in submitting to the "shackles" of marriage (III, 87, 95), despite the fact that he has every intention of continuing to behave as he likes. His assurance that it is women who gain and men who lose by marriage, unsubstantiated by logic, is amply supported by popular jokes and literary stereotypes of his time and ours.[2]

II

Women's alleged need for marriage rests on the assumption that they have no satisfying alternative to centering their lives on a man. Lovelace is sincerely convinced that woman is a feminine earth, dreary and desolate unless shone upon by a male sun (IV, 245). Women must depend on men for their significant relationships, he says, for friendship between women is merely a shuttlecock, "which they are fond of striking to and fro, to make one another glow in the frosty weather of a Single State; but which, when a *man* comes in between the pretended *inseparables* is given up." Moreover, it "never holds to the sacrifice of capital gratifications, or to the endangering of life, limb, or estate, as it often does in our nobler Sex" (V, 274–275). Many men have claimed that women are incapable of friendship, at least within their own sex, because women cannot really care when there is no biological attachment and because their friendships are corrupted by competition for male approval. At best, it is said, female friendship is a stopgap until marriage; at worst, a thin disguise for petty rivalry over men. Through Lovelace's version, Richardson exposes the contempt for women which underlies this traditional charge.

Richardson disproved Lovelace's illusion that women cannot be happy without men by showing them enjoying life independently and by suggesting that they may have more to lose than to gain by marriage. He focused in *Clarissa* upon the friendship between the heroine and Anna, as well as filling Part II of *Pamela* and *Sir Charles Grandison* with similar friendships between women attracted by each other's minds and uninfluenced by jealousy over men. His emphasis upon such friendships is perhaps the most distinctive sign of his ability to see the world from a woman's point of view. It is the hallmark which Virginia Woolf singled out in *A Room of One's Own*, though she failed to mention that, long before twentieth-century women authors, Richardson had presented women in relation to each other rather than to men.[3]

The friendship between Clarissa and Anna is plainly the most significant and satisfying relationship in either woman's life. It is free of petty rivalry, for Anna admires Clarissa without envy, and illustrates in her reaction to her friend's troubles the reckless generosity which was conventionally restricted to the "nobler Sex." Disproving Lovelace's sneer, she is ready to jeopardize her reputation for Clarissa's sake—as important a sacrifice as an eighteenth-century lady could make: if Hickman should reject her for going to London with the disgraced Clarissa, so much the worse for him (II, 306). Instead of fleeing from a woman of damaged reputation, as well-conducted ladies were supposed to do and as Sophia Western does from Mrs. Fitzpatrick, the unmistakably virtuous Anna is all the more eager to be with her friend.

So sufficient is their friendship, and so occupied their minds, that Anna and Clarissa both claim with obvious sincerity that they would prefer not to marry. Their repeated preference for the single life is not the thin rationalization for compulsory spinsterhood which it traditionally has been in literature, for both of them are very desirable women with eligible suitors.

Clarissa longs to settle in a single life, in which she could "defy the Sex. For I see nothing but trouble and vexation that they bring upon ours"; married, "one is obliged to go on with them, treading ... upon thorns, and sharper thorns, to the end of a painful journey" (II, 314). This is the kind of thing that, traditionally, men have said about women. Both she and Anna realize what was and is obvious enough, but has not been generally recognized until recent times: that often women give more than they get in marriage. Anna deflates courtship as a state in which women are "courted as Princesses for a few weeks, in order to be treated as Slaves for the rest of our lives" (I, 191). Clarissa elaborates more moderately on what a woman loses in marriage: "To give up her very Name, as a mark of becoming his absolute and dependent property; To be obliged to prefer this strange man['s] ... humours to all her own—Or to contend perhaps, in breach of a vowed duty, for every innocent instance of free-will—To go nowhither; To make acquaintance; To give up acquaintance; To renounce even the strictest friendships perhaps; all at his pleasure, whether she thinks it reasonable to do so or not" (I, 223). As to the argument that women require men's protection, Clarissa says it is their "way of training-up" rather than their natural weakness which makes them "need the protection of the brave"; and Anna adds that in marriage "this brave man will free us from all insults but ... His own!" (II, 150). Finally, Anna exposes the fundamental flaw in traditional patriarchal marriage by pointing out that there is not one man in a hundred "whom a woman of sense and spirit can either *honour* or *obey*, tho' you make us promise *both*, in that solemn form of words which unites or rather *binds* us to you in marriage" (VIII, 198).

Marriage even to a paragon like Sir Charles Grandison involves some sacrifice of a woman's interests, as his sister explains: "Her name sunk, and lost! The property, person and will, of another, excellent as the man is." She goes on, like Sue Bridehead in Hardy's *Jude the Obscure*, to compare brides dressed up in their wedding finery to "milk-white heifers led to sacrifice" (V, 393, 395). In Fielding it is only the whorish Lady Bellaston and the adulterous peer who cast aspersions upon "the matrimonial institution itself, and at the unjust powers given by it to man over the more sensible, and more meritorious part of the species" (III, 105, IV, 102–103).

Even when Richardson's women want to marry, they are neither eager nor passive. Harriet Byron ridicules Sir Hargrave's complacent assurance that no woman can resist a rich, handsome man who offers her marriage. She thinks a woman should wait until she is twenty-four, so that she can make a reasoned choice (I, 163), as does Sir Charles Grandison, who wants Emily to have an opportunity to "look round her, and make her own choice" (VI, 140). Instead of waiting until she "fulfills her destiny" by falling in love, Harriet coolly considers what qualities she wants in a husband, what qualities will make marriage worth while for her (I, 164). If these are not forthcoming, she would rather not marry; for, though she is well aware of the blessing she has in Sir Charles, she does not share the general opinion "of the dreariness, and disadvantages of a single state: on the contrary," she thinks "the married life attended with so many cares and troubles, that it is rather . . . a kind of faulty *indulgence* . . . to live single" (VI, 244).

Sir Charles Grandison contains several long discussions of the advantages and disadvantages of spinsterhood, remarkable for Richardson's recognition that this subject was worth discussing, for the enlightened thoughtfulness of his consideration, and for his conclusion that many women are better off unmarried. How these contrast with the dehumanized stereotype of the old maid so familiar from Fielding and other novelists. "If no *proper* match ever offers," would it not be stupid "to take an *improper* one, to avoid the ridicule of a mere name? An *unsupported state* is better than an *oppressed*, a *miserable* one" (VI, 228). Through Harriet, Richardson points out that ridiculing old maids confirms the supremacy of men: by deriding single women, men make women dependent on them for the approval which ultimately leads to proposals of marriage (V, 14).

Constantly affirming women's capacity and desire to be independent, Richardson developed in Clarissa the tragic conflict between this potential and the patriarchal society which systematically repressed it. Driven from home by her need to protect her freedom, Clarissa is then subjected to relentless pressure from Lovelace—culminating in the rape—to acknowledge dependence on him.[4] Although she does manage to defeat him morally, the price she pays shows that society would not allow a woman to live independently.

Clarissa is not even allowed to feel independently, for her family insists that, if her heart is free, she can have no good reason to withhold it from Solmes. Only love for a man could "make a creature late so dutiful, now so sturdy" (I, 150); it is unthinkable that she could be resolute without support from attachment to some man. Similarly, the foolish Sir Hargrave in *Grandison* cannot believe that Harriet can reject his proposal when she is not engaged to someone else.

In striking contrast, every one of Fielding's amiable women is emotionally dependent on a man and derives strength from her love for him. When a demonstrative outburst from her father so affects Sophia's "dutiful, grateful, tender and affectionate heart" that she almost agrees to marry Blifil, she is saved only by her word of honor given to Tom and her love for him (IV, 230). However, the freely flowing feelings of Fielding's characters are a sign of freedom only in his men. While the Richardsonian heroine stands as an individual who has at least the potentiality for self-determination, all Fielding's good women are dependent upon masculine approval and love.

In fact, they exist only to serve the men they live with. Sophia's greatest pleasure, before she falls in love, is playing her drunken father to sleep, and Amelia is not "capable of any sensation worthy the name of pleasure" when neither her husband nor her children are present (I, 224). Heartfree in *Jonathan Wild* is rewarded with a daughter who has refused several matches so that "no other duty should interfere with that which she owed the best of fathers, nor prevent her from being the nurse of his old age" (238). Clarissa and Anna, on the other hand, think of the single life as one in which they can fulfill themselves while also fulfilling their obligations to others.

III

Richardson's women can think of fulfilling themselves because they have the same capacities as men. While his views on women's minds and education represented enlightened feminist opinion in his time,[5] his emphasis on the intellectual capacity of women shows unusual commitment. He populated his novels with articulate women who are equal or superior to their male counterparts: Pamela excels both Parson Williams and Mr. B. in ready wit and sound judgment; Clarissa holds her own with the brilliant Lovelace; Anna and Charlotte Grandison are more intelligent than their suitors.

In addition to general criticism of contemporary education, as doing all it could to restrict the intellectual development of girls, Richardson explicitly challenged the entrenched contemporary assumptions that the knowledge of Greek and Latin was what constituted an educated person, qualified to discuss intellectual topics with other educated people; and that this knowledge was a male prerogative. Fielding, accepting these assumptions, has his single female Latin scholar make blunders, and explains that, though a soldier does not need Latin, Booth has been taught it so he should not be a blockhead. For a man like Fielding, the fact that women did not know the classical languages meant that they could never be considered learned and could never talk with educated men as equals.

Richardson combatted this idea by making both Pamela and Clarissa learn Latin and, more radically, by suggesting that one could be an educated person without knowing it. Anna points out the narrowness of men who glory in their superior knowledge of the classics, which they have only because they had educational opportunities from which women were debarred, and satirizes the university graduate who disdainfully smiles "at a mistaken or ill-pronounced *word* from a Lady, when her *sense* has been clear, and her sentiments just; and when he could not himself utter a single sentence fit to be repeated, but what he borrowed from the authors he had been obliged to study" (VIII, 240).[6] In *Grandison*, Harriet and another woman show up such a one as a conceited ass. The man can answer them only with sneers at women's intelligence (I, 69, 71–72, 81).

But the most impressive evidence of Richardson's respect for women's minds appears indirectly in the amount of space he devoted to reporting their discussions of general questions. Clearly he wanted to make the point that women were qualified to consider any topic and that their ideas were worth hearing. He explicitly justified women in having and voicing opinions by the rule which Harriet's grandfather gave her: "Not impertinently to start subjects, as if I would make an ostentation of knowledge; or as if I were fond of indulging a talking humour," but to respond frankly when called upon to give her "sentiments upon any subject" (I, 20). Fielding, in contrast, singled out as a particular excellence Sophia's refusal to express an opinion, even when pressed to do so by Allworthy, Thwackum, and Square. There is no indication in his novels that women can, or if they are good want to, participate in anything like intellectual conversation. When they must defend themselves, Fielding's heroines eschew argument for tears and pleading. It is only his anti-heroine, Shamela, who holds her own with Mr. Booby in abusive argument and reads theology with her lover, Parson Williams.

Fielding's intellectual women are ignorant, conceited, objectionably self-assertive, and unchaste.[7] Fluent Mrs. Fitzpatrick, who is eloping from her husband, declares that women are as intelligent as men. She makes many complaints of her husband's stupidity, to which Sophia pointedly fails to respond. When she exhorts Sophia to make sure that the man she marries will be able to tolerate superior intelligence in his wife, Sophia primly replies: "I shall never marry a man in whose understanding I see any defects before marriage; and I promise you I would rather give up my own, than see any such afterwards" (III, 90). Contrast with this smug evasion Harriet's justification of Charlotte Grandison's disrespect for Lord G: "What can a woman do, who is addressed by a man of talents inferior to her own? Must she throw away her talents? Must she hide her light under a bushel, purely to do credit to the man? . . . it is said, Women . . . must encourage Men of Sense only. . . . But what will they do, if their lot be cast only among Foplings? If the Men of Sense do not offer themselves?" (I, 352).

Fielding, like his Squire Allworthy, assumed that a woman's judgment is crippled by her lack of a man's experience and that one who has and expresses opinions is necessarily dictatorial and immodest. Richardson would not have conceded either point.

Clarissa presented her opinions so modestly that her elders could not be hurt by her superior judgment (IV, 65). Richardson took pains to distinguish between independent, intellectual women and objectionably unfeminine ones. Self-willed Anna Howe contrasts herself with a busybody who constantly manages everything in the house, including her husband (III, 206–207). Articulate Harriet satirizes a Miss Bramber who erred by being obviously "*eager to talk*" (I, 20).

Since another common charge against intellectual women is that they neglect their homes and families, Richardson insisted that Clarissa, Anna, and Harriet were skilled in housewifery, though he did not glorify domestic pursuits. While Fielding finds Amelia at her most amiable when she is cooking a simple supper for her husband (III, 178), Richardson's Mr. B. would rather see Pamela improving her mind than doing routine baby-tending: he would rather hear her "read her *French* and *Latin* Lessons" than see her "ingross'd by those Baby Offices, which will better befit weaker Minds" (IV, 14).

Richardson's intelligent women, aware of their superiority to the average man, are free of that awe of the masculine mind which Fielding considered appropriate. In contrast to Mr. Allworthy, who asserts that "the highest deference to the understandings of men" is "a quality, absolutely essential to the making a good wife" (IV, 182), Sir Charles Grandison says that such submission is necessary to the happiness only "of common minds" (VI, 143).[8] Polly Darnford in *Pamela*, a good woman, knows that if she marries a stupid man she will oppose his wrong-headed actions and be mortified when he makes a fool of himself in company (IV, 261–262). Even saintly Clarissa could not submerge her understanding as Sophia could, but would have to make heroic efforts to avoid despising a husband intellectually inferior to herself.

Richardson's intelligent women are keenly aware of masculine conceit and enjoy puncturing it. While Sir Hargrave displays his witty gallantry before Harriet, and Mr. Walden repeats lines of Tibullus at her "in an heroic accent," she coolly evaluates both of them (I, 65). She enjoys sniping at "the Lords of the *creation*" (I, 65) and can even criticize the peerless Sir Charles for his patronizing attitude (III, 252–253). Charlotte Grandison openly strips the chivalrous veneer off his disparagement of women. When he pompously claims that "we men should have power and right given us to protect and serve your Sex... and, at last, lay all our trophies... at your feet," she tartly rejoins: "you have concluded with some magnificent intimations of superiority over us—Power and right to protect, travel, toil, for us, and lay your trophies at our feet.... Surely, surely, this is diminishing us, and exalting yourselves, by laying us under high obligations to your generosity" (V, 415–418).

Fielding's heroines, on the other hand, are incapable of seeing any fault in the men they love. Sophia is convinced that callous Squire Western is "the best of fathers" (IV, 141); and Amelia, that her weak, incompetent Booth "is the best, the kindest, the worthiest of all his sex" (II, 65). Infinitely more sensible than he, she claims—and believes—that "though my understanding be much inferior to yours, I have sometimes had the happiness of luckily hitting on some argument which hath afforded you comfort" (I, 212).

Not only did Richardson make his most virtuous female characters independent and critical of men, he also presented sympathetically women who rebel against men and marriage, women who would have been presented by his conventional contemporaries as unruly monsters. Anna Howe is less perfect than her friend Clarissa, but she is right-minded, virtuous, and on the whole amiable. She is not castigated for her insubordination to her narrow-minded mother, her reluctance to marry Hickman, her declaration that she will not blindly obey him after marriage, or her outspoken hostility to men. Her unabashed insubordination lays her open to criticism from Richardson as well, but not severe criticism. After Anna has explained to Belford how hard she will find it to bear the subjection of her will in marriage, his reaction is not that she is presumptuous and selfish, but that her failings, if such they are, are "much more lovely... than the virtues of many of her Sex!" (VIII, 204). Though meekness and gentleness like Clarissa's make Richardson's ideal woman, an active, self-willed person like Anna is superior to a meek, gentle domestic animal.

Anna's ultimate justification is that she does, in fact, make a good wife, and without changing her character. Her marriage is harmonious even though she has not sunk her will in Hickman's: "there is but *one will* between them; and that is generally *his* or *hers*, as either speaks first, upon any subject" (VIII, 301). Lovelace, characteristically, would not have believed this possible; for he is sure that "a directing wife" will not stop until she makes her husband despicable and herself "a plague to all about her" (V, 280).

Actually, Richardson verged on over-indulgence to Anna's persistent teasing of Hickman and undermining of his self-confidence. He seems to have recognized that, behind her conscious motive of hoping to make Hickman release her from her engagement, was a generalized hostility toward man developing from her half-conscious anger against a society which oppressed and exploited women. Richardson sensed that there was a warfare in all sexual relationships in his society, with one group oppressing the other, and thus contrasts with writers like Fielding, who would smother the conflict of interests and the oppression with romance. Anna's attacks on the unoffending Hickman are her unfair but understandable response to the overbearing conceit encouraged in men by a patriarchal society.[9]

One wonders why such an apparently conventional middle-class man as Richardson was so sympathetic to women that he radically criticized social thought and institutions in their interest. One reason may be that he *was* middle class and hence, unlike Fielding, an outsider to privileged London society. For most of his life he had been a tradesman, treated perhaps as Lovelace treats the tradesman at whose house Clarissa boarded. He did not have the education of a gentleman; he did not know Latin and Greek. Thus he was not insulated by the complacency which assures the ruling class that it deserves its privileges because of its innate superiority. He could sympathize with women, other outsiders who were told that it was their duty to respect their superiors and that, because they lacked university education, they were not competent to discuss intellectual things. In *Grandison* Richardson explicitly compared women to men such as merchants, who have not received a classical education (V, 407–408). Knowing that one is oneself the victim of unjust discrimination sharpens one's ability to see unjust discrimination elsewhere.

Richardson was free of the illusions produced by romantic love. His cooler relationships with women enabled him to see them as people rather than as idealized beings radically different from himself; nor could he see himself as the traditional romantic hero with his adored but not quite human love object. The morbid fantasies which contributed so much to Richardson's inspiration may also have led him to question conventional roles by increasing his awareness of the negative elements in men's attitude toward women; certainly they would not reinforce complacency about the sexual status quo.

Richardson did not stress romance in his good marriages, and he showed his intelligent women suspicious of conventional romantic adulation, which they rightly consider to be an insult to their intelligence rather than an indication of true rational friendship.[10] His striking exponent of romantic love is the rake Lovelace, who says that "Love that deserves the name, never was under the dominion of *Prudence*, or of any *reasoning* Power" (V, 284), and glories in emotional outbursts such as "Having lost her, my whole Soul is a blank" (VI, 215). Richardson demonstrates that this "love" is in fact centered on self. Though Lovelace constantly calls Clarissa his "goddess" and "empress," he shows no consideration whatever for her wishes and feelings: to him she is an ideal of his erotic fantasy more than a human being.

Lovelace's romantic exploitation of women is normal in our culture, where the mystique of romantic love has traditionally obscured the true relationship between the sexes, and thus obstructed reform. Fielding surrounded Sophia with a romantic haze which, ostensibly raising her above the human level, actually removes her from consideration in ordinary human terms. Since Amelia and Booth love each other, there can be no discussion of their relative rights and obligations; hence Booth's thorough exploitation of Amelia is not apparent to the characters, to Fielding himself, or to the average reader. In contrast, Richardson, seeing women as people like himself, would not have them submerged by love even in a good marriage. Since the wife remains a separate entity, her interests might sometimes differ from her husband's, and they should not be ignored.

Finally, the particular quality of Richardson's imagination enabled him to identify with women, to see things from their point of view. This identification naturally led to the feminist recognition that women have the same potential as men, the same autonomy, the same needs and legitimate claims to self-realization and self-determination. Though this awareness informed all of his work, and is evident in his personal relationships and letters as well, it appears most unequivocally and forcefully where his imagination was most in control. While *Sir Charles Grandison* abounds with admirably enlightened sentiments; its characters and plot do not fundamentally challenge conventional views. (Sir Charles does emerge as a living justification for male supremacy, and the women, however intelligent, are dependent on his approval and love.) In *Clarissa*, on the other hand, where Richardson was more deeply identified with his characters and they controlled the development of his theme, the reader is compelled to share the struggle of a woman against the society which restricts her development and denies her full humanity.

Jane Eyre: Woman's Estate

MAURIANNE ADAMS

The experience of rereading *Jane Eyre* as an adult is unnerving, to say the least. This is not the novel we were engrossed by in our teens or preteens, when we saw in Jane's dreadful childhood the image of our own fantasies of feeling unloved and forever un- loveable, and of fearing that we were "unpromising" girlchildren, whose lack of beauty and unpredictable tempers cut us off from an imaginable and acceptable future. Perhaps I am writing too per- sonally, but I suspect we share, if only in transient fantasy, an attachment to several girlhood books—*Jane Eyre, The Secret Garden, Sara Crewe,* and the many versions of Cinderella's story —and an attachment to the portrait they convey of the unhappy and mostly secret underside of girlhood. I do not mean to over- darken our early readings of Jane's saga, for the other side of that coin, which we latched onto with equal fervor and which also fed our fantasies, was the happy ending, the relief we felt when this homely and stubborn Cinderella also made good, reunited finally with her loving and understanding Edward Rochester.

The reexperiencing and rethinking of this most important novel unnerves the adult reader, I think, because the elements we retain from earlier memories of Jane interact with our more mature understanding of the enormous complications that beset her diffi- cult, strongly willed and ambivalent development from child to woman. Jane *is* (what most of us "merely" fantasize ourselves to be) an extreme case: she is an unloved, unlovely, unpleasant, poor and dependent orphan child, without prospects, and without a hopeful future. It is this daily and daytime nightmare of childhood burdensomeness and of unwelcome and unrelieved dependence—personal, familial, social, and economic—that haunts Jane's slumbers right up to the eve of her marriage to Rochester. Driving her from Thornfield, it is exorcized only by a full replication of her childhood, through a process that takes her to the breast of "the universal mother" (Jane's words, not mine) on the hard ground at Whitcross, and then to a welcomed and beloved recuperation at Moor House, where she grows from the surrogate younger sister into the financial resource of an entire family of equals—a family, *mirabile dictu,* that turns out to be her true family.

To adapt a Wordsworthian and Freudian adage to literal interpretive purposes, the child Jane is mother to the woman. Her hopes and dreams of a happy adulthood, fed by the generous love of Rochester and the perfect fit of his nature to hers, are nonetheless undermined by her conscious recognition of the disparity in their position and her inevitable reliance upon him for everything—money, status, and family. Her anticipation of her situation as Rochester's wife reactivates an unconscious fear that her childhood experience might now be perpetuated into adult life. The recurrent burdensome children who haunt Jane's nightmares on the evenings preceding the intended nuptials, come, with some comment on her own part as to their portentousness if not their literal application, as a warning from within herself, that this marriage, in these terms, simply will not do. "Gentlemen in his station are not accustomed to marry their governesses," warns Mrs. Fairfax. Accordingly, the sudden emergence of Bertha Mason Rochester from her attic hideaway confirms and verifies what Jane had already feared, that as Rochester's wife she would be but his mistress, a kept woman, without any independent social status. Thus, even without foreseeing Bertha, the careful reader of Chapters 24 and 25 will find that the spectre of unrelieved dependency, however beloved and welcome Jane may feel in her lover's arms, gives urgency to her procrastinations and her efforts to find some other way out. She postpones the inevitable wedding day until she can do so no longer, she looks at her wedding dress and the packed trunks labelled with her new name with fear and trepidation, she feels degraded by Rochester's lavish gifts of jewels and satins, and she writes to her Uncle John in Madeira to track down the unexpected hint of her inheritance: "if I had a prospect of one day bringing Mr. Rochester an accession of fortune, I could better endure to be kept by him now." [1]

Not only does the revelation of Bertha's existence verify Jane's fears, that as a dependent wife she would be little better than a mistress; it also reactivates her fears that as a dependent she might with time become burdensome once again, the tiresome successor of Céline, Giacinta, and Clara, of whom Rochester freely admits, "Hiring a mistress is the next worst thing to buying a slave: both are often by nature, and always by position, inferior: and to live familiarly with inferiors is degrading" (p. 274).

Quite simply stated, Jane Eyre's childhood and her efforts to achieve adult womanhood are characterized by two needs, at times in competition with one another: the one to love and be loved, and the other to be somebody in her own right, a woman of achievement and integrity, with an outlet in the world for her passions and her energies.

The major theme is, I believe, the first of these two, the romantic theme, and the novel concludes in romantic terms, although I might note the forested-in, stagnant and physically oppressive atmosphere at Ferndean. (It was too unhealthy to send Bertha there!) I think that the hemmed-in and darkened visual quality at Ferndean indicates the price exacted by domestic romance, the impossibility of reconciling Jane's desperate need to be loved, to be useful, with her less urgent venturesomeness and independent curiosity.

Necessarily, these two major themes have further complications in Jane's narrative, just as they do often enough for women in real life. The first of these, the romantic theme, has interlocking elements I have commented on already—(1) Jane's need to *be* loved (this, I believe, is a more clearly and urgently articulated force in the novel than her direct experience of loving) as it competes with fears of a life without love and is fed by childhood starvation for love; (2) her causal linking of lovelessness and rejection with the continued experience of economic, social, and personal dependence; (3) her alienation from the social and domestic world around her (Reeds, Brocklehursts, Ingrams, and Eshtons) and her fears that they constitute the *only* world, that she will remain alienated by her lack of beauty and unfeminine traits; (4) her uncontrollable outbursts of mutiny and rage which might afford momentary relief to her integrity and sense of outraged justice but which scarcely endear her to the social superiors whose love and approval she craves; and (5) her explicit differentiation of her "real" family (Reeds are all she knows, until her fortuitous encounter with the Rivers) from her "spiritual" kin (first Helen Burns, later Edward Rochester), a split perpetuated until the happy Moor House resolution of the familial elements— blood, spiritual affinity, economic inheritance and interdependence, even religious persuasion and social status.

The second theme, the desire to *be* somebody, complicates integrity with a drive toward upward mobility. This second theme as it emerges in the novel is uneven and inconsistent, characterized by the sporadic outbursts of mutiny and rage mentioned above, but in every instance undermined by regret, loneliness, and an over-eagerness to serve others as a means of earning their approval and love.

Jane Eyre, like other novels about women, traces the competing and possibly irreconcilable needs for perpetual love and perpetual autonomy. Jane's brief stint as a teacher at Morton constitutes her single experiment in autonomy and independence, but even it is marred by loneliness, and by a sense of personal waste in the rural countryside. Clearly, *Jane Eyre* is a developmental novel, a female *Bildungsroman* as it were, and necessarily the interactions of personal and social roles and dilemmas differ from those of a male developmental novel, as they differ in life experience. *Jane Eyre* presents a girl emerging into womanhood, and it does so in essentially domestic contexts, contexts which nonetheless make severe demands upon Jane's person, integrity, status, family, and financial position.

Rereading *Jane Eyre* I am led inevitably to feminist issues, by which I mean the status and economics of female dependence in marriage, the limited options available to Jane as an outlet for her education and energies, her need to love and to be loved, to be of service and to be needed. These aspirations, the ambivalence expressed by the narrator toward them, and the conflicts among them, are all issues raised by the novel itself and not superimposed upon it by an ideological or doctrinaire reader. Now that the burden of trying to pretend to a totally objective and value-free perspective has finally been lifted from our shoulders, we can all admit, in the simplest possible terms, that our literary insights and perceptions come, in part at least, from our sensitivity to the nuances of our own lives and our observations of other people's lives. Every time we rethink and reassimilate *Jane Eyre*, we bring to it a new orientation. For women critics, this orientation is likely not to focus particular attention upon the dilemmas of the male, to whom male critics have already shown themselves understandably sensitive, but rather to Jane herself and her particular circumstances.

We begin, then, with a nine-year-old child at Gateshead. She sits withdrawn into a window-seat, cut off by a red moreen curtain from the Reed family clustered around the drawing-room hearth. The curtain is a barrier which serves to protect Jane, to isolate her, and to reinforce her identification both with interior space (she daydreams over her book) and with the barren landscape on the other side of the uncurtained windowpane. Only momentarily is she secure in her retreat, where her fantasies take an inward journey through the storm-tossed icy landscapes of Bewick's *History of British Birds* and an outward journey into the wet lawn and storm-blasted shrubbery of the wintry afternoon. This is a paradigmatic situation and is recalled later, when the same details of crimson curtain, window-seat, and book separate Jane at Thornfield from the drawing-room society of Ingrams and Eshtons. Again she is a solitary dependent in a great house, and through an apparent paradox, associates her inner resources with her defenses against the humiliations of social class and estrangement from family life.

Jane's continuing dependence, as a child, a poor relation, a charity schoolgirl, and a governess, is primary and it is explicit: "My first recollections of existence included . . . this reproach of dependence" (p. 10). Her alternatives are retreat and rage. Symptomatically, Jane's outburst of mutinous fury in the opening pages of the book is triggered by John Reed's violation of her sole remaining sanctuary. Jane's protective withdrawal thus is not to be confused with total acquiescence. As she notes subsequently in her narrative: "I know no medium: I never in my life have known any medium in my dealings with positive, hard characters, antagonistic to my own, between absolute submission and determined revolt. I have always faithfully observed the one, up to the very moment of bursting, sometimes with volcanic vehemence, into the other" (p. 342).

It does not require great psychological insight to understand Jane's coping devices and their image-equivalents in the inner and outer landscapes of Jane's fantasy and social worlds. Jane's estrangement from social and familial life is imaged by her protective isolation from domestic interiors, while her spirit is constantly vigilant to search out spiritual affiliation in the outer landscape—she meets both Helen Burns and Edward Rochester outdoors. Both interior and exterior landscapes afford important interpretive clues, and the psychic demarcation of the Gateshead drawing room (where Jane is unwelcome) from the fantasy/natural icy landscapes (with which Jane feels at one) is repeated with careful attention to nuance and detail at Thornfield, where Jane meets with Rochester as kin and equal, beyond the orchard wall, screened in by beech trees and sunken fences. This sequestered world, equivalent in some ways to the earlier window-seat retreat, is now mutually shared. Rochester in these early scenes of awakening love, brings together themes which will drive them temporarily asunder: on the one hand he identifies directly with Jane's alienation from the social world and is seen by her as her spiritual kin, on the other hand he is her vicarious means of access to a status far beyond her own grasp.

The recurrent clues afforded by domestic interiors and external landscapes as to Jane's estrangement or her affinities, serve a further visual purpose. They image in the world of society a retreat and alienation from the adults from whose hands Jane must take her daily bread; this, in personal and psychological terms, has consequences for a far more profound and dangerous dissociation of spirit from flesh. This split is revealed in the recurrent references to Jane as a caged bird, an image by which Jane is seen as simultaneously fettered (to her flesh and to her social position) and free (to her inward fantasy and spiritual space). It is in connection with this dissociation or alienation of Jane's psyche from her position in social space that plain Jane, and symbolic Eyre have special interpretive value.[2] Surely one test of Rochester's affinity is his recognition of Jane's duality, in that he sees her as "a curious sort of bird [seen] through the close-set bars of a cage; ... were it but free, it would soar cloud-high. ... If I tear, if I rend the slight prison, my outrage will only let the captive loose. Conqueror I might be of the house; but the inmate would escape to heaven before I could call myself possessor of its clay dwelling-place" (pp. 122 and 280).

The images suggest that Jane's interaction with Rochester in the initial Thornfield phase of their relationship is in spirit only, dissociated from the alternative examples of social womanhood that surround her, those large and fleshly creatures, her Aunt Reed, Rochester's wife, and his presumptive bride-to-be, Blanche Ingram.

It is significant for later developments in the novel to understand the psychogenesis of the ethereal Jane by tracing it back to her early trauma of extreme ostracism, her incarceration in the Red Room, an episode in which her outburst against John Reed's taunts is followed by solitary confinement and an even more extreme psychic withdrawal. It is as if the sole protective retreat available is her inner and non-corporeal self. The terror haunting the Red Room is not the ghost of her dead uncle, nor the shadows in the garden outside, but the image of Jane's self etherealized in the darkened mirror: "All looked colder and darker in that visionary hollow than in reality: and the strange, little figure there gazing at me, with a white face and arms specking the gloom, and glittering eyes of fear moving where all else was still, had *the effect of a real spirit:* I thought it like *one of the tiny phantoms, half fairy, half imp* ..." (p. 11, emphasis mine).

There is an important psychological process implicit in this mirror image, which is related to the relative absence of overt and explicit sexuality in Jane's relationship with Rochester. Jane has pulled inward, and withdrawn from a physical self occupying social and familial space at Gateshead, into a "placeless" or status and space-free spiritual and moral identity, occupying thin air. Jane withdraws into her imagination and her spiritual integrity, a process by which ego is reduced to its irreducible and invulnerable inner core. Withdrawal, however, is not to be understood as simply negative. Although the elfin and visionary mirror image also presents to Jane an image of terrifying supernaturalism, this effect is the pagan antecedent for Helen Burns's mystic and Christian anticipation of that happy day when the spirit would be freed from the fetters of the flesh. Under the influence of Helen's "doctrine of equality of disembodied souls" (p. 208), Jane's terrifying vision of herself is eventually transmuted by the coeval claims of Christian supernaturalism and human justice. Jane can in the same utterance deny both flesh and the social world defined by the flesh, and thus claim Rochester as her equal, as if she were spirit addressing spirit: "I am not talking to you now through the medium of custom, conventionalities, nor even of mortal flesh—it is my spirit that addresses your spirit; just as if we had both passed through the grave, and we stood at God's feet, equal,—as we are!" (p. 222). If the early vision of herself in the Red Room mirror prepares for a spiritualized or elfin Jane born of the cast-off Jane, it also produces a Jane capable of "charming" Rochester beyond the capacities of a mere Blanche Ingram. Indeed, the inception of their love is perceived through a mutual recognition of spiritual affinity that takes us back to the imagery of the Red Room: Rochester emerges before Jane's astonished gaze as a phantom figure, the "gytrash" of Bessie's evening stories whom Jane had *seen* in the Red Room mirror, while she in turn reminds Rochester "unaccountably of fairy tales" (p. 107). Their early love is characterized in the language of fantasy and folk-tale, and the negative and dispossessed qualities associated with Jane's elfin-self are temporarily driven away by Rochester's fond endearments—she is his "malicious elf," his "sprite" and "changeling," "a fairy, and comes from Elf-land . . . to make me happy; and I must go with it out of the common world to a lonely place—such as the moon, for instance" (p. 235).

In the "both/and" manner Jane's narrative has of pursuing a personal and economic dilemma simultaneously, using the psychic mode of fantasy interchangeably with the social mode of realism, Rochester had indeed fortuitously emerged as a spirit-being intimately associated with Jane's most traumatic childhood experience of psychological withdrawal. He is thus Jane's spirit-mate in the sense that Jane appears supernatural to him. The mutual identification and recognition of each in the other suggests a modality of love as fusion.

But the spiritual kinship which is an important dimension of Jane's and Rochester's love—and indeed, an affiliation leading directly to their reunion at the end of the novel, brought together by that otherwise inexplicable spiritual call—is balanced by Rochester's solidity for Jane as a social presence in the outside world. Rochester is introduced into Thornfield mere paragraphs after we read of Jane restlessly pacing the Thornfield battlements, wearied by her passive life, aching for a wider field of activity and for more various experience. This is an important occasion in the novel, for it defines the single moment of understanding that might be called feminist ("women feel just as men feel; they need exercise for their faculties and a field for their efforts as much as their brothers do") and I shall return to it shortly. The point here is that Rochester's entrance to Thornfield at this very juncture affords Jane a domestic and romantic rather than independent and autonomous field for activity, a person to whom she manages to prove useful (note the three-fold repetition of Rochester's request to "lean" on Jane) and who reciprocally serves as a vicarious channel for Jane's yearning for the greater world beyond Thornfield's gates.

The emphasis thus far has been upon Jane's preservation of an irreducible core of personal integrity in the face of social alienation and ostracism. Although her outrage at injustice becomes more explicit as she grows older, only on one occasion are the upheavals of Jane's passionate integrity identified with an overt feminist understanding. What seems to me most significant about her extended psychic explosion on Thornfield's battlements is not so much the fact of its existence within a novel that takes autonomy and action in the real world as at least one of its themes, but rather the various subterfuges by which it is quickly undermined. The recurrent apologies that attend it suggest Jane's uneasiness with her feminist awareness. Further, the passage is actually the second occasion upon which Jane wishes to be up and out in the active world of towns, and to burst through the constraints of domestic service in other people's households. This theme, the wish for an autonomous outlet for her talents, education and energies, her longing, that is, to move out of the confines of her status and place, to the larger and more exciting world "out there," will be treated subsequently. The feminist outburst is in keeping with Jane's earlier mutinies, like them regretted after the fact, and like them undermined by her desperate need to be loved and accepted. It is no accident that this long passage occurs immediately prior to Rochester's emergence on the scene, following which Jane's feminism *per se* is not heard from again, although the issues of independence and integrity, insofar as they too are feminist, of course remain.

This passage, taken as a whole, repeats the early Gateshead outburst in the light of a more analytic understanding. "Children can feel, but they cannot analyse their feelings; and if the analysis is partially effected in thought, they know not how to express the result of the process in words" (p. 19). The new element in the Thornfield passage is Jane's consciously expressed aspiration "for a power of vision which might overpass that limit" (p. 95). This aspiration pursues a double course within the novel. As vision, it becomes internalized into Jane's dreamlife, her surreal paintings, and the tales her imagination creates and narrates continuously. But as a longing for direct action, it belongs to the sequence of thwarted impulses toward "the regions full of life" which Jane experiences for the first time at Lowood following the loss of Maria Temple through marriage. On both occasions, this longing is immediately undermined, first by the humbler aspiration toward a new servitude reinforced by the Lowood dinner gong, and later by Bertha Mason's demonic laughter and eccentric murmurs. Bertha's subhuman voice resonates in Jane's apologies which relentlessly punctuate the Thornfield outburst ("Anybody may blame me who likes," "Who blames me? Many, no doubt").

Bertha's role in undercutting Jane's feminist outrage is not without purpose in that Bertha characterizes the dangers of ungoverned passion and rage, forced into demonic intensity. She is like Jane in the Red Room, a hidden and ostracized figure, locked into solitary confinement and thereby presenting a monstrous equivalent to Jane's "deep ire and desperate revolt." Jane calls our attention to the anxiety that attends her awareness of her own fluctuations between repression and rage. But she does not note what the pattern of her narrative implies, that the rage, indignation and rebelliousness characteristic of Jane the child finds a feminist voice in Jane the woman, and in her longing "for a power of vision that might overpass that limit; which might reach the busy world" (p. 95).

Jane's consciousness of her possible participation in a world beyond her social barriers occurs first at Lowood, where Jane sees in the horizon a space more objective, substantial and inviting than the interiorized and icy wasteland imaged in Bewick. The Lowood landscape is presented in a series of concentric half-circles, with Jane at its center, "the high and spike-guarded" Lowood walls encircled in turn by summits and further encircled by the great dome of the horizon (p. 66). Looking out, Jane longs to explore as far as her eye can see, but firmly represses her desire (at the last moment) "in a manner suiting [the] prospects" (p. 29) toward which her entire Lowood training has been directed. The oscillation in this episode between longing and repression makes the apologies and Bertha's laughter, both of which undercut Jane's more conscious feminism at Thornfield, appear both characteristic and inevitable in retrospect.

> I went to the window, opened it, and looked out. There were the two wings of the building . . . the skirts of Lowood; there was the hilly horizon. My eye passed all other objects to rest on those most remote, the blue peaks: it was those I longed to surmount, all within their boundary of rock and heath seemed prison-ground, exile limits. I traced the white road winding round the base of one mountain, and vanishing in a gorge between two: how I longed to follow it further! . . . I tired of the routine of eight years in one afternoon. I desired liberty; for liberty I gasped; for liberty I uttered a prayer; it seemed scattered on the wind then faintly blowing. I abandoned it and framed a humbler supplication; for change, stimulus: that petition, too, seemed swept off into vague space: "Then," I cried, half desperate, "grant me at least a new servitude!" (P. 74)

Compared with this, the Thornfield scene suggests a final and fully-fledged burst of consciousness—Jane's vision strained yet again along the "dim sky-line" in a last-ditch effort to "overpass that limit" and reach the busy world, towns, "regions full of life I had heard of but never seen . . . more of intercourse *with my kind*" (p. 95, emphasis mine). In each instance Jane is dramatically situated within barriers (spiked walls, battlements) that define her "place," and each time the impulse to reach the horizon and move beyond is vitiated by both inner checks ("a new servitude," "Anybody may blame me who likes") and outer mockery.

Yet it is worth noting that Jane's aspirations are also displaced in their pure form to the other major male character in her narrative. St. John is the male embodiment of Jane's ambitions. Representing the conscience uncomplicated by feeling, and "the ambition of the high master-spirit" (p. 398), he is the type of heroic wanderer which Jane had at moments longed to be and earns the closing paragraph in a tale which presumes to be Jane's narrative of her own life.

The nature and limits upon Jane's capacity for exploration and autonomy are tested at Morton, where she is economically independent, engaged in worthwhile and serviceable work, but bereft of emotional sustenance. Jane's refusal of a loveless marriage, even though it would allow her to fulfill the aspiring and ambitious side of her nature through missionary work, is a further test of her venturesomeness. Although the alleged social impossibility of her accompanying St. John as a co-worker but not wife is an impediment obviously not of her making, it does appear that Jane's feminism is ambivalent at best, and her drive toward autonomy and an independent working life is undermined by her need for a sustaining and nurturing love. Sides of her nature are presented as polar opposites, without an alternative posed by which they might be fused. Jane's life is posed in terms of contrasting locales, opposing imageries, irreconcilable life choices.

But Jane's integrity is quite another matter. She consistently bridles at efforts to exploit her dependent status, whether the motives be sadistic (John Reed), possessive (Rochester), or egocentric (St. John). She will not marry St. John because she is afraid to lose her independence. As his comrade "my heart and mind would be free," and "there would be recesses in my mind which would be only mine, to which he never came... *but as his wife—at his side always, and always restrained, and always checked*—forced to keep the fire of my nature continually low, to compel it to burn inwardly and never utter a cry, though the imprisoned flame consumed vital after vital—this would be unendurable" (pp. 358–359, emphasis mine).

Even the relation with Rochester is characterized by a pervasive word-play on "master" and "governess" in what appears to be, in part at least, Jane's struggle for self-mastery and self-governance at Thornfield. The more unrelenting and competitive struggle between two strong wills and similar temperaments in Jane's parallel conflict with St. John, is expressed with far stronger reference to the "fetters" and "ascendancy" of the male and the

"thralldom" of the female, perceptions which carry the reader
back to the petty tyrannies of John Reed (whose name and initials
St. John Rivers echoes): "as a man, [St. John] would have wished
to coerce me into obedience" (p. 360).

Prior to her flight from Thornfield and experience at Moor
House, Jane's efforts to maintain both independence and integrity
are rendered untenable. Acceptance of her social and economic
dependence on the whims of others proves emotionally intolerable. Even the small sanctuaries to which she retreats are violated
time and again. The avenues open for making her own way in
the world impose restrictions upon her nature, whether as governess for Rochester's ward, as teacher among the poor children
at Morton village, or as St. John's missionary wife or co-worker.
No alternative provided by the first two-thirds of this novel enables her to integrate the dislocated aspects of her nature.

The plot of *Jane Eyre* follows psychic necessity in a way we
have come to expect of dream-work. One characteristic of Jane's
narrative is her inordinate attentiveness to the details of her dream
life. Similarly, the plot, understood as the manipulation of the
world to conform to desire and inner necessity, is complicated by
the censorship exercised by Jane's reason, even while her dreams
and fantasies serve as psychological and interpretive clues to the
reader. Jane's imagination is constantly at work creating a tale
independent of any source other than its own creative and com-
pensatory power, "a tale that was never ended—a tale my imagination created. . . . quickened with all of the incident, life, fire, feeling, that I desired and had not in my actual existence" (p. 96).
Strengthened by reason, it also serves the purpose of admonition.
To master her feelings for her master, Jane draws the exaggerated
portraits of "a Governess, disconnected, poor, and plain" as con-
trasted to "Blanche, an accomplished lady of rank," with her
round arm, diamond ring and gold bracelet—and these form the
pictorial equivalents for "Reason having come forward and told
in her own quiet way, a plain, unvarnished tale" (pp. 140–141).
Similarly, Jane's triptych, painted at Lowood but displayed at
Thornfield, images the ambivalence that accompanies her great
expectations in a series of psychological landscapes which repeat
the elemental language of the novel (air and water, in one case

iced over), with much of the scene submerged below the water-line or horizon in a suggestion of the relationship of Jane's conscious and unconscious life.[3] The first of the series shows a swollen sea claiming all but a partially submerged mast, a golden bracelet, and the arm from which the bracelet has been washed or torn. This symbolic association with Blanche Ingram's jewels and Rochester's lavish wedding gifts prefigures and reinforces the submerged fears expressed in Jane's dream of buoyant but unquiet seas, driving her back from the sweet shores of Beulah: "I could not reach it, even in fancy" (p. 133). The second painting images a female form which Rochester interprets as evening star and wind, an etherealized cluster that anticipates the moon, not moon "but a white human form" prefigurative of the white apparition that warns Jane to flee Thornfield, as well as the wind on which Jane's initial supplications for liberty are lost, but which subsequently carry Rochester's entreaties to her at Moor House at the moment of their greatest crisis and triumph. The third panel depicts the ice-bound landscape of Jane's despair. The triptych's symbolic relevance to Jane's emotional and religious crises at Thornfield and later, suggests a technique of illuminating through pictorial and dream montage many of the implicit personal themes.

Jane's compulsively active dreamlife is further characterized by recurrent, anxiety-ridden, and regressive nightmares, with images of barriers, closed doors and phantom-children. The Thornfield nightmares focus upon the psychic as well as the social obstacles to Jane's imminent marriage, through a recapitulation of Jane's obsessive anxiety over her humiliating childhood and perpetual homelessness. Jane's dreamlife is the dark underside of her rational self-control. Rochester arouses her with talk of their natural affinity and Jane dreams of billows of trouble under surges of joy.

Dreams portending death and still-birth are the grotesque accompaniments of Jane's efforts to envision herself a married woman. Debarred from "the new life which was to commence to-morrow" (p. 241) by internal inhibitions, small wonder at her otherwise inexplicable procrastination until there could be no more "putting off the day that advanced—the bridal day" (p. 241). The dreams explain Jane's procrastination, which is never accounted for directly, beyond the tacit equation of her rebirth as a married woman with a new identity and a new name—Jane

Eyre transformed into Jane Rochester. This transformation is in itself traumatic, a "newborn agony—a deformed thing which I could not persuade myself to own and rear" (p. 214).

Jane's anxiety dreams on the eve of the wedding express her premonitions of rebirth as a deformed adult. Jane's nightmares find symbolic reinforcement in a landscape of separation and division, represented by a chestnut-tree riven to its roots, apples divided (the ripe from the unripe), drawing-room curtain pulled down, moon eclipsed by curtains of dense clouds. The dream motifs are mutually reinforcing: a consciousness of some barrier dividing her from her husband-to-be; the burdensome child; the strain to overtake Rochester, despite fettered movements; then a second dream of Thornfield in ruin, the child still in Jane's arms, impeding her progress, nearly strangling her in its terror while Rochester disappears like a speck on a white track. Two nightmares dramatize a single although complex perception. Associating the adult woman Jane Rochester with the abandoned and alien child Jane Eyre of her earliest memories, they identify the abandoned child with the anticipated yet feared prospect of awakening a "young Mrs. Rochester—Fairfax Rochester's girl bride."

But worse is yet to come. Two nightmares prepare for a third, the nightmare into which Jane in fact awakens to see the apparition of Bertha Rochester looming over the bedstead. Bertha's appearance further confirms Jane's fears of the still-birth of her marriage, for Bertha *is* the real Mrs. Rochester and Jane's hopes now in fact lie dead, "cursed like the first-born out of the land of Egypt," and "my love: that feeling which was my master's... shivered in my heart, like a suffering child in a cold cradle" (p. 260). The grotesque connection of Jane's nuptials with Bertha's marriage is reinforced by Bertha's face seen by Jane in her mirror, an image which serves as the maniacal opposite of the elf seen earlier in the Red Room mirror.[4] The two mirror images render, by polarized extremes, the terms of Jane's spiritual and physical dissociation, on the one hand the asexual self who is spiritually akin to Rochester but cannot be his wife; on the other a passionate and sex-crazed creature, a woman of satin and jewels who tries on (and then destroys) the extravagant veil which (as a symbol of wealth) Jane had reluctantly accepted. Once again, psychic and economic issues overlap. By destroying this symbol of Rochester's wealth and pride, Bertha ironically paves the way for Jane's ultimate reunion with a humbled Rochester in a smaller estate.

But here, in this recognition scene, Bertha and Jane are merged for a single awful moment. The fusion is more than Jane can bear, and her collapse here repeats her collapse in the Red Room under equally severe psychic pressure. The episode concludes in the regressive mode, Jane asleep in Adèle's crib as she had once slept in the dead Helen's arms, the child "so tranquil, so passionless, so innocent.... She seemed the emblem of my past life; and he, I was not to array myself to meet, the dread, but adored type of my unknown future day" (p. 252).

It is clear that marriage at this point in the novel is not a smooth developmental transition so much as a rupture, raising a host of questions which the work, to its credit, does address. There is the question of identity: Who, and what, is a "Mrs. Rochester"? There is the question of continuity: Can one imagine an equal and independent adulthood as female and wife, given the background of one's daily humiliations as someone else's dependent throughout childhood and adolescence? And there is the question of integrity and power: Is there an imaginable mutuality that does not perpetuate the master/subordinate economics of Jane's status at Thornfield?

Jane reaches the threshold of marriage three times in the novel. She cannot cross it until she can meet her "master" as his partner and equal, his equal by virtue of her inheritance and family solidarity, his partner by virtue of their interdependence. Before she leaves Thornfield, Jane's visions of herself as an adult are simultaneously regressive and parental. Her blighted hopes leave "Jane Eyre, who had been an ardent expectant woman—almost a bride ... a cold, solitary girl again" (p. 260). Now, the hope of mature love, a feeling "which was my master's—which he had created" is thwarted. Jane's articulation of her disappointment points to an aspect of her dependence on Rochester not noted earlier—*he makes of her a woman;* she is not a woman in her own right. Without him, she is once again a child, with all the terrors of her situation as a child reactivated. Rochester is not unaware of Jane's fear of, and her resistance to, adult love and its attendant sexuality.

Although her resistance is handled playfully for the most part, Rochester does comment upon her "fear in the presence of a man and a brother—or father, or master, or what you will" (p. 122), and the presence in this catalogue of familial rather than sexual bonds between male and female is noteworthy. Subsequently, in what cannot be ignored as role reversal, Jane's nurturing custodianship of the blinded and maimed Rochester is again parental rather than sexual. The sole distinguishing feature of the child born of their marriage (the dailiness of marital life is scarcely commented on at the end of the novel) is that he is a child-Rochester, his father in miniature.

By now, it is apparent that family harmony, a sense of belonging somewhere and to someone, is identified by Jane with her own psychic "kind" or kindred, and with sympathetic understanding and shared feelings and tastes. Looking out from the Thornfield window-seat at Rochester among his own social set, for example, Jane discovers that she loves Rochester because she finally perceives that "he is not of their kind. I believe he is of mine... I feel akin to him..." (p. 156). This is a woman's narrative in which blood runs thick, but psychic kinship is deeper and more sustaining, so that Rochester can be seen as "my relation, rather than my master.... So happy, so gratified did I become with this new interest added to life, that I ceased to pine after kindred" (p. 129). Similarly, on Rochester's side, the cord of "natural sympathy" which he admits binds him to her, also has subtle umbilical nuances: "a string somewhere under my left ribs, tightly and inextricably knotted to a similar string situated in the corresponding quarter of your little frame... I am afraid that cord of communion will be snapt; and then I've a nervous notion I should take to bleeding inwardly" (p. 221).

Rochester does in fact offer Jane a home after what must have seemed endless wanderings. "A little, roving, solitary thing" to Bessie, a "little castaway," an "interloper and alien" to Brocklehurst, Jane moves from one temporary refuge to another. Rochester recognizes Jane for the "poor orphan child" that she is, for he, like Jane, is also a homeless wanderer, and welcomes her into his heart and hearth as if she were the prodigal returning: "here, come in, bonny wanderer" (pp. 120–121), to which she responds in kind, "I was now at last in safe haven" (p. 85), "wherever you are is my home—my only home" (p. 216).

Rochester's protective and paternal role is particularly apparent in a scene which recalls the earlier domestic grouping at Gateshead which had visually consolidated Jane's isolation; but the Gateshead scene is recalled in this Thornfield instance for the purposes of total reversal. This time around, Jane sits by Mrs. Fairfax's side, with Adèle nearby, in a complex of interrelationships in which Jane is simultaneously daughter to Mrs. Fairfax and mother to Adèle, with Rochester looking on as lord protector and bemused pater-familias to them all. It is important to separate the two elements, the paternal and protective support provided by Rochester as head of the household, and the internal sharing of kinship and support of the essentially fluid motherly-sisterly-daughterly roles and relations among the three Thornfield women, and even more dramatically among the other beneficent and triadic mother/daughter/sisterhoods of the novel: Maria Temple/Helen Burns/Jane Eyre, and Diana Rivers/Mary Rivers/Jane Eyre. In these last two positive "sisterhoods" the paternal figure is absent. His protective role is shared among women, although what is omitted, and what Jane Eyre misses, is, of course, the romance.

We all know, having read *Jane Eyre* many times over, that in the end she seems to have it both ways, or indeed, *all* the ways that the novel presents as worth having. Jane regains her lover, stumbles upon her real family, discovers her status and is showered by an inheritance that gives her far more money than she can possibly use, thus turning her into the protector and head-of-household at Moor House that Rochester had been at Thornfield. All this, with no loss of integrity, and only a slight softening around the edges of her north-of-England orneryness. The "happy" ending, which resolves some issues but sweeps others under the carpet, is presented, as suggested early on in this discussion, in the Cinderella mode, although with important differences. The bare outlines of the plot suggest that Jane *is* Cinderella, supplanting bad foster-parents and sisters with good (from Reeds to Rochester/Rivers) and winning a chastened Prince Charming as well. Cinderella is an essentially girlhood fantasy (although Dickens' *Great Expectations* imagines aspects of the fable along male lines), the fable of a young girl beautiful but exploited, rewarded for her patience, goodness, submission and beauty by the miraculous appearance of Prince Charming to lift her forever out of her misery. This fable, as received along traditional lines, is clearly inappropriate to our Jane, who so passionately values her conscience and her independence, who tends toward action rather than passivity, and who intermittently aspires toward her own life in the larger world. Rather we have in Jane a Cinderella reimagined, unsubmissive and unrelenting on the issues of paying her own way and of being loved for her better moral and personal qualities. No passive capitulation into the arms of Prince Charming for her, but continued governess pay at thirty pounds *per annum*, even after the ringing of the wedding bells. For this impoverished young woman, once again, the social and economic dilemmas of status cannot be severed from the marital and sexual dilemmas of role. Perpetual degradation in poverty keeps Jane from her spiritual kin and kind, while the degradation of a dependent marriage to a social superior would alienate Jane from her better self.

The Cinderella paradigm will carry us a long way in understanding the interaction of personal and social motifs in both Jane's romantic and worldly aspirations. The significance of the Moor House episode rests in the fact that the Cinderella dilemmas are resolved within the family structure in which they initially occur. They are resolved, that is, through the discovery of a nurturant and self-supporting sisterhood. Prince Rochester does *not* lift Cinderjane out of her misery. Looked at in this way, and focussing upon the characterizing domestic and interior housecapes that are the major "landscape" of this novel, cruel stepsisters crop up like the recurrent bad dreams they in fact embody, the perpetual reinforcers of Jane's dispossession at Gateshead, Lowood, and Thornfield. And as if to insist upon this Cinderella equation, the cruel stepsisters turn up wealthy and favored by nature, with a cruel mama in tow, evil female mother/daughter triads of Reeds, Brocklehursts and Ingrams, fortune's darlings, all of them marriageable and promising in the accepted terms of the day and of the novel. But these figures are exorcized by the Rivers sisters, whose fostering sisterhood is anticipated in the earlier triads of Maria Temple, Helen Burns, and Jane Eyre. And as if to further the emerging equation of sisterhood with spiritual kinship, and of sisterhood and kinship with equivalent social status, there is the fact that both pairs of "good" foster-sisters are themselves impoverished governesses, earning their keep while trying to maintain their integrity.

From this analysis, it follows that Jane's transition from poor orphan into secure woman could not possibly be achieved through marriage to Rochester at Thornfield. Instead, at Moor House she reenacts an emotional and psychic equivalent to the experiences of infancy and childhood, moves quickly through the maturational process—becoming a younger, then an older sister, and, finally, an heiress, the cause of her family's reunification, independence, and status in the larger world. As in the way of folktale and fantasy, the evil stepmother is exposed and punished, and the step-sisters who had lorded it over the orphan are cast down; accordingly, the Reeds are destroyed one by one and the Brocklehursts and Ingrams evaporate from the scene, their psychic function now complete.

Despite the careful paralleling of psychic and status motifs in the presentation of Jane's situation, there is a clear primacy established of the personal over the social/economic issue, however much the second might prove a necessary precondition for independence in the first. Jane's inheritance, when it finally comes to her, seems at first only another painful reminder of her isolation. Far more satisfying is the discovery that she is indeed part of a family, a family whom she might now assist. Her joy has all the poignancy of remembered isolation, as she reminds St. John, who, insensitive to the warmth provided by nurturing family love, believes she is throwing her money away: " 'And you,' I interrupted, 'cannot at all imagine the craving I have for fraternal and sisterly love. I never had a home, I never had brothers or sisters; I must and will have them now . . . I want my kindred: those with whom I have full fellow-feeling' " (p. 341). The language here is redolent of the familial and kinship aspects of Jane's attachment to Rochester. Money is related to independence, making possible the relative equality and strength which underpins the rather more forced reallocation of dependence and status at Ferndean: "Are you an independent woman? A rich woman?" (p. 382), with the not surprising rejoinder, "I love you better now, when I can really be useful to you, than I did in your state of proud independence, when you disdained every part but that of the giver and protector" (p. 392).

One can imagine alternative endings to the one offered by this novel. The themes traced out in the Rochester-romance, an aspect of Jane's narrative that receives more than its fair share of critical attention, are in fact resolved at Moor House in a familial scene that provides warmth, kinship, status and shared wealth. A twentieth-century novel might well have ended on this note, with cousins marrying or not as they wish, and with Jane continuing at Morton or finding some larger arena for her energies, her commitments, her education and skill. Some women's lives have always pursued this course, likely enough with similar sacrifice, in Brontë's time and earlier; Charlotte Brontë is herself an instance, in her life, if not in her fiction.

There are, however, determinant characteristics of this novel that make a non-romantic resolution of the personal and social themes out of the question. First, there is considerable ambivalence expressed toward the aspiration to be truly free, to live out as fully as possible one's ambitions and aspirations. Second, Jane's energies are transformed into a form more socially acceptable for a woman, in her desire to serve and be of use. Early on at Lowood, Jane abandons her spontaneous cry for liberty, replacing it with the humbler supplication, "Grant me at least a new servitude!" (p. 74). Service at Thornfield is her new servitude, to Rochester especially, who leans on her time and again, encouraged by her offer, "Can I help you, sir?—I'd give my life to serve you" (p. 179).

But finally, and I think most importantly, questions of estate and position, status, integrity and equality are resolved in the romantic mode, in what is undeniably a romantic novel, which is to say one characterized by fortuitous interventions which enable events and the world to conform to the shape of wish and desire. *Jane Eyre* is marked by the fantasy that love is a fusion of souls, a conception of love out of which it is difficult to imagine an ongoing, humdrum daily adult life. "I am my husband's life as fully as he is mine. No woman was ever nearer to her mate than I am; ever more absolutely bone of his bone and flesh of his flesh" (pp. 396–397). A comparable twentieth-century instance, dealing with similar issues of love and autonomy, sexual passion and sisterhood, is Doris Lessing's *Golden Notebook*, in which the world is far less tractable and more resistant to resolutions between life issues which may, after all, prove to be irreconcilable. But in *Jane Eyre* love and autonomy are at odds, and only "romance" makes some modicum of equality available in so extreme a case.

The Jane/Rochester symbiosis at Ferndean has been commented on in print, with predictable sympathy to Rochester's diminution. At the risk of seeming heartless, it seems important to say that Rochester is not so central to Jane's own story as an easy reading might suggest, and as the neglect of the Moor House episodes in the interpretive and critical literature on this novel appears to confirm. Clearly Rochester's possessive mastery is purged (literal fire putting out symbolic fire) at the same point in the narrative chronology at which Jane is exorcizing the icy wastelands of her moral conscience. Similarly, the decline in Rochester's status is a precondition of their marriage, but it is difficult to determine whether his physical maiming is to be read as the harsh biblical punishment for adultery and pride, or whether its very harshness draws our attention to Jane's extreme, perhaps excessive, need to be needed, as yet another requisite for their married interdependence. The gap between them during the early days at Thornfield loomed very large indeed; thus the measures necessarily taken to close that gap might seem excessive to twentieth-century eyes.

What does seem clear is that to marry prior to Moor House would mean an exchange of childhood for adult dependence, bound this time by diamond fetters. Jane's suspicion, that as his wife she would be his mistress, and as his mistress his slave, is given substance by the unexpected Gothic twist to the plot. What is important is not Jane's moral scruple, but the certain inference that psychic kinship and spiritual equality cannot transcend the social degradation of a dependent relationship.

The novel can imaginatively suggest the necessary adjustments between psychic energy and social limits, but cannot enact them in Jane's status-ridden world except by a fortuitous inheritance and family reunification. With Jane's great expectations and fervent aspirations toward the active life displaced onto the cold figure of St. John Rivers, her prayers for liberty subdued into the search for a new servitude, and her early withdrawal redeemed by the kinship patterns in the novel, there is nothing left for her to do but marry. But to marry both she and Rochester must change— she in her objective circumstances, he in his social pride. To look to marriage merely as an easy escape out of a child's isolation and the fulfillment of girlish dreams would be an emotional lie, an alternative that Jane explores in fantasy but whose complications overwhelm her rational consciousness. To look to a man's world of heroic activity is forbidden and Jane's aspirations subside. Jane will relinquish liberty for new servitudes; she will relinquish the great world for vicarious and useful experience in the small. But she will not accept the degradation of continued dependence, the condition of hireling, slave, or kept woman by which the associational language of this narrative defines the position of a wife with no estate to call her own.

War and Roses:
The Politics of *Mrs. Dalloway*

LEE R. EDWARDS

Two figures dominate Virginia Woolf's fourth novel: Clarissa Dalloway and Septimus Smith. The one buys flowers and gives parties; the second returns from war, goes mad, and dies. This relation—of the perfect hostess and the shell-shocked soldier—is obviously not fortuitous. Indeed, the multiple connections and disjunctions which sustain these figures in a complex, interconnected web have been noticed by virtually everyone who has ever written—or thought—about the book. Clarissa lives. Septimus commits suicide. But life and death are not transacted in a vacuum. To see the characters embedded in a social structure containing possibilities for both limitation and liberation is to discover the beginnings of a new analysis, both feminist and social, not just of *Mrs. Dalloway*, but of all the works of Virginia Woolf.

By way of beginning, let me note that Virginia Woolf, Clarissa Dalloway, and I share two common characteristics: our sex and, in the broadest sense, our class. Shaping and defining us, our status as middle-class women has traditionally served to keep us out of what convention has established as the center of power, that masculine world which we have tended to encircle like so many electrons around a nucleus, in an outmoded diagram. Distrusting this status, we distrust ourselves and the vision of the world that grows out of our condition. Seeing ourselves as insignificant, inconsequential, unimportant outside of the sphere of home, family, and friends, we see our world as both small and trivial. We dislike ourselves because, like Clarissa Dalloway, we fear that we are "spoilt." [1] Like Jane Eyre surveying the world from the top of Thornfield's battlements we are, at best, defensive.

The wish to escape from what we perceive as our social prison, as well as from the confines which our own minds have built around us, has usually taken one of several, by now quite predictable forms. Since our class and sex appeared to us as prison walls, we developed new constructs in terms which would allow us to deny or to transcend these limitations and chose—or discovered, after the fact, that we had chosen—to avoid the traps customarily set for us by adopting the strategies of the other sex. Accepting, that is, the world our fathers and brothers created, we accepted as well their evaluation of the relatively greater import of this world in comparison with our own. Agreeing that the public sphere is haloed with grandeur, we sought to move into it, believing also that no vacuum would be created behind us as we abandoned our old places. Alternatively, we rejected the role of bourgeois man just as passionately as we rejected that assigned to his feminine counterpart and tried to reconstitute ourselves as something entirely new under the sun, as radicals of some new order.

I am not now interested in quarrelling with either of these modes of adaptation or even in evaluating the tactics such strategies call into being. What is to the point, however, is to see that in *Mrs. Dalloway*, as well as in several of her other novels and essays, Virginia Woolf is offering yet another choice. This alternative is arrived at by means of a serious, implicitly political investigation of the strengths and failures of middle-class society. Her perspective, located firmly within that society, is yet original enough to move in a direction that such investigations seldom take. But our distrust of what is middle-class, in combination with our distrust of what is set out or perceived as traditionally feminine, has obscured this subject from us and has prevented critics in general from treating it.

Inventing Septimus Smith and setting him out as both match and foil for Mrs. Dalloway, Virginia Woolf was trying, I believe, to focus our attention on the primacy of her concern not simply with the topics of individual isolation and interaction commonly counted as her subjects, but with a larger framework depicting and examining modes of social organization. In and of themselves, the book suggests, the forms that society chooses to honor, value, and perpetuate tend to foster solitude, fragmentation, abstraction, rigidity, and death on the one side, or communion, harmony, spontaneity, and life on the other. Wars and parties, shellshock and roses, authority and individuality, death and life, "manly" and "feminine" are counters, metaphors, or symbols, but also, Virginia Woolf suggests, the literal facts resulting from a society's choice of particular forms. Thus, in *Mrs. Dalloway*, wars, madness, the love of suffering and pain, adherence to an abstract, hierarchical, authoritarian set of values and means of organisation are linked to death, and frequently, if not exclusively, to a particular notion of masculinity; conversely, parties, roses, joy, and the celebration of the spontaneity and variability of life are tied to and embodied in various female figures. The politics of *Mrs. Dalloway* are such that life is possible only when roses, parties, and joy triumph over war, authority, and death. Clarissa's celebrations—ephemeral and compromised though they may be—are a paradigm of sanity, a medium through which energy can flow in a world which is otherwise cruel, judgmental, and frozen.

The problem with the brief schematization I have just presented is not simply the usual one of demonstrating that the proposed reading is supported by the text, although that necessity must, of course, be faced. The real difficulties, however, are embedded in both the nature and the implications of the stated propositions and account, I think, for the appeal that Virginia Woolf's novels make to close reading, technical analyses, a linking of value purely and solely to what we can comfortably call individual consciousness. For who could seriously entertain these theories on other grounds? If it seems certain that we all condemn war and hope for some alternative, it seems equally certain that most of us are not predisposed to take seriously the notion that giving parties and celebrating life provide viable social or political alternatives. The idea that they might seems at best either stupid or naive and, at worst, so blind to the conditions and possibilities of all but the most privileged lives as to reveal not simply a moral lapse but a total moral blindness. Recommending the politics of joy seems either a piece of cynicism or an attempt at outright fraud.

Furthermore, our whole notion of the meaning of politics, the standard definition of the word, is in terms of precisely those qualities Virginia Woolf denounces or is at least skeptical about: the organisations of government, management, factions, intrigue,

parties whose conventions are most unfestive. To talk easily of
politics and with assurance of being understood, you have to accept the assigned meaning of the word. If you don't, you leave
yourself unprotected, vulnerable to the charge that you fail to
comprehend the meaning of the word at the center of your discussion. Thus, Virginia Woolf is not generally regarded as a political—or indeed even a social—novelist.

But if politics has to do with government, and government has
to do with the systems or policies by which a political unit is
operated, and society is a political unit which is, if not the entire
state, at least one of its aspects, then isn't any discussion political
which considers and evaluates the systems or policies by which
society operates? The problem really has to do with where one
locates systems, how one defines policies, and what, of course, one
imagines society to be. For Virginia Woolf, politics in both a
general and an institutional sense has first to do with people conceived of as individual entities rather than corporate masses. The
values by which people live, the order in which they consent to
arrange these values, determine the shape of social as well as institutional structures.

The gap that she points to, the chasm that her writings both
indicate and indict, is the one that opens up between human and
humane values on one side and systems, bureaucracy, Acts of
Parliament on the other. She identifies that constriction in our
notion of politics which makes it difficult to bridge this gap: we
think too much of abstractions, not enough of single cases; we
assume, too quickly and with much too little evidence, that all
people are, at base, alike and can thus be "handled" most "effi-
ciently" by appeals to generalities; we think of politics and government at an increasing distance from individuals, human values,
ethical, emotional, even sensuous considerations. Therefore, she
suggests, all revolutions have always been betrayed because, at a
certain point, the makers of the revolution came to have more regard for the system they installed than they did for the less
tangible beliefs initially responsible for installing that system. The
solution is not simply to make another revolution, but to change
the bases on which revolutions are made, not merely to shift the
power balance within society so that those who make war no
longer have power, but to imagine a society in which the having
of power is no longer paramount.

The adjustment of vision and of imagination required by these premises is, however, of such magnitude that the call for such measures in the novels of Virginia Woolf has been, for the most part, overlooked. Even those who concede that she might, perhaps, think of herself as a social novelist tend to fall into two more or less dismissive categories. The first finds her vision bound by snobbishness or psychic narrowness; the second sees her characters as embodiments of transcendent archetypes, thus undervaluing the worldly reality Woolf is at such pains to establish.[2] The author herself seems to indicate her awareness of this situation and of its genesis in the following passage from her essay, "Women and Fiction" (1929):

> For a novel, after all, is a statement about a thousand different objects—human, natural, divine; it is an attempt to relate them to each other. In every novel of merit these different objects are held in place by the force of the writer's vision. But they have another order also, which is the order imposed upon them by convention. And as men are the arbiters of that convention, as they have established an order of values in life, so too, since fiction is largely based on life, these values prevail there also to a very great extent.
>
> It is probable, however, that both in life and in art the values of a woman are not the values of a man. Thus, when a woman comes to write a novel, she will find that she is perpetually wishing to alter the established values—to make serious what appears insignificant to a man, and trivial what is to him important. And for that, of course, she will be criticized; for the critic of the opposite sex will be genuinely puzzled and surprised by an attempt to alter the current scale of values, and will see in it not merely a difference of view, but a view that is weak, or trivial, or sentimental because it differs from his own.[3]

The paradox inherent in the critical treatment generally accorded *Mrs. Dalloway* is implicit in the general analysis Virginia Woolf provided in her essay. The greatness of the book has been acknowledged, while its scope has been largely ignored or overlooked by critics of both sexes, for conventions, the conventions of power and, if you like, of men, govern women, too. We would feel—or at least believe that we would feel—something amiss if critical consensus gave top honors to *King Lear,* while resolutely insisting that its greatness lay in its fidelity to the details of royal succession in the Dark Ages; but no such check has operated on the assessment that Virginia Woolf wrote her novels in "the subjective mode . . . the only mode especially designed for temperaments immersed in their own sensibility, obsessed with its movements and vacillations, fascinated by its instability" [4] and that "despite its grounding in social and political life, then, *Mrs. Dalloway* is designed as the fictional biography of a single character." [5]

But the values and visions of a woman may not be those of a man. And the subject of *Mrs. Dalloway* is not the same as its technique. There is a world in the work as well as a self, and the world is one which, recovering from one war, obsessed with the memory and the horror of it, is even yet hurtling blindly onward toward the next. The seeds of war make the roots of that society and are nourished by its tears. In these circumstances war comes as a disaster, certainly, but not as a surprise. In the middle of post-War London, on a beautiful day in June, five years after hostilities have ended, Peter Walsh encounters soldiers marching. There is no reason for the presence of this vision in the book, no reason for the entire network of references to war which includes in experience, memory, or association almost every character in the novel from Lady Bexborough and Clarissa's Uncle William at the beginning to old Miss Parry at the end, and certainly no reason for the particular rendering of the character and the dilemma of Septimus Smith unless we see and acknowledge that these visions, references, and characters constitute a significant portion of anything we might wish to call the subject of the book. Thus, when Peter Walsh finds his way through the city blocked, he looks up to see, out of the infinite things an author might have created as impediments to individual progress, specifically "boys in uniform, carrying guns," who "marched with their eyes ahead of them, marched, their arms stiff, and on their faces an expression like the letters of a legend written round the base of a statue praising duty, gratitude, fidelity, love of England" (p. 76). Watching the small procession as it passes out of view, Peter Walsh meditates on what he sees:

[T]hey did not look robust. They were weedy for the most part, boys of sixteen. . . . Now they wore on them un-mixed with sensual pleasure or daily preoccupations the so-lemnity of the wreath which they had fetched from Finsbury Pavement to the empty tomb. . . .

[O]n they marched, . . . as if one will worked legs and arms uniformly and life with its varieties, its irreticences, had been laid under a pavement of monuments and wreaths and drugged into a stiff yet staring corpse by discipline. (Pp. 76–77)

Important in itself, this meditation on the metamorphosis that sixteen-year-old boys undergo when they become imprisoned in the carapace of armor gains additional significance in the context of a web of references interweaving war, mechanism, and human beings who have shifted their allegiance to some set of monu-mental abstractions. Thus, for example, the long grey car which appears in the book prior to the soldiers is important not simply because it provides a convenient way for Virginia Woolf to move through time and space. It is important precisely because, unlike a conventional plot, the device *is* arbitrary, is not connected with human motivation, makes individuals feel, for the most part, in-significant, makes them feel that because the car is powerful who-ever rides in it must be powerful as well. The explosion of the motor provokes thoughts of "the voice of authority" and of the hymns of "the spirit of religion . . . abroad with her eyes bandaged tight and her lips gaping wide" (p. 20). The spirit of this re-ligion is connected with Churches, with organizations, with a Westminster containing buildings and memorials—the Cathedral and the Tomb of the Unknown Warrior—with prayers and ritual, the Reverend Whittaker and Miss Kilman; it is in direct contrast to the Westminster inhabited by the almost offhandedly spiritual Mrs. Dalloway, who returns home, like "a Goddess, having ac-quitted herself honourably in the field of battle" (pp. 43–44) to improvise transitory celebrations, whose powers and forms must always be freshly generated. Unlike Mrs. Dalloway, the human agency responsible for the agitation the car produces will not be known until Judgment Day, but the emotion created proceeds without such knowledge or attachment: "for in all the hat shops and tailors' shops strangers looked at each other and thought of the dead; of the flag; of Empire" (p. 25). Impressive mechanism divorced from specific individuals quickly becomes associated with figures embodying the power of the state—the Queen, the Prince of Wales, the Prime Minister, and finally, significantly, Sir William Bradshaw. The association, in turn, provokes a community of response which leads, finally, to action: "in a public house in a back street a colonial insulted the House of Windsor which led to words, broken beer glasses, and a general shindy..." (pp. 25-26). Even Moll Pratt, who "would have tossed the price of a pint of beer—a bunch of roses—into St. James's Street out of sheer light-heartedness and contempt of poverty" (p. 27) is prevented from doing so by her regard for a constable, another symbol of the state's authority. The car moves along a route that goes from a dissociation of personality and power, to reverence for power in the abstract, to fighting and damming up of life. While the particular instances here are trivial, the scale can all too easily enlarge, the consequences become more sinister indeed, as happens in the case of Septimus Smith and the doctors, Holmes and Bradshaw.

When Peter Walsh looked at the soldiers, he saw them first as boys, then as corpses, and finally as artifacts, statues who had renounced life in order to achieve "at length a marble stare. But the stare Peter Walsh did not want for himself in the least..." (p. 77). Septimus Smith, too, might have preferred to retain his capacity to blink and cry. But nobody asked him and, in any event, nobody cared what his preference was. There was a war, and the war needed men. "Septimus was one of the first to volunteer. He went to France to save an England which consisted almost entirely of Shakespeare's plays and Miss Isabel Pole in a green dress walking in a square" (p. 130). The experience of war, however, smashed this vision; the reassembled pieces made hideous patterns. In addition, those who had sent Septimus to war had always been suspicious of that early dream. Culture made Mr. Brewer, Septimus' employer, as nervous as it later makes Dr. Holmes and Dr. Bradshaw. Imagination was not healthy. Miss Pole was not fit company for a rising young clerk. Exercise was what was needed, porridge more to the point. And "in the trenches the change which Mr. Brewer desired when he advised football was produced instantly; [Septimus] developed manliness..." (p. 130). Now only the birds talk Greek. The Classic world, the world of culture and, more importantly, the world which had served Septimus by giving his imagination form died in the War and can now exert itself only as part of the paraphernalia of madness.

How odd that what a man is should not be sufficient to define him as a man, and that "manliness" should be seen as a quality to be learned. We do not, after all, have to teach a horse to be horsely or a rose to be a rose. How odd, too, that for so long we have not noticed, much less condemned, this oddness. But these observations are merely parenthetical. What is most interesting in *Mrs. Dalloway* is to see the lesson Septimus learned when he became a man: he must not feel. Thus, when his best friend, Evans, "was killed, just before the Armistice, in Italy, Septimus, far from showing any emotion or recognizing that here was the end of a friendship, congratulated himself upon feeling very little and very reasonably. The War had taught him. It was sublime. He had gone through the whole show ... and was bound to survive. He was right there" (pp. 130–131).

Surviving, unfortunately, killed him; for Septimus was finally unable to turn himself into a statue by a simple exercise of will. He told himself he could not feel. He wished himself into insensibility. "He would shut his eyes; he would see no more" (p. 32). He lied. He did feel

himself drawing towards life, the sun growing hotter. ... The trees waved, brandished. We welcome, the world seems to say; we accept; we create. Beauty, the world seemed to say. ... To watch a leaf quivering in the rush of air was an exquisite joy. Up in the sky swallows swooping, swerving, flinging themselves in and out, round and round, yet always with perfect control as if elastics held them; and the flies rising and falling, and the sun spotting now this leaf, now that, in mockery, dazzling it with soft gold in pure good temper; and now and again some chime ... tinkling divinely on the grass stalks—all of this, calm and reasonable as it all was, made out of ordinary things as it was, was the truth now; beauty, that was the truth now. Beauty was everywhere. (Pp. 104–105)

Of the person who can entertain these perceptions, it is simply silly—or mad—to say he cannot feel. Septimus dies because the

War has acted on him, as the possessor of such feelings and responses, trapping him between anguish and guilt and giving him
no way out except through his own death. He feels anguish because of the discrepancy between his feeling that the natural
world is beautiful, the human world corrupt, and guilt because
despite the discrepancy the feeling for the goodness and the
beauty of life persists. He feels anguish because he thinks he cannot feel, guilt because he wishes not to feel, and both because he
cannot admit what, in fact, he does feel. He feels anguish
because he cannot love and guilt because, in not loving, he has
deserted the fallen, betrayed his love and betrayed, as well, an
ideal of humanity which values love. Yet he feels equally tor-
mented because he has, indeed, loved Evans and because this love
violates the standards of manliness which the War and the
trenches have taught him to honor. If he truly did not feel anything when Evans died, then he would not need to punish himself
for this lack of feeling: the ability even to imagine the need for
such punishment would be beyond his capacities. He feels anger
because he has fallen and been deserted by those from whom he
had hoped for help—the government, the doctors, his wife—anguish because, since he is also a deserter, he can, in justice, expect
no better treatment, and guilt because he feels anguish at being
unable to live in a cold, just world.

Trying to deny his feelings by trivializing them, he thinks of
himself and Evans as two dogs romping in front of the fire. His
feelings, however, refuse to be denied and avenge themselves by
making him see dogs turning into men, giving him a vision of a
world where such trivialization, such denial need not occur but
making that vision appear, in the terms of this world, a grotesque
one. He wishes to "escape . . . to Italy" (p. 139), the place where
Evans died and was betrayed, where Rezia was married and betrayed, so he can live through these experiences again without
betrayal. This wish is both literally and psychologically impossible; therefore, it is mad. Septimus' madness, then, is not so much
the result of his misperceptions as it is of his inability to reconcile
the conflicting—but accurate—information he perceives. What is
worst, of course, is the failure of those around him to admit that
they, too, are implicated in producing these contradictions and
that what they ask of Septimus is either the impossible denial of
their existence or, failing that, his death. Even Rezia must bear a

portion of this burden, for in wishing to see herself as "the English gentleman's good wife" she would force Septimus to be "an English gentleman," a version of Hugh Whitbread. Because Septimus can only fleetingly provoke in Rezia the awareness that this vision is hollow at its core, Rezia persists in wishing that Septimus could manage to be simultaneously the good soldier and the loving, philoprogenitive husband. So she, too, contributes to the depth of the chasm at his feet.

There is a terrible logic behind Septimus' suicide. There is logic as well in the mental colloquy that precedes it, in Septimus' final statement, and in Dr. Holmes's response. Septimus is sitting on the window sill, feeling once again that, on the one hand life is good, nature beneficient, and on the other that the human world makes life horrible, desires death in general, his own death in particular. In flinging himself "vigorously, violently down on to Mrs. Filmer's area railings" (p. 226), Septimus believes he is taking the only action possible to him, escaping from his double bind by giving Holmes what he wants without also betraying his own vision of the possibilities of life.

Septimus is, in very large measure, correct in thinking that Holmes and Bradshaw desire his death. Ostensibly purveying cures, the doctors are themselves part of what has caused Septimus' disease, part of the machinery of destruction whose unacknowledged presence Septimus perceives but cannot conquer. Critics have often noted that the portraits of the two doctors—and particularly of Dr. Bradshaw—constitute an oddity in the entire canon of Virginia Woolf's fiction. Nowhere else can one find characters rendered so simply in a single dimension, so deprived of any inner life or light which might act to save them from total villainy. In *Mrs. Dalloway*, even Hugh Whitbread, Miss Kilman, and Lady Bruton, flawed though each of them is, emerge out of shadows and highlights which serve to endow them with a certain measure of human dignity and to generate, on the part of reader and observer, some measure of fellow feeling which the characterization of Holmes and Bradshaw totally denies to them. This observation is true, but hardly, I think, as puzzling as is sometimes made out. Remembering that Septimus' madness is caused by his inability to find a way in which he can both respond to war and continue to live, and remembering, too, that the authority which bolsters the state in its martial appeal has sheltered

Sir William Bradshaw as well, we can see that the reduction of Holmes and Bradshaw to counters symbolizing Proportion and Conversion, the deities they worship, is neither accidental nor a flaw in Virginia Woolf's technique. Both Holmes and Bradshaw are rendered crudely, emerge harshly and without shadows because Virginia Woolf wishes us to see them literally as vampires who feast "most subtly on the human will" (p. 152). They have done to themselves, she suggests, what they wish to do to Septimus. The thinness with which they are characterized corresponds to the thinness of their existence.

To be a soldier, a man must be persuaded or, if necessary, compelled to surrender his self. He must leave home, put on a uniform, forget that those he kills are individuals like himself, and, hearing only the assigned tune must march in the assigned rhythm to his predetermined and bloody destination. No one would do this, the book suggests, if there were no social imperatives sanctioning both means and goals, diverting attention from the real issues and consequences by appeals to what, in *Three Guineas*, Virginia Woolf would call "unreal loyalties." Holmes and Bradshaw embody these sanctions and imperatives. In a supposedly peaceful society theirs is the cause that makes war not simply possible but inevitable. They leave one no choice, no room to maneuver. One must, like Lady Bradshaw, succumb "to the craving which lit her husband's eye so oilily for dominion, for power..." (p. 152), give up one's claim to a personal vision and so die to oneself; or, if one refuses, one must simply die and be condemned by the system which has caused one's death in the language expressive of the system's categories. " 'The coward!' cried Dr. Holmes," (p. 226) as Septimus leapt out the window. Virginia Woolf is using Holmes and Bradshaw to show in fictional terms the linkage she treats more abstractly in *Three Guineas*, a network that ties all forms of oppression to each other, that has at its roots a love of power, an egotistic craving to stamp the world out according to the pattern that exists in one's own head or, failing that capacity, simply to stamp out the other patterns in the world.

Virginia Woolf is not denying Septimus' madness by showing it as provoked by what society calls sanity. Nor is she offering a simple-minded or romantic endorsement of suicide as a solution to the problems posed by Septimus' dilemma. She is, however, suggesting that for one trapped as Septimus is, unable to find either

a form which can adequately contain feelings or a mode of action
to extend them, pressured by a society which covertly demands
denial of both feeling and the necessity for feeling at the same
time as it will not allow the admission that this denial has taken
place, then death in order to preserve the integrity of feeling may
be preferable to a life which offers no such possibility. Death is
not, in these circumstances, a solution, but a statement that—for
the dead one—solution was impossible. A solution, however,
would be the discovery of a mode of being which enhances feeling and which develops a mode of action or a plot which can
harmonize feelings by accepting their fluidity and multiplicity
rather than by attempting to endorse some and banish others.

In *Mrs. Dalloway*, Virginia Woolf provides such a solution,
such an action, such a plot most clearly through the figure of
Clarissa herself and the parties she creates. Defined throughout
the book by her love of life, by her capacity to preserve this attitude in the face of war, death, sickness, age, and the limiting
demands of her own personal ego, Clarissa sees her parties as a
prism, a medium through which the lives of others may pass un-
obstructed and be combined:

> [W]hat did it mean to her, this thing she called life? . . .
> Here was So-and-so in South Kensington; someone up in
> Bayswater; and somebody else, say in Mayfair. And she felt
> quite continuously a sense of their existence; and she felt
> what a waste; and she felt what a pity; and she felt if only
> they could be brought together; so she did it. And it was an
> offering; to combine, to create; but to whom?
> An offering for the sake of offering, perhaps, Anyhow, it
> was her gift. . . . that one day should follow another . . . it was
> enough. (Pp. 184–185)

This delight in diversity, "in people's eyes, in the swing, tramp,
and trudge; in the bellow and the uproar: the carriages, motor
cars, omnibuses, vans, sandwich men shuffling and swinging; brass
bands; barrel organs; . . . London; this moment of June" (p. 5)
marks the separation between Clarissa and what she represents,
and what Holmes and Bradshaw are and stand for in the book.
Where Bradshaw proposed to deal with Septimus' suicide through
legislating "some provision in the Bill" (p. 279), Clarissa contends
that "the veriest frumps, the most dejected of miseries sitting on

doorsteps . . . can't be dealt with . . . by Acts of Parliament . . ."
(p. 5). They love life, too, she says; they must, therefore, be allowed to live it as they feel it and not as some external agency
would interpret it for them.

Virginia Woolf validates Clarissa's view throughout the novel
by pointing particularly to women who appear not as fully developed characters, but as images embodying Clarissa's sense of how
people, in fact, proceed through the universe. Thus we see Moll
Pratt wishing to toss roses; Rezia Warren Smith building up a
world out of odds and ends, appearing triumphant as "a flowering
tree" (p. 224) invisible to those "judges . . . who mixed the vision
and the sideboard" (p. 225); and old Mrs. Dempster, touching,
but indomitable: "Roses, she thought sardonically. All trash,
m'dear. For really, what with eating, drinking, and mating, the
bad days and good, life had been no mere matter of roses, and
what was more, let me tell you, Carrie Dempster had no wish to
change her lot with any woman's in Kentish town! But, she implored, pity. Pity, for the loss of roses" (p. 40). Most notably
and vividly, of course, we see the old woman standing in the
street opposite the Regent's Park Tube station, singing with a
"voice of no age or sex, the voice of an ancient spring spouting
from the earth; which issued . . . from a tall quivering shape, like
a funnel, like a rusty pump, like a wind-beaten tree for ever barren of leaves which lets the wind run up and down its branches
singing . . . and rocks and creaks and moans in the eternal breeze"
(p. 122). This figure, humanity pushed as far as possible toward
the eternal and the disembodied, sings of a love which is impersonal—as Clarissa's was for Sally Seton, as Septimus' might have
been for Evans could either of them have acknowledged the bond
that lay between them. It is unmarred by the self-regard and possessiveness that makes Peter Walsh, for example, wish to stamp all
women with the indelible imprint of his own private vision of
them and so flaws his passion for Daisy and, earlier, for Clarissa;
that rots Miss Kilman's feelings for Elizabeth as well, and is,
indeed, responsible for much of Clarissa's general hostility toward
passion.

These presences, these brief glimpses of lives lived, these particularly pointed references to love are not invoked in aid of some
feeble statement asserting the innate superiority of women over
men, any more than Septimus' suicide was used to assert the vir-

tues of insanity. Indeed, in order to prevent this sort of overly simple reading, Virginia Woolf is at pains to show Richard Dalloway
bringing roses to Clarissa and including Ellie Henderson in the
world of Clarissa's parties, Peter Walsh inventing the world which
he inhabits and inventing the shape and values of "compassion,
comprehension, absolution" (p. 86) which console the solitary
traveller at the end of his ride, and Miss Kilman, Lady Bruton,
Rezia, and even Clarissa participating in the rigid universe ruled
by Proportion and Conversion, bolstered by egotism and by spiritual "contraction," marked by churches and by letters to the
Times. On the other hand, one must also notice that neither Peter
Walsh nor Richard Dalloway is, judged by the standards of
society, quite "manly" or "successful," that Miss Kilman is as she
is because the War took away her work, and society, declaring her
ugly, also declared her outcast, that Lady Bruton's obsession with
emigration is not quite in proportion and that she herself cannot
finally produce—or even draft—the necessary note to the newspaper, that no man can fully understand why Clarissa gives her
parties or what they mean.

If Virginia Woolf would not imprison the world in a code of
feminism lest she be guilty of a crime on the order of Holmes's
or Bradshaw's, she can, nevertheless, not ignore the presence of
certain tendencies in the world she anatomizes. Not much interested in first causes, she never snarls herself in arguments about
sex as an inevitable determinant of action. Her focus, instead, is
always on the social, on the ways in which individuals respond to
the roles assigned them by the world, and on the nature and significance of the roles themselves. Freedom in her books is measured by the degree to which individuals can manipulate their
socially assigned and defined roles. Clarissa and Sally Seton survive in Mrs. Richard Dalloway and Lady Rosseter. The guests
refrain from laughing at the Prime Minister not because his political function makes him awesome, but instead because he is "so
ordinary. You might have stood him behind a counter and bought
biscuits. . . . And to be fair, as he went his rounds . . . he did it very
well" (p. 261). Conquering hatred of the idea of Miss Kilman by
recognizing that Miss Kilman is both more and less than simply
an idea, Clarissa inspires us to "be as decent as we possibly can"
and do "good for the sake of goodness" (p. 118) even though our
ethical notions are inevitably primitive and the world full of seem-

ingly incomprehensible disasters. Finally, in those situations where a choice must be made, we can endorse the heart rather than the brain, choose roses and not war. Such freedom, Virginia Woolf suggests, is more easily available to women precisely because they have less power in society and therefore less of a vested interest in either society or power.

Having reached these conclusions I can, even now, feel an inward churning of those emotions which the novel raised in me when I first read it, and flung the book away with expressions of dismay. Had we—women, that is—come so far, I asked, merely to be confronted with a vision of woman as goddess, an endorsement, however complex or ambiguous, of our sex as maintainers of some ineffable "life," a vision of the world which suggested hostess as an honorable profession? Hadn't women been goddesses and hostesses long enough? Wasn't that the problem? How could Clarissa's life bring pressure to bear against harsher realities not included in a vision which, like Peter Walsh's saw civilization as a collection of "butlers; chow dogs; girls in their security" (p. 82) and of people assembled from London's better addresses? Clarissa's query that because "she loved her roses (didn't that help the Armenians?)" (p. 182) seemed frivolous, even shocking. Obviously, the answer would be negative, if such response did not dignify the question beyond its worth.

Suppose, however, we alter slightly the terms of Clarissa's interrogation, asking now not specifically about roses, but instead about what, in general, might help those like the Armenians "hunted out of existence, maimed, frozen, the victims of cruelty and injustice" (p. 182). The usual answers are: money, letters, and other signs of support to institutions which aim to aid the downtrodden and marshall the opinions of others in their favor; expressions of hostility toward those individuals or institutions which seem to be responsible for the conditions we deplore; in the last resort, some violent act which would heave out the agents of repression and make way for new agencies closer to our hearts' desires and, with any luck, closer to those of the Armenians as well.

Versions of this plan have been at work for as long as history has recorded the deeds of human beings. To some extent, one can only suppose that they have worked, that we are all in some sense better off for the various social, intellectual, and technological revolutions that bloodily accompanied our progress from the cave. Perhaps such motion really does require blood to feed it. And yet, if the study of economics is a dismal science, so too is the study of politics, filled with quarrels about the definition of progress, leading only to the conclusion that war follows war and revolution, revolution. Is it not possible, which is to say initially, simply conceivable, to find another way? Could we create an alternative motion and set of social patterns based neither on systems nor on power but deriving instead more directly from individuals, from a notion that people are quite various and variable and that therefore we must learn to live leaving the ideas of others alone, learn to live with their solitude and our own as well? Imagining such a notion could we adhere to it so that Clarissa's parties might extend themselves beyond the boundaries of a single house, a single evening, a small number of involved participants? Could we learn to value joy as much as we now treasure suffering and learn, as Virginia Woolf suggests in *Three Guineas*, that when the mulberry tree makes us dance around it too fast the only thing to do is sit down and laugh? Could we see that the perfect hostess has a history and a heritage both honorable and, at least potentially, political? And if we could do any or all of these things, would it matter? Would the Armenians be helped?

Maybe.

I wish I could be more positive, but the difficulty of an easier affirmation is again pointed to by Virginia Woolf when she shows us Clarissa standing at her party "drenched in fire" (p. 255), knowing Septimus is dead and knowing, too, that nothing she has done has been sufficient to prevent this death or the War which preceded it, or to change Bradshaw into someone who would not force one's soul. Faced with such knowledge it is easy to give up, difficult to have any faith in the efficacy of individual belief or action, simpler to die or to work for a cause or to locate reality somewhere else than one's own life. And yet we can say with certainty that the known routes of Religion or Love or War do not seem to have done the hypothetical Armenians much lasting good either. These ways have been tried repeatedly, while the way of the hostess has been confined to the private house. Perhaps we should open the door and let her out rather than deny that she

ever existed or that we, men and women alike, might have anything to learn from her. Surely a society having at its center a
"figure, made of sky and branches... risen from the troubled
sea... as a shape might be sucked up out of the waves to shower
down from her magnificent hands compassion, comprehension,
absolution" (p. 81), a woman "lolloping on the waves and braid-
ing her tresses..., having that gift still; to be; to exist;... her
severity, her prudery, her woodenness... all warmed through
now,... as if she wished the whole world well" (pp. 264–265)
might be more pleasant to live in than one organized around "all
the exalted statues... the black, the spectacular images of... soldiers" (p. 77). Virginia Woolf is suggesting that we damn ourselves if, in constructing a view of the world we deny a connection between politics and feelings or values, and so create a politics
lacking both beauty and joy. She may be right.

"Out of the chaos, a new kind of strength":
Doris Lessing's *The Golden Notebook*

MARY COHEN

Reputedly, Doris Lessing bristles when asked about her role in the women's liberation movement, or when named as first in importance among feminist writers of our day. She insists that the waste of women's lives has never been her main concern. But her readers won't take no for an answer; moreover, they trust the tale. So, for countless readers, her novels—*The Golden Notebook* chief among them—recreate the dilemmas they live through as women. While Lessing offers them bleakly realistic pictures of the battles they will have to fight and fight again, she also manages to make the struggle seem worth the toll, and that is the point to which this essay will primarily direct itself.

Before turning to this question, however, it might be well to say a word for Lessing's side of the argument, that her focus has never been turned exclusively on women. The anger that the feminist label rouses in Lessing comes from the fact that what has seemed to be special pleading for women has been only a part of a larger plea, that humanity reexamine its directions. It is no wonder that Lessing dismisses her concern with "the sex war," a single facet of the struggle, when critics like Frederick Karl are capable of such diminishing statements as the one which follows: "Like Persephone, her women emerge periodically from the underworld to tell us what went awry—and it is usually sex." [1] Her women, like Lessing herself, tell us that much more is awry. Karl quotes an interview in which Lessing says: "I'm impatient with people who emphasize sexual revolution. I say we should all go to bed, shut up about sexual liberation, and go on with important matters," and comments, "Her turn upon herself is curious, for this conflict between collective politics and personal matters had been the crux of her work for the last two decades," [2] thereby slanting her comment deliberately and distorting the thrust of her thinking. He neglects to add that Lessing's remark followed an expression of her fear of world-wide nuclear destruction. Immediately after the quotation given by Karl, she goes on to say: "We must prevent another major war. We're already in a time of total chaos, but we're so corrupted that we can't see it." [3] It is necessary, then, to admit that the role of women in Western society is only one of Lessing's concerns; yet, despite her protests, it is equally clear that Lessing's fiction adds significantly to our understanding of what it means to be a woman in contemporary life.

It is vitally important that the protagonists in Lessing's longest and most significant works—*The Golden Notebook* and *Children of Violence*—are women, women whose personal lives have been painful and at times even debilitating. But she has never given us merely the diaries of mad housewives; her women have been involved with the larger political and social issues of their time: Anna Wulf's volunteer work is work for the Communist Party (until the Party so disillusions her that she regretfully withdraws her hopes and energies from it); similarly Martha Quest awakens from her first marriage to reexamine the political realities of her time; when Martha can admit that her life within a large suburban house tended by black servants is an outrage, she then can involve herself with the problems of the color bar in Africa, with the Communist Party, and later, when she goes to England, with anti-war and nuclear disarmament committees. The fight out of the "women's world" *is* significant to Lessing; she is indeed aware of the energy and talent squandered by women's submission to a conventionally inferior social position. Outside both the man's world and the traditional woman's world, Lessing's protagonists have a clearer vision of the changes necessary to permit individuals to grow, humanity to survive.

Turning to *The Golden Notebook*, it is perhaps instructive to begin with a second complaint, again one that the author has turned on her critics. Lessing says of the novel, "the way it's constructed says what the book is about—which very few people have understood." [4] Critics too often fasten on the fragmented structure and find in it the suggestion of its meaning: Selma Burkom would have the key to the novel turn on the statement, "Everything's divided and split up" [5]; Jonah Raskin asks in his interview with Lessing, "The form suggests the disintegration of contemporary life, doesn't it?" [6] To be sure *The Golden Notebook* mirrors much of the chaos and fragmentation of life in post-war Britain and particularly of the life of the protagonist, Anna Wulf. But the critics have been too easily satisfied with this assessment. *The Golden Notebook* goes beyond the mere picturing of disintegration; rather, it moves toward reintegration, of Anna, if not of her society. The victory is reflected in the structure of the novel itself, of course, when, in the end, Anna relinquishes her four separate notebooks—each of which had contained a fragment of her life—for a single, golden notebook. The novel records (as the structure demonstrates) the impediments set in the way of becoming a whole person. In it, Lessing charts the progress of Anna Wulf, herself a writer, as she fights her way out of a life which is badly fractured, to the point where she achieves a hold (albeit precarious) on herself and feels at least some sense of connection between herself and her society. In her essay "The small personal voice," Lessing outlines the goal she sets for herself and, I would assert, for Anna as well:

> I believe that the pleasurable luxury of despair, the acceptance of disgust is as much a betrayal of what a writer should be as the acceptance of the simple economic view of man; both are aspects of cowardice, both fallings away from a central vision, the two easy escapes of our times into false innocence. One sees man as the isolated individual unable to communicate, helpless and solitary; the other as collective man with a collective conscience. Somewhere between these two, I believe is a resting-point, a place of decision, hard to reach and precariously balanced. It is a balance which must be continuously tested and reaffirmed.[7]

Lessing uses Anna to test and reaffirm, for Anna battles against personal despair and against the Communist lie. She rejects the forms or institutions—such as marriage or a conventional job—

which society offers as ways of preserving oneself by narrowing the possibilities for experience. Ultimately she fights in herself the need for order which has caused her to fragment her life and record each fragment in a separate notebook. We watch Anna struggle to keep herself open to experience and to make herself whole.

The novel is composed of a running narrative or "conventional novel" which takes place in the "present"; the first four sections of the narrative, "Free Women," are followed by a series of entries from the four notebooks Anna keeps. The first notebook, the black, deals with Anna's first novel, *Frontiers of War*; it describes the novel itself, the African experiences from which the novel was drawn, and the continuing business details of its success. This account is followed by that of the red notebook, Anna's experiences with the Communist Party. The yellow notebook contains Anna's novel drawn from her own experience, an affair of five years, now over; the blue notebook is Anna's diary which records this affair and others, her role as mother to a young child, and her despair of capturing in words the "truth" of her experiences. The fourth series of notebook entries is followed by the golden notebook, where, finally, Anna is able to put all of herself in one book. The novel concludes with a final "Free Woman" section. I would like to trace Anna's battle—against the need in herself for order which causes her to split herself into manageable pieces, and against the forms and institutions which limit or falsify human response.

Midway through the novel Anna is questioned by her best friend's son, Tommy, then nineteen, who has been reading her notebooks:

> "Why the four notebooks? What would happen if you had one big book without all those divisions and brackets and special writing?"
> "I've told you, chaos."
> He turned to look at her. He said sourly: "You look like such a neat little thing and look at what you write. . . . Are you afraid of being chaotic?"
> Anna felt her stomach contract in a sort of fear, and said, after a pause: "I suppose I must be."
> "Then it's dishonest. After all, you take your stand on

something, don't you? Yes you do—you despise people like
my father, who limit themselves. But you limit yourself too.
For the same reason. You're afraid. You're being irresponsible. . . . And you aren't even honest enough to let yourself
be what you are—everything's divided off and split up. So
what's the use of patronising me and saying: You're in a bad
phase. If you're not in a bad phase, then it's because you can't
be in a phase. You take care to divide yourself up into com-
partments. If things are a chaos, then that's what they are. I
don't think there's a pattern anywhere—you are just making
patterns, out of cowardice." [8]

Anna is afraid of being chaotic. To provide herself the order she
needs she accepts herself as splintered, but gives form to each
splinter-Anna by capturing the piece in a notebook: Anna, past
and present, Anna, political and personal. What she gains by
this strategy is detachment. In her novel, particularly, by drawing the fictional affair between Ella and Paul, Anna can examine
her own affair with Michael with greater penetration than she
is able to in her own diary. But the cost of the intensive self-
examination which the notebooks allow is never being able to
see herself whole: her life is divided, bracketed, broken. Oddly
enough, it is Tommy, the adolescent son of her closest friend,
Molly, the novel's other "free woman," who sees that, despite
Anna's desire to become a free woman, her tendency to split
herself up is as limiting as the conventional person's willingness
to preserve the forms.

Anna and Molly have prided themselves on remaining free of
forms. They have won their status as free women primarily by
rejecting compromise marriages. They had both been married
briefly to men with whom they could never have been happy.
When the book opens, they have lived not altogether happy without them, but scornful of loveless marriages. Both have several
affairs, casual and serious, and both fight against the growing conviction that they would never meet men "who were capable of
seeing what they really were" (p. 178). In resisting safe marriages,
Molly and Anna are resisting self-limitation. Most of the other
characters in the book, male and female, have accepted the limitations of marriage or other institutions; they are provided with a
way to live but remain cut off from the richer possibilities of life.

Richard, Molly's former husband, is one of these limited characters. (His current wife, Marion, in her desperation, drinks too
heavily, but Richard excuses himself by asserting, " 'I've had half
a dozen unimportant affairs. So do most of the men I know who
have been married any length of time. Their wives don't take to
drink' " [p. 29].) Anna and Molly are critical of Richard because
he has so nearly destroyed Marion, apparently no longer loves
her, yet refuses to deal with his situation. Richard, of course,
returns their antagonism. Early in the novel the three argue.
Richard charges: " 'Well, Anna, I've had the privilege of getting to know you better than I did before, and I can't say you
impress me with knowing what you want, what you think or
how you should go about things.' " Anna counters, " 'Or perhaps
what it is you don't like is that I do know what I want, have
always been prepared to experiment, never pretend to myself the
second rate is more than it is, and know when to refuse.' " Molly
asks if Richard isn't attacking them for the way they live: " 'The
less you say the better, what with your private life the way it is.' "
Richard responds, " 'I preserve the forms' " (pp. 25–26). Lessing
surely asks: preservation to what end, for what purpose?

Richard is drawn as the women's opposite. Again it is Tommy
who makes the distinctions: Tommy explains first to his mother
and Anna, " 'You didn't say to yourselves at some point: I am
going to be a certain kind of person. I mean, I think that for both
you and Anna there was a moment when you said, and you were
even surprised, Oh, so I'm that kind of person, am I?' " He turns
to his father and continues:

> "The thing about mother and Anna is this; one doesn't say,
> Anna Wulf the writer, or Molly Jacobs the actress—or only
> if you don't know them. They aren't—what I mean is—they
> aren't what they *do*.... People like Anna or Molly and that
> lot, they're not just one thing, but several things. And you
> know they could change and be something different. I don't
> mean their characters would change, but they haven't set into
> a mould. You know if something happened in the world or
> there was a change of some kind, a revolution or something.
> ... They'd be something different if they had to be. But
> you'll never be different, father, you'll always have to live
> the way you do now." (P. 36)

From the beginning chapter, then, the division is drawn between those who are open to experience and those who hedge their lives with limitations. Anna's struggle to remain open and truthful is set against a backdrop of lives which are closed and unexamined.

The novel offers a number of clearly drawn but sympathetic portraits of characters who become less than they might have been. Marion, Richard's wife, is shown initially as a pathetic society woman, still in love with her husband and therefore crushed by his infidelities. She first appears, drunken, and envious—she thinks—of the lives of free women. Later, when Tommy is blinded, she finds, in helping him, a way of getting outside herself and of seeing Richard more clearly. She explains to Anna: " 'I've made scenes, and been a fool and been unhappy and . . . the point is, what for? . . . Because the point is, he's not anything, is he? I don't care if he is ever so important and a captain of industry. . . . I thought, My God, for that creature I've ruined my life. I remember the moment exactly. I was sitting at the breakfast-table wearing a sort of negligee thing I'd bought because he likes me in that sort of thing. . . . I've always *hated* them. And I thought, for years and years I've even been wearing clothes I hated, just to please this *creature*' " (p. 398). Marion's discovery should open her up. Unhappily, she immediately assumes another set of constrictions which prevent her from moving toward her own emancipation. First she is Tommy's "coy little girl" cohort in "political" projects (which amount to offering succour to various "poor things"), later she becomes a shop owner, who is, in Molly's words, "surrounded by a gaggle of little queers who exploit her, and she adores them and she giggles a lot and drinks just a *little* too much, and thinks they are ever such fun" (p. 665).

The more painful failure is Tommy, who has seen the choices so clearly but who cannot cope with the limitlessness of his mother's and Anna's way of life. Shortly after he questions Anna about her notebooks and chides her about her inability to accept the chaos around her, he attempts to kill himself. During his conversation with Anna, they had talked about what lay ahead of him; his father could offer him a host of jobs, his mother or Anna could find him as many or give him the money he needed to travel or to live at home without working. Anna points out his problem: he has too many choices. In fact, that does seem to be

Tommy's problem, and he tries to avoid it by committing suicide. Tommy succeeds in blinding rather than killing himself, and his maiming leads to unexpected results. Tommy adjusts, without any apparent difficulty, to his condition. Moreover, his aimlessness is gone. (One of the problems in the novel is that it is very difficult to decide precisely what career Tommy does take up; the fault seems to lie with Lessing rather than the reader.)[9] The new Tommy is far from pleasant; he becomes a sort of tyrant in his mother's house. As Anna and Molly discuss this, they hit upon the essence of the change: " 'He's happy for the first time in his life. That's what so terrible. . . . you can see it in how he moves and talks—he's all in one piece for the first time in his life.' Molly gasped in horror at her own words, hearing what she had said: *all in one piece*, and matching them against the truth of that mutilation" (p. 378). When the whole range of choices lay before Tommy he could not act; by closing off the number of possibilities Tommy could take hold. The cost, Lessing makes clear, is more than a literal loss of sight.

The greatest loss to the world of rigidity—and it comes at the end of the novel, leaving Anna standing alone—is Molly. Throughout the novel, the reader watches Anna and Molly strengthening each other, each proof to the other that the tough choice to become free women was the right one. At the end, however, Molly gives up the battle. Molly is somewhat older than Anna and the strain of Tommy's suicide attempt and recovery has sapped her strength. So, finally, she takes herself out of the "emotional rat race" and accepts a safe marriage. In the last conversation Molly says sardonically, " 'There's nothing like knowing the exact dimensions of the bed you're going to fit yourself into' "; then annoyed with herself, " 'You're a bad influence on me, Anna, I was perfectly resigned to it all until you came in' " (p. 666). Unlike Tommy or Marion, Molly has no illusions about her decision. Lessing has the reader see that she fought the good fight until her strength finally gave way.

The focus of the book is Anna's attempt to become a "whole person," which, in Anna's case, means coming to terms with her emotional and political life as well as with her writing. At the outset, in the narrative section, we learn that Anna has recognized that the prospect of life with Michael is a false hope; but she admits to feeling incomplete without a man in her life. In the course of the narrative, she falls into a depression, deepened by her daughter's leaving for boarding school. Since Anna had previously given up her membership in—and consequently her work for—the Communist Party, and since she suffers a writer's block which prevents her from doing more than recording her various selves in her notebooks, Anna finds her last prop removed when her daughter—and with her the external demand for a stable, controlled Anna—goes off to school. The fourth, and next to last, narrative section leaves Anna in a precarious emotional state. In the notebooks which follow the narrative sections we are made to feel the pain of Anna's experiences more intensely; yet, from these notebooks we also discover what Anna gains from her introspection.

In reading over the novel she's been writing in the yellow notebook Anna realizes what happened to her in her affair with Michael:

> And so now, looking back at my relationship with Michael ... I see above all my naivety. Any intelligent person could have foreseen the end of this affair from its beginning. And yet I, Anna, like Ella with Paul, refused to see it. Paul gave birth to Ella, the naive Ella. He destroyed in her the knowing, doubting, sophisticated Ella and again and again he put her intelligence to sleep, and with her willing connivance, so that she floated darkly on her love for him, on her naivety, which is another word for a spontaneous creative faith. . . .
>
> Sometimes when I, Anna, look back, I want to laugh out loud. It is the appalled, envious laughter of knowledge at innocence. I would be incapable now of such trust. I, Anna, would never begin an affair with Paul. Or Michael. Or rather, I would begin a deliberately barren, limited relationship. (Pp. 211–212)

In fact Anna had ignored the "warnings" Michael had given her, that he would not marry her. She had accepted his refusal to assume responsibility for her and for her daughter without letting herself know the meaning of his lack of commitment. Her affair with Michael was better for Anna than her marriage had been. She had married Max Wulf without having any real emotional relationship with him, so, it seemed to her later, the marriage had never happened; he had never touched her. With Michael she had known times of deep sympathy but, as she comes to see, Michael put her intelligence to sleep.

Anna feels the need for social commitment. She was drawn to the Communist Party twice in her life. When she lived in Africa during the war most of her energy was in the service of a small idealistic circle of communist sympathizers. Later, in London, she joins the Party and works for them. She gives several reasons for joining: the Party offered her an occupation which, when compared with the blatant commercialism of the literary world, seemed significant. Moreover, it offered her activity which in itself engendered a sense of purpose. Most importantly, the Party gave her "the company of people who have spent their lives in a certain kind of atmosphere, where it is taken for granted that their lives must be related to a central philosophy." She thinks with regret as she decides to leave: "There is no group of people or type of intellectual I have met outside the Party who aren't ill-informed, frivolous, parochial, compared with certain types of intellectual inside the Party. And the tragedy is that this intellectual responsibility, this high seriousness, is in a vacuum: it relates not to Britain; not to communist countries as they are now; but to a spirit which existed in international communism years ago" (p. 343). She realizes her own need for a "personal myth"; "Koestler. Something he said sticks in my mind—that any communist in the West who stayed in the Party after a certain date did so on the basis of a private myth. Something like that. So I demand of myself, what is my private myth? That while most of the criticisms of the Soviet Union are true, there must be a body of people biding their time there, waiting to reverse the present process back to real socialism" (p. 160). What Anna comes to see is that neither her personal myth nor the official party line are true to what is going on. Instead of a healthy, growing philosophy sensitive to the need for change, Anna realizes, "there's a group of hardened fossilised men opposed by fresh young revolutionaries as John Butte once was, forming between them a whole, a balance, and then a group of fossilised hardened men like John Butte, opposed by a group of fresh and lively-minded and critical people. But the core of deadness, of dry thought, could not exist without lively shoots of fresh life, to be turned so fast, in their turn, into dead sapless wood" (p. 344). But the final shattering of Anna's illusions about the Party comes in her discussion with a Party mem-

188 · MARY COHEN

ber whom she admires. He insists that alienation cannot be coun-
tered—at this point in history: " 'throughout history, there have
perhaps been five, ten, fifty people, whose consciousness truly
matched their times. And if our consciousness of reality doesn't
fit our time, what's so terrible about that' " (p. 359). Anna is ap-
palled: " 'All you are saying is, we must submit to being split. . . .
That's treachery. . . . to humanism. . . . [Because] humanism stands
for the whole person, the whole individual, striving to become as
conscious and responsible as possible about everything in the universe. But now you sit there, quite calmly, and as a humanist you
say that due to the complexity of scientific achievement the human being must never expect to be whole, he must always be
fragmented' " (p. 360). Anna is disappointed in the Party, then,
for two reasons: on the political level the Party is devoid of
promise, given as it is to in-fighting, dogmatism, and deceit; on
the personal level the Party accepts rather than resists fragmentation of the individual. Anna rejects the Party for these failings
at least three years before Tommy forces her to see her own
fragmentation or before she can resolve to end it.

Anna's loss of faith in the Communist Party leaves her adrift.
Her personal life is fragmented, her political life lacks focus. Her
dissolution reveals itself in still another area of life: she is unable
or unwilling to write. Her dissatisfaction with writing is closely
linked to her dissatisfaction with herself: her writing and her
personal life fail to connect with the greater social concerns. Several years before the narrative begins, Anna had gone through a
period of therapy with a woman psychoanalyst, Mrs. Marks. She
is grateful to her, but she is not altogether comfortable with the
aims of psychoanalysis. A conversation she records reveals her
reservations. She describes the diary she has been keeping—clip-
pings of various disasters rather than a personal account: " 'I
glanced over them the other day: what I've got is a record of
war, chaos, misery.' 'And that seems to you the truth about the
last few years? . . .' She was saying without words that our 'experience' has been creative and fructifying, and that I am dis-
honest in saying what I did. I said: 'Very well then; the newspaper
cuttings were to keep things in proportion. I've spent three years,
more, wrestling with my precious soul, and meanwhile. . . . It's just
a matter of luck that I haven't been tortured, murdered, starved to
death, or died in a prison' " (pp. 250–251).

Although she tried throughout the course of Anna's therapy, Mrs. Marks had not been able to break through Anna's writer's block. She failed, in part, because she had, to Anna's way of thinking, a false view of art. Anna remembers her anger at Mrs. Marks' acceptance of the idea that "the artist writes out of an incapacity to live" (p. 62). Elsewhere she considers the atmosphere of the doctor's office: "it is almost like an art gallery.... It gives me pleasure, like an art gallery. The point is, that nothing in my life corresponds with anything in this room—my life has always been crude, unfinished, raw, tentative; and so have the lives of the people I have known well. It occurred to me, looking at this room, that the raw unfinished quality in my life was precisely what was valuable in it and I should hold fast to it" (pp. 236–237). Anna deplores the thoughtless reverence for art (Mrs. Marks's office Anna describes as being like a shrine to art) and the idea that art and artist exist somehow apart from ordinary life. In order to write again, Anna will have to draw on the raw unfinished quality of her life, which will mean relinquishing the several notebooks and the attempt to create order. Not until she meets someone who shares her ideas about art's connection with the life of individuals and the society they live in will Anna have the courage to return to writing.

The novel draws a picture of Anna scattered in notebooks, without significant connection to society, barely recovered from an affair which had been damaging because it had not permitted the involvement of her whole self, and unable to write because what she wrote seemed both untrue and unconnected to the larger world. Early in the novel Anna tells Molly she fears the loss of resilience: " 'Both of us are dedicated to the proposition that we're tough ... a marriage breaks up, well, we say, our marriage was a failure, too bad. A man ditches us—too bad we say, it's not important. We bring up kids without men—nothing to it, we say, we can cope. We spend years in the communist party and then we say, Well, well, we made a mistake, too bad. ... Well don't you think it's at least possible, just possible that things can happen to us so bad that we don't ever get over them?' " (p. 53). The reader begins to fear that Anna has finally reached the point of giving up. It is her experience with Saul Green that puts Anna together again.

Anna, now living alone, takes in Saul Green, a very much

troubled American leftist and writer, as a boarder. That someone in Saul Green's beleaguered mental state can do Anna any good is difficult for the reader to accept, but the way has been prepared. In the third yellow notebook, Lessing has Ella work out the ideas for the affair between Anna and Saul: "I've got to accept the patterns of self-knowledge which mean unhappiness or at least a dryness. But I can twist it into victory. A man and a woman— yes. Both at the end of their tether. Both cracking up because of a deliberate atempt to transcend their own limits. And out of the chaos, a new kind of strength" (p. 467).

The idea works, but unfortunately the last blue notebook, the golden notebook, and the final "Free Women" chapter, the sections which detail the affair from which Anna emerges with new strength, are the least satisfying in the novel. In these sections Lessing is careless, and the novel becomes confusing, apparently without good reason. Tommy and Marion are got rid of; how they parted and why they took up their separate positions are matters left unexplained. Saul Green becomes—or seems to—Milt in the final narrative. Most bothersome is Anna's denial in the last "Free Women" narrative that she will write again; the reader must see her response as evasive, since Anna's decision to write again, which occurs at the conclusion of the golden notebook section, is the climax toward which the novel moves.

Moreover, Lessing's portrayal of Saul Green works against his function in the novel. He is meant to lead Anna into breakdown and exorcize her fear of formlessness. While he seems to do so, he is so little different from other men in his treatment of Anna that it is difficult for the reader to accept him as her mentor. He uses her sexually, ignoring her emotional needs, in fact, tormenting her further by seeking out other women—or at least seeming to. (His journal shows him to have moved callously through the lives of countless women, in countless cities.) Apparently these failings are not intended to interfere with the reader's recognition that his perseverance through madness and his faith in literature and its value to a reordered world are crucial to Anna's recovery and growth.

In the course of the novel Anna's examination of herself and others had yielded several ideas essential to her sense of herself. In considering her affair with Michael she learned about the naive Anna; the Anna who meets Saul Green will not put her intelligence to sleep. Anna knows the day will come when she will ask him to stay and he will have to leave. She accepts that knowledge and goes into the experience despite it. From her observations of Americans, she finds she understands the prevailing tenor of the times: one must limit emotions, "Of course, emotion is a trap, it delivers you into the hands of society, that's why people are measuring it out. . . . How old-fashioned of me to seek a witch-doctor to be taught to feel. . . . In a world as terrible as this, limit emotion. How odd I didn't see it before" (pp. 544–545). Anna has already counted the pain her own emotions have caused her: "women's emotions are all still fitted for a kind of society that no longer exists. My deep emotions, my real ones, are to do with my relationship with a man. One man. But I don't live that kind of life, and I know few women who do" (p. 314). Nevertheless, Anna refused to submit to blocking herself off; rather, she comes to terms with what her decision to keep herself open will mean: " 'It is possible that in order to keep love, feeling, tenderness alive, it will be necessary to feel these emotions ambiguously, even for what is false and debased, or for what is still an idea, a shadow in the willed imagination only . . . or if what we feel is pain, then we must feel it, acknowledging that the alternative is death. Better anything than the shrewd, the calculated, the noncommittal, the refusal of giving for fear of the consequences . . .' " (pp. 545–546).

Anna is revitalized through her affair with Saul Green, and it is the golden notebook that heralds her triumph. She goes into the experience with Saul knowing its limitations, and when he leaves she is not unprepared. She emerges stronger, open, and with her resilience confirmed. The first sign of health comes at the end of the final blue notebook section when she resolves to put all of herself in one book. The golden notebook is a record of chaos perhaps, but also of strength growing from the facing of chaos. Without a society which fosters wholeness, without men who can deal with free women—or be free men themselves—Anna can hardly hope to find herself whole, but the golden notebook gives a sign that she will at least continue to fight against fragmentation in herself.

Saul encourages Anna to write again. He doesn't seem to answer the questions Anna had posed directly, but he shares her commitment to self and society and their agreement about the im-

192 · MARY COHEN

portance of literature is understood. He explains his desire for her to return to work in terms of his own needs: " 'You're part of a team. . . . There are a few of us around in the world, we rely on each other even though we don't know each other's name. But we rely on each other all the time. We're a team, we're the ones who haven't given in, who'll go on fighting. I tell you, Anna, sometimes I pick up a book and I say: Well, so you've written it first, have you? Good for you. O.K., then I won't have to write it' " (p. 642). Saul gives Anna the first sentence for her novel: "The two women were alone in the London flat"—the first sentence of *The Golden Notebook*, thus a promising sign.

It is significant that Lessing leaves the reader with the idea that Anna herself can, at the end of her struggle, write a novel like *The Golden Notebook*. If she can, then it means that Anna has overcome her fear of formlessness and that she will never again write a novel, like her first, which falsifies the experience from which it is drawn.[10] It is in her final dream in the golden notebook section, her last experience within the madness she has shared with Saul Green, that Anna learns how to take in the substance for her fiction. A projectionist is directing her film-like dream; in it she sees the events which went into *Frontiers of War*: "And because of his directing me, I watched even more closely. I realised that all the things to which I had given emphasis, or to which the pattern of my life had given emphasis, were now slipping past, fast and unimportant. . . . Then the film went very fast, it flicked fast, like a dream, on faces I've seen once in the street, and have forgotten, on the slow movement of an arm, on the movement of a pair of eyes, all saying the same thing—the film was now beyond my experience, beyond Ella's, beyond the notebooks, because there was a fusion; and instead of seeing separate scenes, people, faces, movements, glances, they were all together" (p. 634).

Having faced whatever chaos exists in her life as she does by committing all of herself to a single notebook, Anna is then able to go on, to write again. She will draw from the raw unfinished quality of her life, the part of her life which will be most valuable if in fact she is, as she once insisted to an unbelieving Mrs. Marks, " 'living the kind of life women never lived before' " (p. 472). She is no longer part of the Communist dream, since it was a dream that failed. She still lacks a man at the center of her life; her struggle to escape fragmentation will probably always be with her. Still, she hasn't lost her resilience, and she will write again. She will continue to stand for humanism, "for the whole person, the whole individual, striving to become as conscious and responsible as possible about everything in the universe."

Eve among the Indians

DAWN LANDER

Landscape
After all anybody is as their land and air is.
Anybody is as the sky is low or high,
the air heavy or clear
and anybody is as there is wind or no wind there.
It is that which makes them and the arts they make
and the work they do and the way they eat
and the way they drink
and the way they learn and everything.
Gertrude Stein

"This new creature with the long hair is a good deal in the way."
Mark Twain, "The Diary of Adam and Eve"

I

I suppose I began to compose this essay on women in the wilderness long ago, when I was a girl living in the desert and dust of Southern Arizona and later in the irrigated central valley at Phoenix, and I suppose that now I am not in the beginning of consciousness, but somewhere in the middle, and am only elaborating upon an earlier response to the flat landscape and coarse uninhabited mountains.

I lived for a period in the tiny town of Douglas, situated in copper mining country near Cochise's stronghold, a mile from Mexico, where the road suddenly became dirt at the border entrance to the adobe village of *Agua Prieta*. I went yearly to Tombstone Helldorado Days and wondered at the Boot Hill inscriptions, "Hanged by the neck until dead, 18—" and watched the re-staging of the battle at the O.K. Corral. I went to the rodeos and watched the cowboys rope the cows and wrestle the bulls, and to the State Fair and the County Fair and looked at the jams and prize sheep and Indians painting with sand. I caught catfish in the cattle ponds and watched the red slag from the smelter pour down the mountain at night.

I lived a while in Phoenix, situated in a valley and ringed by mountains which erupt abruptly like purple sentinels out of the valley floor. The valley is green and irrigated at the heart, and dry and brown on the skirts, or spotted with yellow cactus flowers. There were rabbits and quail and acres of cotton and caterpillars, and the cold irrigation water that forced me out of bed at three in the morning. I wore high boots and opened the dikes in the citrus grove, and the gophers, wet and looking like rats, swam out of their flooded tunnels, and my father killed them with the shovel. I carved Indian Kachina dolls out of balsa wood and stuck pigeon feathers on their heads. I squinted hard to find the "needle's eye" which led to the lost Dutchman's gold mine in the Superstition Mountains. I swam with my dog in the river and shot my father's pistol at beercans. I loved the desert, the rugged mountains, the sunsets, the night sky. I did not identify myself with houses, churches, and fences. I loved to be outdoors. I loved the space, energy, and passion of the landscape.

Ten years after I left Arizona, I began graduate studies in American literature and, not surprisingly, my interest focused upon literature of the wilderness. Repeatedly, however, I could find no place for myself and for my pleasure in the wilderness in the traditionally recorded images of women on the frontier. Tradition gives us the figure of a woman, strong, brave and often heroic, whose endurance and perseverance are legendary. It may seem strange that I find it difficult to identify with this much-praised figure. But I can almost hear her teeth grinding behind her tight-set lips; her stiff spine makes me tired and her clenched fists sad. Victimization and martyrdom are the bone and muscle of every statue, picture and word portrait of a frontier woman. She is celebrated because she stoically transcended a situation she never would have freely chosen. She submits to the wilderness just as—supposedly—she submits to sex. But she needn't enjoy it, and her whole posture is in rigid opposition to the wilderness experience: to the land, to the Indians. Her glory, we are told, is that she carried the family, religion, fences, the warmth of the hearth and steaming washtubs inviolate to the middle of the American desert.

I did not see myself in this image and could not believe that it fully communicated the character of the frontier woman. I felt that if my feelings about the wilderness were not those assigned to women by custom, then perhaps other women did not fit the stereotype either. I began in scholarly earnest to read the feminine voices in the literature of the American frontier, and I found recorded experiences which substantially alter the composite figure tradition has handed down.

Some American women writers have tried to go beyond the stereotypes. Alice Marriott repeats "all this history" of the cattle country from a woman's point of view in her book, *Hell on Horses and Women*. Concerning the title, she says, "Never once . . . did I hear a *woman* acknowledge the truth of the statement that 'The cow business is . . . hell on horses and women.' . . . I have come to the conclusion that that oft-quoted statement originated with a man. . . . And, manlike, they said the words and attributed them to women, without asking women how they really felt." [1]

Other women have satirized traditional assumptions. Sarah Lippincott, interviewing Greeley, Colorado, women in 1873, writes:

> The women of Greeley seem to me to have spirit and cheerfulness. Yet I felt . . . they must be discontented, unhappy, rebellious; and I tried to win from them the sorrowful secret. I gave them to understand that I was a friend to the sex, ready at any time, on the shortest notice, to lift up my voice against the wrongs and disabilities of women; that I deeply felt for wives and daughters whom tyrant man had dragged away from choice Gospel and shopping privileges. But the perverse creatures actually declared that they were never so happy and so healthy as they are here, right on the edge of the great American desert. [2]

Caroline Kirkland, in 1839 in *A New Home—Who'll Follow?*
wrote of a heroine who believed "that people, nay, women alone,
can live in a wilderness. . . ."[3] Agnes Smedley lived in the farm-
lands of the plains and in the mining communities of the South-
west and, although in her fictional autobiography, *Daughter of
Earth*, she rejected the traditional roles assigned to women in these
frontier settlements, she did not reject the wilderness; she em-
braced the landscape and identified herself with its native inhabi-
tants, the Indians:

> Arizona penetrated my spirit and I felt no friendship for the
> American soldiers who had hunted and fought the Apache
> leader, Geronimo, until they had captured him and sent him
> and his warriors to the swamps of Florida, most of them to
> die. I understood why Geronimo had fought for so long to
> hold the land he loved. The deserts were indeed gray and
> sinister wastes . . . but . . . lay there, calling to you to come
> on and on . . . just beyond was something still more beautiful
> in the moonlight. . . . The Arizona desert came closer to my
> spirit than has any place I have ever known.[4]

She rode a horse almost everywhere she went, often with a gun
slung at her side, and writes that she rode safely, for "it was a
land where women were strong."[5]

Once I knew that my own feelings about the wilderness were
duplicated in the experiences of historic and contemporary
women, I began to speculate on the reasons for the discrepancy
between women's actual feelings and the received tradition. White
women like Agnes Smedley identified with the American wilderness and saw it as a refuge from socially assigned roles. Nevertheless, American tradition has regarded the white woman as an
intruder into the landscape and has treated the drama of the New
World as the reenactment of the myth of the Fall of Eden. As
Eve's appearance in the garden assured the corruption of Eden,
so was "the American Earthly Paradise, lost when the first White
women entered."[6] "Two paradises/'twere in one/To live in paradise alone," Andrew Marvell wrote in "The Garden," only a few
years after the first white woman landed in the New England
wilderness. If the New World was viewed as a potential Second
Paradise, as a return to Marvell's "happy Garden-state,/while man

there walked without a mate," it was also eventually regarded as a Paradise Lost.

If New World literature and criticism imitated Old World patterns, there was an apparent modification: the scapegoat in the New World Garden[7] was not simply the woman, but the white woman. And as if to convince white women that they were anomalies in the landscape, most books about frontier America report only that they hated to leave civilization, were repelled by the rugged landscapes, and hated and feared Indians. All in all, it is said, the wilderness life was too rough for women. About 1848 Francis Parkman described the women in a group of emigrants on the Oregon Trail: "The women were divided between regrets for the homes they had left and fear of the deserts and savages before them."[8] In 1940, William Sprague, in a study entitled *Women and the West: A Short Social History*, restates the three themes in Parkman's writing:

> It is a *well known fact* that women, as a rule, find it harder to leave friends, relatives, and associations than do men.[9]
> Perhaps it is *needless to state* that it was the wives of the first arrivals who suffered most severely. *Certainly* they could hardly share their husbands' apparent enjoyment of the aboriginal features of their existence.[10]
> ... in the plains-mountain West, the physical features of the country which women generally find so repugnant....[11]
> This Indian danger was one which sent fear into the hearts of women *in particular*.[12]
> (Emphases mine)

Tradition identifies women with the home, fences, churches, towns, and civilization. This identification is almost a cliché in the literature of the American frontier. Men, on the other hand, we are told, prefer a horse to a house, an open prairie to a fenced yard, nature to religion, and the wilderness to civilization. The woman is stationary; the man is mobile. She is waiting at the lighthouse cliff, searching the sea for the return of the sailor, or in the sod house on the prairie, looking into the horizon for the frontiersman, isolated from the landscape and from human beings outside her immediate family.

"Women are ... the civilizers of mankind. What is civilization? I answer, the power of good women,"[13] wrote Ralph Waldo

Emerson in 1855 in an essay entitled "Woman" and delivered to a woman's group in Boston. Emerson also said:

> ... there is usually no employment or career which they will not with their own applause and that of society quit for a suitable marriage.[14]
>
> And they ... lose themselves eagerly in the glory of their husbands and children. Man stands astonished at a magnanimity he cannot pretend to.[15]

Above all, women want to be in the home, not in the wilderness.

II

Because, as Emerson specified, civilization was the power of "good" women, women cannot be civilized and sexual at the same time. White women who refuse to restrict their behavior to what society intends for them find the wilderness a natural habitat for a forbidden sexuality, and for them, separation from the male, and solitary wandering in the wilderness are considered equivalent to the fall. Thus, for example, the traditional single female in the literature of the American wilderness is a promiscuous savage, black or Indian, or a white prostitute.

In Nathaniel Hawthorne's classic American novel, *The Scarlet Letter*, Hester Prynne, exiled to the wilderness because of her adultery, was

> for so long a period not merely estranged, but outlawed, from society.... Her intellect and heart had their home, as it were, in desert places, where she roamed as freely as the wild Indian in his woods. For years past she had looked from this estranged point of view at human institutions, ... criticizing all with hardly more reverence than the Indian would feel for the clerical band, the judicial robe, the pillory, the gallows, the fireside, or the church.... The scarlet letter was her passport into regions where other women dared not tread.[16]

After having been an agent in what Dimmesdale considers to be his moral downfall, Hester has the audacity to suggest a further voluntary penetration into the wilderness, and habitation with the Indians. "Whither leads yonder forest track? Backwards to the settlement, thou sayest! Yes; but onward, too! Deeper it goes, and deeper, into the wilderness, less plainly to be seen at every step! until, some few miles hence, the yellow leaves will show no vestige of the white man's tread. There thou art free! ...Be, if thy spirit summon thee to such a mission, the teacher and apostle of the red men." [17] But it is a moral wilderness to which Hester beckons Dimmesdale, and he rejects the temptation. It is only because Hester has given in to an outlawed sexuality and is alienated from civilization that she is able to contract an intimacy with the wilderness, and it is, finally, a wilderness which, according to the narrator, "taught her much amiss."

The good women on the frontier stay at home, psychologically if not physically. Earlier, I have suggested that the tradition of the American woman's submission to the wilderness experience has the same psychological overtones as the tradition of her submission to sex: her husband has forced her into the wilderness, but she needn't enjoy it, and because she transcends the experience, she is celebrated for her sacrifice. The "wilderness" taboo denies feminine wanderlust and has a dynamic similar to the sexual taboos which deny feminine lust. The home-loving figure is repelled by all forms of wildness, including sexuality and other peoples.

The American white man, on the other hand, loves the wilderness and belongs in it. His image in the wilderness is that of the hunter, from Leatherstocking to Ike McCaslin to the protagonists of James Dickey's *Deliverance* or Mailer's *Why Are We in Vietnam?* Thoreau wrote, in *Walden*:

> Thus far I am of the opinion of Chaucer's nun [sic], who
> "yave not of the text a pulled hen
> That saith that hunters ben not holy men."
> There is a period in the history of the individual, as of the race, when the hunters are the "best men," as the Algonquins called them. We cannot but pity the boy who has never fired a gun. ....[18]

Hunting is a sacred and exclusively masculine activity and hence it seems the wilderness as an exclusively masculine domain is the theme of most American wilderness literature.[19] White women are absent in this world, populating Cooper's settlements, holding the fort in Dickey's suburbia, defending the two-car garage and backyard barbecue.[20]

Nick Adams, in Hemingway's story, "Fathers and Sons," remembers that his father was a hunter, lived among Indians, and was not successful sexually: "He [Nick] was very grateful to him [his father] for two things; fishing and shooting. His father was as sound on those two things as he was unsound on sex...."[21] But when Nick's own son asks him: "What was it like, Papa, when you were a little boy and used to hunt with the Indians?" Nick is startled. "'It's hard to say,' Nick Adams said. Could you say she did first what no one has ever done better and mention plump brown legs, flat belly, hard little breasts, well holding arms, quick searching tongue... and hemlock needles stuck against your belly...."[22] Nick's first memory of the wilderness is of sex with an Indian girl.

Contrary to its surface appearance, America promises not a land of men without women, a Paradise without Eve, but a wilderness where the white man will have the best sex of his life. The assertion that wilderness life is too difficult for women, and the subsequent insistence upon the exclusion of white women often assumes, unspoken, the retention of a non-white female sexual object (not peer or partner) and a sexuality which is without responsibility. Trudy is a nutbrown maid, unashamed: "'You think we make a baby?' Trudy folded her brown legs together happily and rubbed against him. '...make plenty baby what the hell....'"[23] In the wilderness, the "otherness" of sexual opposites, of the male-female polarity, is reinforced or even replaced by polarities of class or race. In fact, the foreignness of class or race is an indispensable component of eroticism in the wilderness.

Thus, in American literature, only white women are considered too frail for frontier life. For example, Cooper gives Cora dark blood to insure her indigenous relationship to the wilderness and to permit even the imagination of her union with the Indian Uncas, in *The Last of the Mohicans*. Cora's pure white blonde half-sister Alice wilts and faints in the wilderness and is finally returned to the settlements and a domestic environment more suited to her nature. In A. B. Guthrie's *The Big Sky* (1947), Boone, the trapper hero, muses: "...it gave him a pinch when he thought back to last year and remembered the white women that a couple of crazy preachers had brought to rendezvous on Horse Creek.... Damned if they weren't on wheels.... *White women! And wheels!* They figured to spoil a country, except that the women would leave or die. Ask any *hunter* who had fought In-

dians and gone empty-stomached and like to froze, and he'd say
it was no place for women, or for preachers, either, or farmers"
(italics mine).[24] Here is the unrelenting identification of white
women with religion and civilization and the insistence that, like
civilization, the white woman is antithetical to the wilderness.

Above, in the trapper's second reflection, he falls back on a
generalized myth: the wilderness is too rough for delicate feminine nature, is "no place for women." But immediately thereafter,
with no sense of contradiction, he fantasizes about the Indian
women he will seek at the rendezvous: "And he would play some
hand and drink some whiskey and have himself a squaw, and then
he would be ready to go on." [25] Earlier, in his *first* exclamation,
the trapper had been precise and true to the deeper reality of the
male antipathy: the wilderness is no place for ladies. The only
women who are permitted in the wilderness are of subordinated
class and race: blacks, Indians, and white whores. In the novel,
Indian women are promiscuous, prostituted by their husbands who
trade them, with their willing consent, for a piece of red cloth.
After a trade an Indian asks, "ain't there any squaws in the land
of the Long Knives [i.e., whites]?" Later, Boone reflects on the
question which it is said he will remember "as long as he lived":
" 'No squaws in the land of the Long Knives?' In a way it was
so simple it made a man want to laugh." [26] Another character, Jim,
decides that women are for a man's pleasure: ". . . when a man
pleasured himself, he was doing what God expected all along. . . .
Why were squaws so many and so easy, if not for a purpose?" [27]
And why were white women absent if not for a purpose, perhaps
so simple it "made a man want to laugh," but so complex and
personal, it makes a woman want to think.

Men who have sexual relationships with non-white women in
the wilderness indulge a passion which is lustful, savage and prohibited. The adult white male, exiled from the pre-sexual garden
of youth, carries his new sexuality into civilization, but he comes
to feel as well that his passions are incompatible with civilized behavior. Sexuality itself is exiled to the wilderness, which man re-
enters, this time in order to escape the taboos of society and to
seek an outlawed sexuality, generally with a male or female of
subordinate class or race. Nature is no longer the pre-sexual garden
of innocence, but an untamed wilderness of desire. But to extenu-
ate his departure, the white man creates and leaves behind him a

moral and prohibiting figure. His *intentions* are secured within the white woman, his female peer, who he insists behave always in the subjunctive mood, as he should or would. He, then, is free to act in the indicative and to pursue not his intentions, but his inclinations.

III

These inclinations have not always been lyric nor as innocent as, for example, Leslie Fiedler, in *The Return of the Vanishing American*, suggests in his picture of the loving white man and his Indian companions. As the white man's racist and imperialist atrocities increase, so does his need to idealize the white woman, to symbolize his finer intentions. The mere presence of the married white female is considered to be sufficiently potent to dispel the wilderness and to constitute the establishment of civilization. In the American tradition the white woman is a prohibitive moral figure, and the fury the white male may feel against his own passions and prejudices is vented against the white female: she becomes the cause of racism, of the destruction of the wilderness, and of the psychic crippling of the American male. The figure which was, in civilization, on an asexual pedestal, becomes, in the wilderness, a scapegoat. Latent in the composite image which the wilderness tradition has drawn of white women is the assumption that they are innate racists. For white civilization the direct embodiment of the sexual character of the wilderness is the native, in America the Indian. The woman who loves home and hates sexuality and the wilderness is represented, by extension, to hate Indians. This popular image has led recent writers to identify the "invasion of feminine sentiments" into the wilderness as the major cause of historic racism in America. Thus, what began as a seemingly innocuous assumption that women are home-loving, develops into the assertion that they are the cause of racism. This charge of feminine racism is becoming manifest, at a time when racism itself is under attack in the works of the sociologist, historian, and literary critic, and may be a reaction to a fear that racial barriers are weakening. The wilderness theme that women *in particular* hated and feared Indians reinforces contemporary racial taboos which *in particular* separate white women from non-whites.

Although in the literature of the frontier the racial ban most prominently separates white women from Indians, it is only part of a larger interdiction which separates white women from all nonwhites. Herbert Moller, in an article entitled "Sex Composition and Correlated Culture Patterns of Colonial America," published in 1945, sets out

> to explain the growth of racial *repugnance* heavily charged with emotions of horror and disgust. The emergence of an attitude of moral indignation can psychologically be explained, however, by the presence and influence of white women. As a matter of fact, only a very few cases are on record of a white woman brought into court for illicit relations with a Negro. On the other hand, the number of male offenders was large. . . . Moreover, through their enhanced influence on family and community life, women become more or less unintentionally the foremost agents in the establishment of racial barriers. Thus the development of aversion to racial miscegenation in the thirteen colonies can be traced to the invasion of feminine sentiments into colonial society.[28]

Moller places the burden of responsibility for racism in wilderness America upon white women, and he uses a slave society, where miscegenation is forbidden by law, as a model for his thesis.[29] Relying upon a narrow source of evidence, the courts, he concludes that white female offenders of anti-miscegenation legislation were few; and that white women must therefore have been repelled by black men.

However, another scholar, James Hugo Johnston, using a much broader base of evidence, including the legislation itself, divorce petitions, executive correspondence, and census returns, demonstrates that female offenders were far more common than is generally admitted.[30] Nevertheless, that the slave states initially assumed that the greater proportion of offenders would be white males is indicated by the prevailing legislation—such as the Virginia Act of 1662—wherein the children follow the condition of the mother.[31] But, because white women did beget mulatto children, most colonies enacted further legislation addressed to this problem. A Maryland Act of 1681, re-enacting a 1664 statute, reads: "And for as much as divers English or white women ... do intermarry with negroes or slaves, by which means divers inconveniences, controversies, and suits may arise, touching the issue of the children, of such freeborn women aforesaid, . . . be it further enacted [continuing from the 1664 law] . . . shall serve the master of the said slave during the life of her said husband, and that all issue of such freeborn English women shall be slaves as their fathers were." [32]

The legislation operated, as Harriet Martineau pointed out, as "a premium on licentiousness among white men. . . ." [33] At its worst, the legislation "was sometimes used for the purpose of enslaving the white woman" [34] and, even at its mildest, must have served to make white women particularly reluctant to enter miscegenous relationships. When he offers his limited evidence, Moller does not pause to consider these circumstances. Johnston, however, in his study, does:

> The white woman that followed the example of the white man and helped to bring mulatto children into the world had to fear the consequences of her conduct. There was, for her, always fear of the embarrassing responsibility of the white mother of the mulatto—a responsibility that, too often, was nonexistent in the case of a guilty white man. Natural fears of the physical consequences, together with the forces of law and public opinion, must have served to limit the number of mulattoes born of white mothers. [35]

Although the law prohibited miscegenation, society *de facto* tolerated miscegenation involving white males; it did not tolerate that involving white females. A double standard applied to sexual and racial behavior in Southern slave society. Black women were compelled into relations with white men; black men, on the other hand, might be murdered for the slightest indication that they related sexually to a white woman. White women were implicitly taught to accept their husbands' adultery; but they, unlike their husbands, were to feel no physical passion and to feel a particular repulsion toward black men. [36]

Many white southern women submitted to their oppression, became acculturated to their roles, absorbed the sentiments society attributed to proper white womanhood, and were obedient to the taboos which bound them. [37] And the acquiescence of these white women to their own subjection effectively constituted support of the slave system. Other women did not submit [38] and these, it would seem, suggest that an asexual, racist, xenophobic sensibility was not innate to white women but that, when it did (and does) occur, it is a result of a socialization process begun in childhood.

I would like to step back for a moment and suggest a logic with which to consider Moller's thesis. David Hackett Fischer, in *Historians' Fallacies* (1970), writes: "A fallacy is not merely an error itself but a way of falling into error. It consists in false reasoning, often from true factual premises, so that false conclusions are generated." [39] Some of Moller's facts may be valid: racism increased *when* white women appeared. But to thus imply that white women are therefore the source of racism is distorted; their presence might equally well have activated fears and prejudices in male minds.

The social dynamic of the taboos affecting white women in the wilderness communities of New England and the Far West was the same as that of the more transparent ones in a slave society. In the Rockies, the white trappers usually took Indian "wives," but white men would not tolerate any physical contact between an Indian and a white woman. George Bent, son of a Cheyenne woman, writes of the trouble created when military posts were established on the frontier: "The first trouble was at Fort Atkinson in 1853. Lean Bear, a young Cheyenne, was visiting the fort and took hold of an officer's wife's hand, to look at her ring. The lady's husband rushed up and attacked Lean Bear with a big whip." [40] The first trouble occurs *when* a white woman appears, but her reaction is not mentioned and we do not know that it was racist. We only know that her husband had his own definition of what her relationship to Indians should be.

This spontaneously violent response of the white man to potential contact between the white woman and Indian male is also expressed in fiction. In the story cited earlier, "Fathers and Sons," Hemingway suggests that at the slightest possibility that the white woman might imitate his behavior in the wilderness, the white man seems ready to murder. First, the promiscuous Indian maid is sexually aggressive with the white male; the Indian girl Trudy has her hand in Nick's pocket "exploring" while her brother Bill and Nick argue. Meanwhile Billy tells Nick that his own older half-brother wants to sleep with Nick's sister Dorothy. Nick responds: " 'If Eddie Gilby ever comes at night and even speaks to Dorothy you know what I'd do to him? I'd kill him like this.' Nick cocked the gun and hardly taking aim pulled the trigger, blowing a hole as big as your hand in the head or belly of that half-breed bastard Eddie Gilby. 'Like that. I'd kill him like that.' " [41] Who sets up a white woman's attitude? In this instance, Dorothy is not permitted even close enough to speak to Eddie Gilby. The racial and sexual barriers between Dorothy and Eddie, the white woman and the Indian man, are created and enforced by Nick, the white man. Dorothy's attitude, whatever it may be, is not even considered.

Perhaps because of such strong racial feelings, the facts Johnston sets forth concerning miscegenation involving white women almost never appear in traditional American literature. Virtually all fictional mulattoes derive their white blood from a male ancestor. In William Faulkner's *Go Down Moses*, the black blood in the McCaslin-Edmonds-Beauchamp genealogy is all from the female line. The fear, however, of not only the landowner, but of the poorest, smallest Southern white man that his daughter would go to bed with a black is expressed in Faulkner's *Light in August*. It doesn't matter, finally, whether the father of the protagonist Joe Christmas (and therefore Joe) was black. What matters is the fear of the poor white, Hines, that his daughter has slept with a black. Once the idea is planted, events move with an energy not necessarily derived from any particular reality, and the consequences have an inevitability independent of the objective condition: was Joe's father black or was he not?

Hines's fear, the broader and prevailing southern white prejudice, and finally the fascination of the white spinster Joanna Burden hiding nude in the garden—*not* the house—and yelling "Negro, Negro," create Joe's blackness. Joanna Burden, the single white female, imagining herself sexually involved with a Negro, finds at the hands of the novelist a sterile death which in part is the consequence of such a fantasy.

It has been suggested that in most societies miscegenation most often occurs between the male of the dominant group and the female of the subordinate group(s).[42] Thus, in American society, the male white of the ruling classes imposes himself upon the nonwhite or the oppressed female. Threatening promiscuous behavior is embodied in male oppressed nonwhite, in America represented by either the Indian or black slave. On the other side of the paradigm, constrained to abide by another code of behavior, is the female white *lady*. Her most prominent stereotype in American culture is the white southern lady. There is also the white *lady* of the frontier who, it is said, imposed her ethical and moral behavior upon the white males, non-whites, and other generally savage and uncultured elements around her.[43] In the current literature about the American frontier, one author writes, ". . . the term 'lady,' was accorded to most women . . . western men were careful to use the term in speaking even of women belonging to the laboring classes." [44] But the same author also asserts that, "Of course, there were few *ladies* around. There were women, to be sure, and that seemed to satisfy Denver's men who took 'very freely to the charms of negresses and squaws.' " [45]

Herbert Moller, in the article cited above, writes, "Aversion to so-called 'hypogamy' is considered a normal trait of feminine psychology and its existence can be taken for granted in any stratified society." [46] Moller's thesis concerning "feminine psychology" and the origin of racism in America, rather than being allowed to grow dusty on the bound periodical shelf, was restated by Louis Ruchames in 1970 in *Racial Thought in America:* "Moller explains the very strong racial repugnance as being due to 'the presence and influence of white women.' " [47]

Leslie Fiedler, in *The Return of the Vanishing American,* writes of "what Second Paradise was lost when White women entered the American woods that are forever hostile to them to scalp the woodland scalpers with whom the American artist [white male] identifies himself." [48] Fiedler repeats two popular wilderness themes: the woods are hostile to white women; white women hate Indians. He tells his readers, "Your fathers may be foolish or confused, absent always in time of trial [*i.e.,* guiltless of massacre] but your WASP mother is there, tomahawk in hand. . . ." In the introduction to his own essays, Fiedler writes: ". . . these books have become for a new generation of teachers in universities, colleges and high schools, the basis for a new understanding of our classic books and of our culture in general. . . ." [49] And when a student is challenged concerning his ideas, he can protest that he got them in the "Assigned Reading." Fiedler's false conclusions are not simply bad history, but dangerous to the image young women are forming of themselves, when they take as gospel that women are innately homeloving, racist, and fearful of adventure or change. The implications of the stereotype for women now are serious. It is not that women are not racists, but simply that they do not *have* to be. This may seem obvious and unnecessarily stated if it weren't for statements like the following from Fiedler: "Our White mothers... have always dreamed themselves and Indians irreconcilable enemies. . . ." [50]

Fiedler, like Moller, generates false conclusions from historical facts. Women on the frontier seldom left the homestead, whereas men were away for long periods of time to gather wood, hunt, fish, trade. Thus, the men were often absent when Indians attacked and women were obliged to seize a weapon and protect the home. However, this did not mean that white women and Indians were natural enemies. Eliza Farnham, writing in 1846, described a woman, left alone, "protected, if danger came, only by the dog." Indians came, but "she knew they were not enemies, and felt secure in her very helplessness. They had not lived much among the whites, and it requires some teaching to induce the savage to fall on a helpless person who is not his foe." [51] It seems that hostility between white women and Indians, which Fiedler implies is innate, when it does occur, has been learned by both parties.

Fiedler also suggests that female hostility to Indians originates in women's fear of capture: "The male imagination... substitute[s] the male dream of joining the Indians for the female fantasy of being dragged off by them." [52] The man *joins* the Indians; the woman is *dragged* off. Fiedler describes the statue of Hannah Duston which stands today in Haverhill, Massachusetts: "the stone figure of a long skirted, sunbonneted woman with a tomahawk raised aloft in her delicate hand—so like the standard Freudian dream of castrating mother that it is hard to believe it has not been torn down long since by some maimed New England male just out of analysis." [53] Mrs. Duston was taken captive by Indians in 1697. While her captors were sleeping, she reportedly killed ten Indians, including six children, took their scalps and returned to the settlements. Generalizing from the image of Mrs. Duston, Fiedler sees the archetypal white frontier woman as an ax-wielding Indian hater, who will murder ruthlessly in order to return to the comfort of her own hearth.

In 1755, another white woman, Mary Jemison, was captured by Indians, but unlike Hannah Duston, she not only remained with the Indians, but married into the tribe. Still intent upon the figure of Hannah Duston, Fiedler writes that Mary Jemison ". . . remains

as irrelevant as those eccentric males who resented rather than re-
joiced in their captivity. . . . Just as the deep male memory returns
compulsively to stories of men hailed as sons by dusky chieftains
. . . so the female memory lingers *not* on . . . Miss Jemison." [54] My
memory does. Fiedler's false assumption relies upon the taboos I
have described earlier: the wilderness taboo identifies women exclusively with Hannah Duston's murderous passion to return to
the settlements; the racial taboo denies Mary Jemison's integration
into the Indian community; and an implicit sexual taboo enjoins
female memory to forget that Mary Jemison took Indian husbands. Fiedler fails to analyze the experiences and narratives of not
only the women who returned from captivity, but of the many
white women like Mary Jemison who, through circumstance or
choice, became part of an Indian community and, in their own
lifetimes, became legends as the 'white squaws' of the American
frontier.[55] These women form a counterimage to the image of the
victim in the wilderness and to the aggressive inversion of that
image in the figure of Hannah Duston.

Fiedler also accepts the attitudes of fictional characters as the
de facto attitudes of their real life counterparts; he assumes that
American white male literature expresses the reality of the sensibility of the American white female. One example will illustrate:
"A frequent image in frontier literature is that of an Indian dashing an infant's head against a tree: How that bloody picture has
possessed the female imagination for more than three centuries,
and how it appears over and over everywhere in our literature:
from Cotton Mather himself . . . to Anna Eliza Bleecker . . . to
Robert Penn Warren." [56] Two of the three authors cited are
male, and the images they draw are used to substantiate an instance of "female imagination." Throughout his work, from predominantly male writers, Fiedler makes such assertions concerning the real feelings of American women; the *male* view of the
female view is, according to his conclusions, identical to the actual female view.

Fiedler, like Hemingway and Guthrie, betrays an implicit confusion between all women and simply white women. Thoreau, a
typical good companion, "is, we know, at his mythological core
an Indian himself, at home in the unexplored regions where
women flinch." [57] The statement ignores the fact that some Indians
are women. When Fiedler remembers to include the adjective

"white," he does so only to assert that the white woman, sometimes scalping and sometimes flinching, threatens the good companions. Just as he excluded women from the category of Indians above, Fiedler neatly excludes white women—and, for that matter, the American Indian—from the category of American artist. He further claims that the white man is an ingenuous innocent and that women committed all the carnage. And finally, because the white man is hostile to having the white woman in the wilderness, he insists that it is the wilderness itself, the very "American woods that are forever hostile to them (the white women)." In this last phrase, Fiedler at once sums up and perpetuates a tradition.

The contemporary significance of the received tradition concerning white women in the American wilderness is that it denies feminine wanderlust, keeps women in the home, and reinforces contemporary racial taboos.[58] Nevertheless, neither fear of the landscape nor aversion to miscegenation are of necessity feminine traits. Both primary and secondary literature by women significantly modify the traditional image. More research needs to be done, the findings of which are likely to alter the self-consciousness of white women who are accustomed to seeing themselves represented fearing the wilderness, victims of rape and massacre by the nonwhite men who lurk there.[59]

What If Bartleby Were a Woman?

PATRICIA BARBER

Except in one respect, Herman Melville's "Bartleby, the Scrivener: A Story of Wall-Street" (1853)[1] is an oddly timely story
not only in its theme of office alienation but also in its setting. The
lawyer of today—like the story's narrator—might well have offices on New York's Wall Street; he might well have recalcitrant
help; he might well be familiar with the still barbaric city jail, the
Tombs; he might well have windows looking only onto blank
walls. But today's lawyer would not have men doing his copying
for him: by historical circumstance the male scrivener has given
way to that office commonplace, the female typist.

At first thought this recognition seems merely nice, a device,
perhaps, for reminding undergraduates, especially women, that the
oppressiveness of the office world is still with us, that one of them
could be a Bartleby. Then, if one plays further with the idea of
Bartleby as a woman, the sex-changed story seems to contain the
makings of a farce. A Hollywood treatment might involve an unconsciously sexy young thing who moves right into the office of
a middle-aged, but eligible lawyer, hangs her undies across the
window, makes his clients wonder what is going on, and coolly
refuses to do the least bit of work. And at the end they would
marry, or at least fall into bed.

But let us not succumb to the Hollywood version entirely—
which could not, after all, encompass the suicide that closes the
scrivener's story—but rather consider seriously the story of a fe-

male Bartleby. In fact, how would a dignified gentleman like the lawyer of Melville's story respond to a woman who "prefers not to," who refuses, say, to make coffee, or answer the phone, or talk pleasantly to her boss's clients, or do anything other than merely copy documents? And, more drastically, who sets up housekeeping there in the office behind no more than an opaque glass screen, then refuses to do even her copying, and finally refuses to leave?

Is it even legitimate to ask these questions when, in fact, Melville did not write a story about a man and his secretary? To change the sex of a centrally placed character in a story might seem to amount to an act of critical violence. If Hamlet—to take one example—has been played *by* a woman, he has never, so far as I know, been played *as* a woman, and the very idea is a staggering one. What would happen if Ulysses or Oedipus or the Redcrosse Knight or—to jump space and time—Ahab or Huck Finn or any male Hemingway hero became women? What if Eve were a man? The gender of a character would seem to be a given with which a critic cannot tamper, unless, however, we understand the tampering as a heuristic device.

If a female Ulysses or Ahab seems only an impossible joke, this "joke" may serve to point up the separate boundaries we have imposed around our expectations regarding men and women. We might better understand, for one thing, to what a vast extent people's genders have determined their social roles. In considering, say, the absurdity of a sex-changed love story, Cleopatra or Jane Eyre as men, for example, we might realize how largely one's gender and resulting social role determine the emotional life. One might try to imagine Faustus as a woman and if that seems impossible, go on to consider how gender may affect the style and intensity of a person's intellectual life.[2]

It might also happen—as I suggest it does with "Bartleby"— that changing the sex of a character would not turn the story into a joke. The change might suggest new possibilities of human experience, create, in a sense, new role models. Or we might recognize how we do sometimes participate in certain situations in the same way, particularly in those situations arising from social roles which either are open equally to men and women or else—as with Bartleby's job—have become over time open to the other sex. For the critic, the technique of the sex-change might help to expose elements in a literary work which previously were obscure. Our

conventional expectations regarding sexual behavior create a kind
of critical myopia in us: we do not perceive what we do not
expect to find, and thus we may miss seeing, to take Bartleby and
the lawyer as an example, the intensity of feeling of one person
for another of the same sex.

I would like therefore to present a synopsis of the story of Miss
Bartleby in order to show both the insight Melville's story has into
the contemporary relationship of a male boss with his female employee, and also the way the sex-changed story reveals that "Bartleby, the Scrivener" is a story of failed love, a love the lawyer
conceals by adopting a rhetorical tone of genial detachment
toward his experience. To "write" Miss Bartleby's story I have
done no more to Melville's version than change 'man' to 'woman'
or 'lady,' alter the pronouns, and add the title to Bartleby's name.
For brevity's sake I have ignored the other office help in the story:
in a fuller version of Miss Bartleby's story the three other quirky
scriveners would also, I feel, be women, the "girls" in the office.

The story opens with the lawyer explaining to the reader that
in all his many years of law practice he never met with so strange
a copyist as Miss Bartleby. He describes his comfortable professional circumstances at the time he hired this woman and then returns to her story: "In answer to my advertisement, a motionless
young woman one morning stood upon my office threshold, the
door being open, for it was summer. I can see that figure now—
pallidly neat, pitiably respectable, incurably forlorn! It was Miss
Bartleby" (pp. 45–46). He tells how she worked without stopping, how she "seemed to gorge herself on my documents" (p. 46).
"I should have been quite delighted with her application," he says,
"had she been cheerfully industrious. But she wrote on silently,
palely, mechanically" (p. 46). Up to this point Miss Bartleby is a
mysterious, Jamesian figure. She is a young woman with some
secret sorrow that makes her seem, both in her lack of vitality and
her desperate industriousness, old before her time. As the lawyer
relates the story in retrospect, we learn that at first he was not
sensitive to Miss Bartleby's troubled soul.

One day, however, he was seated at his desk in that archetypal
posture of the busy boss: his head was bent over his papers, his
hand extended waiting to be relieved of the document in its grasp.
Without looking up he calls out to Miss Bartleby to proofread the
document with him: "Imagine my surprise, nay, my consterna-

tion, when without moving from her privacy, Miss Bartleby, in a singularly mild, firm voice, replied, 'I would prefer not to' " (p. 47). He is silenced for a moment, finally repeats the question, and again hears her say that she would prefer not to. He gets up "in high excitement," asks if she is "moon-struck" and insists that she help him (p. 47). For a third time she answers, " 'I would prefer not to' " (p. 47). Annoying as it is, Miss Bartleby's extraordinary refusal to do anything but simply copy documents intrigues him. He begins watching her closely, not sure what action to take, but to his every request for an office task other than silent copying, she answers that she would prefer not to.

He is not, however, at first totally dismayed by Miss Bartleby's terms: "Her steadiness, her freedom from all dissipation, her incessant industry (except when she chose to throw herself into a standing revery behind her screen), her great stillness, her unalterableness of demeanor under all circumstances, made her a valuable acquisition. One prime thing was this—*she was always there*—first in the morning, continually through the day, and last at night" (p. 53). His satisfaction with these Protestant-ethic virtues of his "acquisition" is shaken shortly thereafter when he happens by his office one Sunday morning before church. He is startled to find the office door locked from inside and Miss Bartleby there. She comes to the door "in a strangely tattered deshabille" (p. 54) and coolly tells him to go away for a while and then come back. Astounded, he does so and begins wondering why she is there, quickly dismissing the idea that anything "amiss" (p. 54) was going on.

When he returns to his office, she has gone, and he discovers that she has made the office into her living quarters. He looks through her desk and finds a bandanna with her money knotted in it. In good lawyer-fashion he then methodically counts the evidence regarding her mysterious life: he recalls that she never initiates conversation, never reads, that "for long periods she would stand looking out, at her pale window behind her screen, upon a dead brick wall" (pp. 55–56), that she never goes out to eat or to walk or for any other reason, that she never said who she was or where she came from, that she never complains of ill health. He recalls in particular "a certain unconscious air of pallid —how shall I call it?—of pallid haughtiness, say, or rather an austere reserve about her" (p. 56), a reserve which awes him. He then reaches the conclusion that she "was the victim of innate and incurable disorder. I might give alms to her body; but her body did not pain her; it was her soul that suffered, and her soul I could not reach" (p. 56).

He decides to give her another chance at self-explanation, and this time will try direct interrogation. Several times he asks if she will give him some information, but to each request she replies that she would prefer not to. Despite these refusals, the lawyer cannot yet bring himself to do as he had planned—to fire her. The next day Miss Bartleby informs him that she will do no more writing. When he asks why, she stares at the wall: " 'Do you not see the reason for yourself?' she indifferently replied" (p. 59). He does not see any reason, although he does notice, when he looks closely at her, that her eyes are dull and glazed. He decides that she must have strained her vision by writing in a poor light, and assumes that in a few days she will be back at work.

But after a few days she tells him she has given up copying for good. His anxiety mounts: he wishes he could write to her relatives and ask that they take her away "to some convenient retreat" (p. 60). But he knows of no relatives and she seems to him alone —"absolutely alone in the universe. A bit of wreck in the mid-Atlantic" (p. 60). He finally tells her she must go in six days time. But six days later she is still there. Again he tells her to leave and tries to give her some extra money, but still she stays. Finally he resorts to stern fatherly reproval and tells her that she must either do some work or get out. But still she silently refuses.

Miss Bartleby's impassive response drives the usually temperate lawyer to thoughts of murder. Shocked by his own passion, he struggles to maintain a charitable view. But gradually he becomes worried about what his clients and fellow lawyers must be thinking about the strange silent creature in his office. The thought of what her presence might do to his professional reputation finally resolves him to rid himself forever of "this intolerable incubus" (p. 66).

Knowing that Miss Bartleby will not leave of her own accord, he decides that it will actually be simpler if he leaves her. He rents a new office for himself, says goodbye to Miss Bartleby, and then "strange to say—I tore myself from whom I longed to be rid of" (p. 67). Though he is surprised that he was reluctant to leave her, he is relieved to find that she does not follow him. But the new tenants of his office find that they are now stuck with her. She sleeps, it seems, in the entry and sits all day on the banisters of the stairs.

The lawyer tries once more to persuade her to leave, but when he proposes several different jobs he might find her she is quite uninterested. Finally he asks her if she will come home with him "not to my office, but to my dwelling," and there they will work out "some convenient arrangement" (p. 69). She refuses and the lawyer is so dismayed by the whole situation that he leaves town and for the next few days does nothing but drive around out in the countryside, avoiding his office altogether. When he finally returns, he finds a note saying that the police have taken Miss Bartleby to the Tombs as a vagrant.

He goes down to the jail to see her. She is allowed to go outside in the prison yard, since her offense is so trivial and her manner so mild. Feeling guilty now, he tries to defend himself: " 'It was not I that brought you here, Miss Bartleby,' said I, keenly pained at her implied suspicion. 'And to you, this should not be so vile a place. Nothing reproachful attaches to you by being here. And see, it is not so sad a place as one might think. Look, there is the sky, and here is the grass.' 'I know where I am,' she replied, but would say nothing more, and so I left her" (p 71). He arranges for her to get some decent food, but she refuses to eat. The next time he comes to see her, a few days later, he finds her lying next to the stone wall out in the courtyard. She is dead, and he closes her eyes. The lawyer notes that he later heard that she had once been a clerk in the Dead Letter Office in Washington, an occupation he finds fitting to "a woman by nature and misfortune prone to a pallid hopelessness" (p. 73). And he concludes his tale, "Ah, Miss Bartleby! Ah, humanity!" (p. 74).

Melville's story clearly, I think, loses none of its power when Bartleby becomes a woman, a woman who refuses with such a dignified—but suicidal—emphasis. We have an all too plausible portrait of a young woman of great, if pathological, dignity who refuses to accommodate herself to a sterile world of meaningless office work. Her copying tasks offer no means of self-expression or creativity; she can declare her existence only by her passive but determined resistance. Her dignity does not permit either fist-shaking rebellion or the petty carelessness and insolence of the rightfully resentful office employee. For reasons we do not know, her outside life offers no compensating satisfactions, and even though her inner malaise is great, the failure of her office life to offer any relief at all is a devastating commentary on our modern office-bound existence.

Although no feminist would advocate suicide as an appropriate method of protesting one's working condition, still those conditions of office life are a part of what feminist agitation is all about. The lawyer in this story is no Simon Legree, but he still might be called a Mr. Shelby, the kindest of all possible slaveholders, a tactful, polite, patient boss, as decent a boss as one might expect to find; by any ordinary standard he goes out of his way to accommodate Miss Bartleby. We note that at first she seems to him a "valuable acquisition" (p. 53), hard-working, uncomplaining, quiet, like a machine that never causes trouble, the ideal office worker. "One prime thing," he says, "*she was always there*" (p. 53)—like a faithful servant or slave. At least a part of the lawyer's good feeling for her, then, rises from this initial view of her as a useful acquisition or piece of property, an attitude any worker might resent.

It is when she stops doing her work and thus ceases to be a useful acquisition to him that he vaguely realizes by his inability to fire her immediately that he has become attached to her not just because she did his copying for him, but because her loneliness and mysterious sorrow as well as her persistent refusal to leave him express her need—and his need—for human connection. He would like to help her, but his sense of what the employer-employee relationship *should* be—no work, no wages—prevents him from letting Miss Bartleby use a part of the office as a refuge. And in any case, I suggest, he would like their relationship to be more than that: when as a last resort he asks her to come home with him, he does so not only to get her out of the office, but also, one feels, as a way of expressing his own loneliness in a situation where his only relationships are with clients or office workers, relationships necessarily limited by being basically exploitative.

This story about a boss and his secretary speaks perceptively to the difficulties of making satisfying relationships in an office context.[3] In a state of despair a person who is valued only for her machine-like abilities—copying documents—rebels: she refuses, as so many would like to do but being more realistic than Miss Bartleby, do not do, and thereby expresses the hollowness of that situation in which both employers and employees suffer, but the employees, I think, suffer the most. This theme inheres in both Melville's story of the male scrivener and the sex-changed version, but since such a large part of the lower-grade office employees are now women—and their bosses men—the economic exploitation has taken sexist overtones, and by making Bartleby a woman we reveal how Melville's story explores a situation the author could not have known about.

Changing Bartleby to a woman not only serves as a device for bringing the story closer to a contemporary condition of life but also works to reveal an otherwise hidden erotic quality in the original. One of the striking aspects about the sex-changed story is how gracefully it works: the story, one can say, in fact hardly changes, surprising as this seems in view of the radical change to Bartleby. There are, I think, two reasons why Miss Bartleby's story is so similar to Mr. Bartleby's. In the first place the story is not really so much about Bartleby as it is about the lawyer who narrates the story, about passive, affluent complacency shaken by passive, irrational refusal. We never, after all, really do find out what makes Bartleby act as he does, even though we recognize the psychological realism of that suicidal refusal. Instead, as we identify with the lawyer's quiet reasonableness, the story evokes our sense of pity and helplessness in the confrontation with this isolato. That we do not really know Bartleby, that he hardly develops beyond the cadaverous figure staring at the dead brick wall, leads to the second reason why his sexual gender makes so little difference to the story.

Bartleby, whether male or female, is, by the nature of his mysterious ailment, so devitalized, so unerotic, that he becomes for us essentially sexless. This awful sexlessness and seeming absence of any erotic drive are most clearly apparent in the Miss Bartleby version. Let us take the scene where the lawyer unexpectedly encounters her one morning in, as he puts it, "deshabille" (p. 54). The staid man is taken aback both by her undress and her cool behavior, her "wonderful mildness" which "not only disarmed me, but unmanned me, as it were" (p. 54). Naturally enough he wonders what she is up to, half-dressed there in his office. The lawyer's tension here has an obvious erotic element not obvious in the male

Bartleby story and hints at the possibility of the office farce. That possibility is cut short, however, not so much by the lawyer's propriety as by Miss Bartleby's stubborn opposition to any sort of social intercourse, an opposition which, in view of her loneliness, seems startling and abnormal.

Clearly, however, Miss Bartleby intrigues the lawyer, partly by her mystery and solitude, partly by that dignified passivity which he semi-consciously recognizes in himself, and also by the very strength of her defiant stance. That strength has, I think, a distinctly erotic aspect. Here is a woman who in cold and silent anger has pushed her past life away, is pushing her present life away because it is beneath her dignity, and apparently is trying to confront only what is essential, a task few risk. The blank wall she stares at is a *tabula rasa*, Locke's image of the mind prior to experience, the mind at the beginning, the starting-point of knowledge. She is a woman who is alone: perhaps more obviously than a man alone would be, a man like the original Bartleby, she is a figure of pathos, a figure whose solitary state seems to call out for human contact, sexual bonding.

Part of the lawyer's frustration with Bartleby has to do with Bartleby's inaccessibility in his loneliness. As the lawyer narrates the story in meticulous detail, recalling whole conversations, lengthy sequences of thought, nuances of complex feelings, we understand that his experience with Bartleby was a significant one. From the time he first saw Bartleby at his office door the young man made a sharp impression on him, one that stays with him—"I can see that figure now . . ." (p. 45). In the sex-changed story we cannot help but read this distinct recollection as the first hint of erotic interest on the lawyer's part. This reading is then reinforced when the lawyer tells how closely he observed the girl's working habits and living arrangements, and becomes strong when he tells us that her "austere reserve" had "positively awed" him into a "tame compliance" with her ways (p. 56). Miss Bartleby may not be a likely object of erotic interest, but the point is that she is young and female and does live and undress and go to bed right there in the office, activities which can only be sexually provocative. In any case this lawyer does not apparently have ordinary tastes: he is not married though well along in years, himself leads a safe, austere life, and his interest in the other office workers amounts to little more than bemusement. And he is lonely.

As Miss Bartleby more and more withdraws from ordinary office activity, she forces the lawyer to regard her as not just another girl in the office but rather as a special human being. As the lawyer does so, his interest in her intensifies so that when he finally moves out he realizes he does not entirely want to leave her. When he then reaches the point of asking her to come home with him, we cannot help hearing an echo of what is usually a seductive invitation: the lawyer is thoroughly frustrated, finds himself most uncharacteristically "fairly flying into a passion," and is about to walk out "when a final thought occurred to me—one which had not been wholly unindulged before," that is, asking her to come "not to my office, but to my dwelling" (p. 6). We realize here that the lawyer has thought before of asking her to come home with him, and however proper the man is, the wish for a more domestic, a more erotic connection is apparent. When Miss Bartleby coldly refuses, this middle-aged man rushes from the building, runs up the hill on Wall Street toward Broadway, and jumps onto the first passing bus to escape the whole situation. The unusual energy he exhibits plus what follows—heading for the country to spend several days driving aimlessly around—suggest that to him her refusal was an emphatic rejection of him in every respect, including the sexual, a rejection enraging and even somewhat deranging.

The scenes of the lawyer with Bartleby at the Tombs are plainly tender ones, but when Bartleby is a woman the lawyer's tenderness takes on a romantic quality. He tells us that he saw the "wasted" Miss Bartleby "huddled at the base of the wall, her knees drawn up, and lying on her side, her head touching the cold stones," and that when he felt her hand, "a tingling shiver ran up my arms and down my spine to my feet" and he realized she was dead (p. 73). The man at the jail asked if she was asleep and the lawyer murmured, " 'With kings and counselors' " (p. 73), thus quoting *Job* and playing wishfully on his own occupation as a counselor-at-law. The lawyer, then, gives the effect of being a lover at the graveside, the figure of his loved one making him shiver and invoking in him thoughts of her afterlife.

If little of this erotic quality seems apparent in the tale of the male Bartleby, there are, I think, two explanations—one, that the lawyer's propriety and language tend to lead us away from seeing that element, and two, the more important, that we simply do not expect to find a man having an erotic feeling for another man, no matter how familiar we are with Melville's scene of Ishmael and Queequeg in bed.

To take up the first explanation, let us consider the passage midway through the story where the lawyer describes his feelings for Bartleby. For the first time in his life, he says, he was overpowered by "a stinging melancholy" (p. 55) when he contemplated Bartleby's small, lonely life in the office: "The bond of a common humanity now drew me irresistibly to gloom. A fraternal melancholy! For both I and Bartleby were sons of Adam" (p. 55). This talk of a fraternal bond, of a bond between two men, or between men in general, is the jarring note in the sex-changed story, for a fraternal bond would seem to preclude an attachment to a woman, an erotic attachment. The lawyer here seems to see himself and Bartleby in a rather rarified way, as two among all those cast out from Eden, bound, perhaps, by a sort of spiritual loss. If we recognize, however, that this elevated rhetoric is associated with an emotion as rare—for him—and as sharp as a "stinging melancholy," we can see that the lawyer is responding not merely to a vague, generalized sense of humanity but rather to a specific one-to-one relationship. The exalted rhetoric here, along with the frequent use of juristical terms and the heavy use of the passive voice, all serve as the lawyer's linguistic defenses against what would be a too painful understanding of the depth of his own feeling. And because he tells us at the outset what an "eminently *safe* man" (p. 40) he is, how tame his emotions are, we tend to feel he is incapable of strong feelings.

If the lawyer's language and propriety conceal the intensity of his feeling for Bartleby, it is also true that this feeling is concealed by our own unreadiness to see it. We only dimly feel the strength of the lawyer's feeling for Bartleby, in part simply because we do not expect such a respectable, middle-aged type to have such feelings, feelings that are basically homosexual. Our conventional attitude which does not expect to find erotic impulses between "normal" mature people of the same sex is, of course, a denial of the facts. In turn, the effect of this denial is to prevent us from understanding the roots and power of "fraternal" feelings and from understanding that these feelings are the basis of a necessary sense of common human bondage regardless of sexual gender.

The point here is that this element of fraternal passion in the lawyer is nowhere so clearly exposed as when we imagine Bartleby as a woman and therefore a more "appropriate" object of an erotic impulse. By imagining the story of Miss Bartleby, we realize that the story of the lawyer and Bartleby—for all its oddity, dry humor, and stuffy rhetoric—is essentially a love story, a story about a man who is confined in an office setting that forbids intimacy and who comes to love a person he cannot save. Melville's story of human loneliness and ineffectual compassion does not, I think, become merely an office farce.

Old Critics and New:
The Treatment of Chopin's *The Awakening*

PRISCILLA ALLEN

I

The rehabilitation of Kate Chopin began in 1952, over half a century after publication of *The Awakening*, with a translation by Cyrille Arnavon of the novel into French. Edmund Wilson's remarks in *Patriotic Gore* a decade later helped to reintroduce the work to readers of English on a wide scale. There have been other favorable commentators, but already the tide of well intentioned appreciation seems to have turned and we have had a backwash of detraction. The book has had adventures in the past fifteen years, enough to match in effect, if not in dramatic intensity, the adventures that broke its author's heart and career.

When Kate Chopin's third novel was published in 1899, critics of the day, still laboring under the Dickensian canon that fiction should not be such as "to bring a blush to the cheek of a young person," proscribed it as "sensual and devilish." It was "too strong drink for moral babes and should be labeled *poison*." According to some of them, it never should have been written. What they saw in the novel was a story of "a Southern lady who wanted to do what she wanted to. From wanting to, she did, with disastrous consequences." Or less archly, a "detailed history of the manifold and contemporary love affairs of a wife and mother." Since *The Awakening* was so far ahead of its times, it is no wonder that Victorian critics, preoccupied with matters of sex, condemned it.

The fact of Edna's adultery blinded them to other aspects of the novel.

What may seem at first strange and anomalous, however, is that modern critics, liberal and enlightened on sexual matters, applaud the novel and urge its reading, but still see no further essentially than their predecessors. This anomaly reflects the shortcomings of the sexual revolution, when two main rights, it now seems, were won. First was the right to do a lot more of what people were already doing in the way of sex and second was the right to talk about it. No studies exist to show how much sexual activity has increased, but there is no doubt about the talk. We have had a steady torrent of talk about sex since the twenties. Since no fundamental change in the status of the sexes resulted from that revolution, the talk begins to get boring in its predictable sameness, an oppression in itself. And the mode of relating, oppressive to women when it was shy or sly, is all the more oppressive when it is boomed about. This new oppression is reflected in the modern criticism of Chopin's *The Awakening*.

The modern critics' general descriptions of the novel make a resounding chorus.[1] Leary approvingly quotes Eble, the first modern critic: "As Kenneth Eble has said, 'quite frankly the book is about sex.'" In between, others have said the book is: "about the adulterous experiments of a married woman" (Ziff); "a grand orchestration of the symphony of imperative Eros" (Seyersted); "simply a sensuous woman who follows her inclinations without thinking" (Wilson); "an account of a young woman ... who after six years of marriage and two children gradually awakens to the truth that her relationship to her husband is not fulfilling to her as a woman" (Spangler); "the story ... of a wife who becomes increasingly alienated from her husband" (Arms). Eble later equates Edna's "struggle with elemental passion" to Phaedra's. Ziff adds that the book is a "most important piece of fiction about the sensual life of a woman." Arms's plot summary sketches only the coupling aspects of the story. Spangler seems threatened by Edna, when he speaks of her "passional nature's drive for fulfillment."

Their overstatement and isolation of Edna's sexual activity causes them to misread. Spangler's talk of the "ruthless determination" of Edna's "passional nature" leads him to err in saying that she "seeks a lover" in New Orleans. Wilson says of Alcée, "the lover does not satisfy her" and later "she lets Robert know she is prepared to have with him a serious affair." Arms says, in his usual derogatory way, she "uses [Alcée] merely as a convenience"; Berthoff that she "contemplates divorce"; and Ziff that her fantasies in New Orleans "are dominated by the figure of a naked man standing in hopeless resignation by a rock on the seashore." [2]

Eros rules all—on this there is general agreement among these modern critics. They have differences, of course, sometimes depending upon their own critical schema for the book. For example, Arms is mainly interested in exploring sets of oppositions such as romance versus realism to show the artistic complexity of Chopin's treatment. Of all the critics, he pays the least attention to purely sexual concerns; it may be his lack of enthusiasm for Edna's sexuality that makes him denigrate her as an aimless, adolescent, anti-intellectual, who falls asleep reading Emerson (surely the most futile blow delivered against her). In any case, no other critic, aside from Spangler who has opposing reasons, is so harsh in his estimation of the protagonist.

Berthoff's schema is "the conflict between two distinct ways of life," democratic individualism and pastoral simplicity. He finds Edna (and all of Creole society) exemplary of "languor, sensuality, frankness and erotic sophistication"; he identifies the "deeper undercurrents of life" with "animalism" and "the body's life."

Seyersted's set of opposing themes is perhaps the most confused, despite the fact that he sees more of the book than any of the other critics. He says that the "theme of sex and procreation is played off against that of illusions about love and independence." Moreover, he later identifies love and independence as "chimeras" pursued by the "heroine"—the only "villains" in the story. The trouble with these oppositions will be shown fully below. Suffice to say here that the contradictions lie for Edna between the parts of his pairings, between sex and procreation, between love and independence, rather than between the combined pairs. (And would one really be willing, on other occasions—say for a protagonist like Stephen Dedalus—to call love and independence "chimeras" and "villains"?)

The opposition between Presbyterian and Creole attitudes toward sexual matters provides another way of analyzing Edna's passions in an intellectual context. Many of the critics use this subject with an almost personal urgency to explain the heroine's actions. In all the schemata, however, the assumption that the book is "about sex" is fundamental.

II

Modern critics are also surprisingly similar to the turn-of-the-century critics in their judgments of Edna's "failure to her duty" as wife and mother. This is a negative way to approach Edna's real and important actions—to emphasize what she doesn't do instead of focussing on her real accomplishments. The actions are related, of course, in their very opposition: to do one means not to do the other. More important both dramatically and spiritually, however, is that one alternative is negative, passive, and docile while the other is positive, active, and courageous. Ziff demonstrates the negativity in describing Edna's first alternative: "she must *accept* the *termination* of her development and must *arrest* her awakening" (my italics). Berthoff speaks of Edna's "withdrawal from her duties"; Spangler of her "denial" of "social custom, conventional morality or domestic obligations," or, as he phrases it in a later passage, "the restraints of conventional morality, social custom, and personal obligation." Seyersted says that Edna "does not hesitate to throw off her traditional duties towards her family." Arms goes wildest in pursuing this aspect of the story; he claims that Chopin "endorses" the husband's and mother-in-law's accusations that Edna "neglects" her children. (It takes great distortion of the text to support that point, as I will show below.)

While the critics are usually attracted to Edna's sexual activity, their emphasis on the negative aspect of her total struggle ("withdrawal from," "denial of," "neglect of," "restraints") indicates the contradictions they labor under. All of their errors and distortions belong to a particular view of Edna that combines an attraction to or interest in her sexuality with a revulsion before her active strivings. Hence the modern ambivalence: Edna must be both praised and condemned for her sexuality.

Some of the critics make explicit the larger social implications of their judgment of Edna. Arms, for instance, says with hostile tartness: "I suppose that those who look upon the novel as a defense of the New Woman would feel that Mrs. Chopin regards freedom from children as a necessary basis for complete freedom." Milder in tone is Ziff's observation: "Whether girls should be educated free of illusions, if possible, whether society should change the conditions it imposes on women, or whether both are needed, the author does not say." [3] One falsifies and the other misrepresents Chopin, but at least the larger issues are here exposed to daylight.

Other critics demonstrate only by implication that they are Edna's antagonists in the "war of the sexes" and as such judge the sexual issue. On one occasion Spangler takes a point of view he attributes to Léonce (but not the Léonce we meet in the novel), the aggrieved husband of the "ruthless" Edna, who must "confront the evidence" that he is "no longer of consequence to his wife." He adds: "For a man who clearly wants nothing more of home than that it should be comfortable, a wife who longs for 'life's delirium' is no minor trial." I will take a different and longer look at Léonce below; here it is relevant simply to note that Spangler has not only taken liberties with the text and point of view in constructing a character, but he has generalized his observations for wider application. He is similarly inventive in dealing with Robert. Taking a note perhaps from Wilson's observation that Robert, in avoiding consummation of the love affair, was "an all too honorable young fellow," Spangler opines that his "conventionality" is a "mask to hide a severe deficiency of masculine force." This notion fits in with his earlier assertion that "none of the men in the novel is prepared to cope with Edna." Is the novel about *men* coping with Edna, one might ask, or are Edna's problems with them central?

Even small errors such as Berthoff's that Edna "contemplates divorce" reveal a switched point of view. Berthoff interpolates this because he is unconsciously thinking like Robert, who has a "wild dream" of making Edna his wife. [4] These changes in point of view have the effect of taking us outside the novel, not to ask the stock literary question, "how many children had Lady Macbeth?" but to raise social questions of male-female relations. They do by implication what the other two critical comments do openly. The choice of ground was inevitable, perhaps, but let it be said that it was chosen first by male critics.

III

Ordinarily a character's struggle for freedom would touch a responsive chord in all readers. The phenomenon has a universal heart-warming appeal. A success thrills us; a failure in the struggle is tragic. Even slaves who hopelessly revolt are not then castigated for having made a bid for freedom. If anything, their low status makes their attempt all the more poignant. However, these responses do not seem to operate on the critics in the case of *The Awakening*. Edna is not accepted as representative of the human spirit simply because she is female. As female she must be dehumanized. It is a universal of our culture that she be designed solely to fit biologic functions, to be sex-partner and mother, mere agent to the needs, sexual and nurturing, of others—the real human beings. The critics' two main concerns about Edna, her sexuality and her neglect of her duties, exemplify this cultural staple. They have not yet seen her as human.

We might begin the process of rescuing *The Awakening* by modestly requesting critics to take Edna seriously, even though she is female, as a human being. If her youth, beauty, and sexual accessibility render this feat difficult (and Mary Ellmann has shown how male responses to beautiful women in the literary world impede seriousness[5]), they may need the artificial aid of imagining Edna as ugly. Let them, though it may shock their sensibilities, switch the physical appurtenances of Mlle. Reisz and Edna for a moment. (They are able to take a Mlle. Reisz seriously—though with a different sort of hostility.) It is an artificial aid, and a temporary one like orthodontia we would hope, but there is another logic to justify it.

Both women are artists, Reisz in music and Edna in painting. It is their seriousness about and sensitivity to art that draw them together. Early in the novel Reisz recognizes the artist in Edna and chooses her as a kindred spirit. The tone of their relationship is set by the first occasion that Reisz plays for the group at Grand Isle. Afterwards she approaches Edna:

> "Well, how did you like my music?" she asked. The young woman was unable to answer; she pressed the hand of the pianist convulsively. Mademoiselle Reisz perceived her agitation and even her tears. She patted her again upon the shoulder as she said:

"You are the only one worth playing for. Those others? Bah!" and she went shuffling and sidling on down the gallery toward her room. (P. 67)

Reisz, already firmly established in her independence as a musician —and as a "disagreeable," even "demented," woman, according to various male characters in the novel—acts as Edna's mentor. Edna's feelings for Reisz are at first ambivalent, but her feelings for Reisz's music are not. The power of the music, one of the important metaphors of the novel, cannot be overestimated. There are parallels here to the sentiments expressed in Chopin's poem, "To Mrs. R." [6]

> I do not know you out upon the street
>   Where people meet.
> We talk as women talk; shall I confess?
>   I know you less.
> I hear you play, and touched by the wondrous spell—
>   I know you well—

It is Reisz who contributes the wounded bird image (which Spangler finds sentimental), feeling Edna's shoulder blades to see if her wings are strong. The full meaning of this image cannot be appreciated without noting its source. Birds there have been before in the story, birds in cages signifying the spirit bound, wild birds generally signifying freedom from earthbound conditions, but the identification of Edna with a bird and with the possibility of broken wings comes first from her fellow artist, an ugly bird perhaps but with sound wings.

Some critics will object that Edna's art is nothing—a mere extension of the eternal sketching that genteel heroines have indulged in since Jane Austen's day. There are two kinds of answers to this objection. Edna, though she is as modest about her work as Chopin was about hers, continually sells it. She thinks of making her living by it. That fact alone in Business America makes her painting a serious act. Secondly, the quality of her work is not relevant to her need and right to pursue her art. Competence alone does not distinguish the dilettante from the artisan, the amateur from the professional. And for Edna, the impulse to create has all the greater social and public significance for the personal and private obstacles it must overcome. Unlike the drawing of Emma Woodhouse, Edna's drawing is a revolutionary act.

Chopin does not belabor this matter. She gives Edna a skill that she might realistically be imagined to have had and to have had training in. For the rest she is concerned to show Edna's sensuous response to physical reality, the world about her, to her own emotions and yearnings, responses which express her personhood, her precious individuality. Because freedom, individuality, self-expression are not rights to be reserved for gifted artists alone, Chopin shows us that Edna, conventionally brought up, conventionally becoming wife and mother, spontaneously—without contact with blue-stockings or feminist "agitators"—pursues her right to self-expression and cannot feel wicked for doing so. Instead she has a feeling, after setting up her own house, "of having descended in the social scale, with a corresponding sense of having risen in the spiritual." Male critics who delight in Stephen Dedalus' watchwords "silence, exile, and cunning" should applaud Edna's boldness as another triumph of the human spirit. But as we have seen, they do not.

IV

Though critics call him kind, lovable, long-suffering, and so on, Léonce acts as the immediate oppressor of Edna. Her first step towards independence means freedom from his rule, first in his house and then in escape to her own. Chopin explicitly describes the nature of Léonce and dramatizes his oppressiveness in three "nagging" scenes. When we first see them together, he is "looking at his wife as one looks at a valuable piece of personal property." His possessiveness is underscored when we are told "he greatly valued his possessions, chiefly because they were his." In keeping with this quality, he is mainly concerned with making money and showing off his wealth. He is fiercely conventional and supremely insensitive to feelings. He sees his wife's role as caring for him and his children. Not openly forceful in his demands, his most violent act is to leave the dinner table in disgust when he is displeased and go to his club. But he is capable of insidious forms of oppression when he feels, as he seems often to, that Edna's services are not up to the mark, that she has somehow under the surface of her manner detached herself.

Chapter Three contains the first "nagging" scene. Léonce comes in from Klein's hotel after Edna is asleep. He is full of gossip and wakes her to talk with him. But "she was overcome with sleep, and answered him with little half-utterances." He is piqued at her lack of response, and, though he has forgotten the bonbons he promised his boys, he suddenly is concerned about them; shifting them in their beds, he is obviously trying to waken them. He does not succeed, but he returns to tell Edna that one of them has a high fever and needs "looking after." Against a background of repeated past accusations of her neglect, Edna leaps to go see the child, even though she is sure he is all right. She has been fully wakened now and sits on the bed when she returns "leaning her head on the pillow." Léonce finishes his cigar and promptly goes to sleep, as Edna cannot. She goes out to the rocking-chair on the porch, listens to the noises of the night and of the sea, and suddenly she is crying. Male critics looking on this scene see Edna's anguish as "a discontent ... for no apparent reason" which leads to her "unreasoning, stubborn resistance to the will of her husband" (Spangler) or as "no sound reason for the discontent she feels" (Ziff). Many wives, more articulate than Edna perhaps, could define the discontent and its reasons. Chopin leaves interpretation of the ironies and of the personal dynamics to them or to other readers capable of seeing. It is not a case of wife-beating, but the actions of Léonce say, "I am going to punish you for not paying attention to me. I woke you up to talk and you're not talking. It is your job to talk when I want to talk." The chapter ends with Edna's response to praise of her husband: "Mrs. Pontellier was forced to admit that she knew of none better." A grudging and negative tribute, that—with a devastating relativity.

When Edna's consciousness has risen a notch because of her deeply felt experiences on the night when she learns to swim, when she conquers her "ungovernable dread" of water and fear of death, her demands are higher. She needs desperately to be alone to digest her experience, away even from Robert, her swimming instructor, but Léonce nags her about staying in the hammock. Finally he orders her to go in the house. She simply refuses. Secure in the hammock, she wonders "if her husband had ever spoken to her like that before, and if she had submitted to his command. Of course she had. But she could not realize why or how she should have yielded, feeling as she did then." At first there appears to be a stalemate: Edna will not go in and Léonce will not let her be alone as she wishes. He bustles about getting wine and cigars. She succeeds in ignoring him until finally she feels like "one who awakens gradually out of a dream, a delicious, grotesque, impossible dream, to feel again the realities pressing into her soul . . . the exuberance which had sustained and exalted her spirit left her helpless and yielding to the conditions that crowded her in."

Léonce has prevailed again, but this time Edna has had a few moments of resistance. This is the scene that offends Spangler because he sees Léonce as acting merely in concern for Edna's welfare, and her ingratitude as caused by his failures in bed. Chopin shows us that Léonce is more aware of what really is happening. When Edna, exhausted, gives up and enters the house she asks Léonce if he is coming in. He replies, "Yes, dear. Just as soon as I have finished my cigar." Which is to say "*this* time you'll wait for me!"

The third "nagging" scene is also the third and final stage of Edna's "consciousness-raising"; it occurs when the family is back in New Orleans. She has neglected her social duties on her "at-home" day, and Léonce is taking her to task for her failures. She is perfectly cool, casual, and indifferent before his criticisms—so much so that he becomes furious and after criticizing the dinner goes to his club. Again Edna realizes that she has reached a new stage.

> She was somewhat familiar with such scenes. They had often made her very unhappy. On a few previous occasions she had been completely deprived of any desire to finish her dinner. Sometimes she had gone to the kitchen to administer a tardy rebuke to the cook. Once she went to her room and studied the cookbook during an entire evening finally writing out a menu for the week, which left her harassed with a feeling that, after all, she had accomplished no good that was worth the name.
> But that evening Edna finished her dinner alone, with forced deliberation. Her face was flushed and her eyes flamed with some inward fire that lighted them. After finishing her

dinner she went to her room. . . . She was seeking herself and finding herself in just such sweet half-darkness which met her moods. (Pp. 133–134)

No more can Edna be touched by Léonce's tantrums. It is after this scene that she begins to "do as she likes and to feel as she likes," to paint with serious intent and great happiness. Léonce concludes that she is ill, but Chopin tells us that "she was becoming herself and daily casting off that fictitious self which we assume like a garment." It is only a short step from this place to her own house.

V

Edna's oppression by her children is of a very special sort. Its nature has been confused by critics raising the issue of Edna's neglect. Arms's claim that Chopin "endorses" Léonce's accusations of Edna's neglect is based on a distortion of the text and muddies the water further. Before we can approach the question of Edna's oppression we must clear away the false one of her neglect.

Arms's assertion is based on Chopin's definition of Edna as "not a mother-person." Nowhere, however, does Chopin equate not being a "mother-person" with neglect of children. Almost the opposite is true. She pokes fun at the "mother-persons," who could be seen "fluttering about with extended, protecting wings when any harm, real or imaginary, threatened their precious brood. They were women who idolized their children, worshiped their husbands, and esteemed it a holy privilege to efface themselves as individuals and grow wings as ministering angels." And she describes in tones of approval the independence of Edna's children: "If one of the little Pontellier boys took a tumble whilst at play, he was not apt to rush crying to his mother's arms for comfort; he would more likely pick himself up, wipe the water out of his eyes and the sand out of his mouth, and go on playing. Tots as they were, they pulled together and stood their ground in childish battles with doubled fists and uplifted voices, which usually prevailed against the other mother-tots" (p. 18). The children owe their self-reliance to the fact that Edna is not a "mother-person." As for Léonce's accusations, we have already seen what selfishness motivates his expressions of concern. It might be said that Chopin's ideas about child care were far in advance of those of our modern critics who seem, judging from their misogynist strictures on Edna, to favor over-attendance on children. In any case, it is not the physical care of her children that oppresses Edna, for she is remarkably free of that burden. Not only has she a servant who attends them, she has also a mother-in-law who is delighted to take them off her hands for weeks at a time.

There are two explanations for the extremity of the language that Edna uses in "thinking of the children": "the children appeared before her like antagonists who had overcome her; who had overpowered and sought to drag her into the soul's slavery for the rest of her days." One explanation requires that we recapture a historical view of a woman's duties to her children, of her responsibility to their honor and reputation. Edna, in freeing herself from the immediate oppressions she felt, had reached a point where she could have damaged the future of her children publicly, in the community. So far Léonce had put a saving public face on her actions, and though rumors had already reached Mme. Ratignolle about Edna's friendship with Arobin, no irrevocable damage had yet been done. But Edna has reached a turning point in her life; the scene where she assists at the birth of Adèle's child contributes to and culminates in this moment. She must think about her future, which means that she must think also about the future of her children, about her relations with Robert, and so on.

Her strong expression of the children's power over her is based on her knowledge that consideration for their future could force her return to her husband's house, to his bed and board, to the oppression she has just escaped. Divorce is not a consideration, for in the 1890s this right had not been recognized generally or won. Though Edna's revolt in itself still has a revolutionary relevance, we must see that as a matter of historical fact her options were different from modern ones.

Failure to appreciate this fact, along with the critics' emphasis on the sexual aspect only of Edna's struggle, has led to a complete inability to understand the conclusion of the novel. This criticism applies not only to Spangler, who finds the ending "perplexing," "fundamentally evasive," with "inconsistent characterization," a failure in short; but to others as well who accept the ending without seeing its inner dynamic and inevitability, its relation to all that came before.

In their descriptions, plot summaries, recapitulations of the novel, not one critic I have found has noticed a crucial scene. It holds the key to an understanding of the second reason that Edna is oppressed by her children and also soundly motivates her way of "eluding" them. Coming home from Adèle's house after the birth, Edna does *not* rush into her house to meet Robert. She does not yet know that he has gone, but she sits alone on the porch steps to think. The doctor had just observed that sexual love is an illusion designed by Nature, "a decoy to secure mothers for the race." Immediately before this conversation, Edna had come through a scene of "tearing emotion," caused by observing the consequences of sexual love. Even for Adèle, the doting wife and mother, childbirth is a kind of destruction. Edna has to think about the practical results, for women, of sexual activity (contraception does not figure here); she has to think about giving up her life to that inevitable function. She does not want to. And yet a life without love and the full (including sexual) expression of it cannot be life for her, nor can her art without a full life be genuine. She cannot be and does not want to be a Mlle. Reisz. As she sits on the steps she thinks not only of her boys; "the children" is a subject that includes her boys, Adèle's children, and all the possible offspring of her liaison with Robert. She thinks of childbirth, in short, and of children in general.

She goes into the house, not having come to a conclusion, but having decided to think about the problem the next day. "Tomorrow would be time to think of everything." She cannot deny herself the long-yearned-for night of love with Robert. But Robert or no, she promises herself—"that determination had driven into her soul like a death wound"—to resolve the question of her future the following day. The simile of "death wound" indicates the grim nature of the decisions that lie before her. And her resolution is formed *before* she has discovered that Robert has gone out of her life. By ignoring this scene, critics have made a soap-opera of the novel's ending and have led Spangler to believe that Edna rushes to her death "out of a disappointed, illicit love." One could feel greater sympathy for Spangler's dissatisfaction if he had paid less attention to the critics' version of the ending and more to the novel itself. One wonders how they can explain Chopin's placing of the birth scene—or the inclusion of it at all—in the story, especially in a novel so artfully and economically structured. Furthermore, simply to ignore the scene's crucial after-effects on Edna is to make drivel out of art.

Characteristically, Chopin shows us the results of Edna's thinking in her actions. She has already arrived at Grand Isle when we learn more specifically what Edna had thought as she lay awake on the sofa all the night before. She has considered her love affair with some objectivity. Of Robert she has realized that "the day would come when he, too, and the thought of him would melt out of her existence." She can conceive of other affairs like the one with Arobin: "Today it is Arobin; tomorrow it will be someone else." She cannot bear the idea of returning to her husband and her infidelities to him make no difference to her so far as he is concerned ("it doesn't matter about Léonce Pontellier"); but they would make a difference to her children. For her children, she repeats, she is willing to give up "the unessential," but "she would never sacrifice herself for her children." One of the "unessentials" to her children is her being. She has recently visited them and found that they have no need of her; they are perfectly happy with their grandmother. They have need only of her honor and good reputation, which she cannot give them without sacrificing daily her independence and full life. The only way that she can escape her "soul's slavery for the rest of her days" is to die.

It is because she cannot sacrifice herself to the consequences of sexual activity and at the same time is not willing to live without sensuous experience that Edna drowns herself. That is her precise contradiction: not some abstract opposition between "romance" and "realism," as Arms would have it; not a choice between marriage and free love, as Ziff defines it; neither is it sexual deprivation in the form of Robert's rejection that motivates her ultimate act, as Spangler says. It is a contradiction that involves her whole being as a woman, artist, person, a contradiction not of her making but of a society so at the mercy of biology, despite its vaunted technology and democratic claims, that it keeps over half its members in chains.

Critics have said that Chopin's novel is about a woman's sexual awakening. Today, when we have so many female characters portrayed as natural experts in the bedroom, that is hardly a revolutionary theme. My quarrel with the critics is as much on what they fail to see and say as on what they define as the core and totality of the book (a bit as if, treating *Moby Dick*, they called it a book about the whaling industry). The heroism of Edna is that she is able to pursue her felt needs with so little guilt and that rather than settling for less than a chance to fulfill them she chooses instead to die. For so young a woman, she shows tremendous strength in discovering, defining, and following her natural human needs, despite all the societal pressures on her to conform to a set pattern. *The Awakening* is a far more revolutionary novel than any of the critics have realized. What gives it its shock effect today (for it still has that power) and its relevance is that it is a portrait of a woman determined to have full integrity, full personhood—or nothing.

Winning:
Katherine Anne Porter's Women

BARBARA HARRELL CARSON

In Katherine Anne Porter's "Old Mortality," Miranda Rhea watches her uncle's horse, Miss Lucy, win a race in a hundred-to-one long shot. Seeing the animal's bleeding nose, her wild eyes and trembling knees, Miranda thinks in anguish, "That was winning, too." [1] In many ways, the painful victory of the old mare (including the odds against it) epitomizes the victories of the human females in Porter's Miranda stories. For them, too, triumph and defeat are virtually indistinguishable. As if to underline the significance of the metaphorical race, Porter often presents her women on horseback, galloping for all they are worth toward Mexico or away from death or just around the farm, to convince themselves of their undiminished vigor. But whether they are involved only in symbolic contests or in literal races as well, her women—Miranda, Miranda's Grandmother (Sophia Jane Rhea), her Aunt Amy, her cousin Eva, and even, in her own way, the Grandmother's old servant, Nannie—all, with varying degrees of awareness, seek the same prize. We would call it, in the worn phraseology of our day, a valid selfhood. Porter herself speaks of it as entry "into ... an honest life" (p. 336). If the words are vague, the concept is not. At its center are the recognition and use of one's own powers and abilities even in the face of custom, the discovery of truth for oneself (including the truth of one's own desires), and the strength to face that truth and act from that basis. It is, in short, the creation of an essence for oneself through self-initiated actions, rather than the passive acceptance of a role assigned by others.

Porter deals with the struggle for literal self-possession by the women of the Rhea family in nine stories: the seven sketches gathered under the title "The Old Order" in *The Collected Stories* and the two longer works, "Old Mortality" and "Pale Horse, Pale Rider." Although the stories (except for "Pale Horse, Pale Rider") are set in the South, the problems faced by these women apply beyond those geographical limits. The region that had, with such a hyperbole of lofty sentiments, elevated woman to a pedestal, convinced her of her own sacredness, and walled her in a crinoline prison, offered to the writer a perfect crucible for the study of what happens in general when the lady decides to abdicate her throne—or at least gets the feeling that it is not, after all, a very comfortable seat.

The black servant Nannie did not, of course, occupy the feminine pedestal (although as "Mammy" she did share in the "matriarchal tyranny" exercised by the Grandmother [p. 351]). Nevertheless, she is important to Porter's treatment of women for several reasons. For one, Nannie suggests Porter's view of woman's true condition. Although different in complexion and status, the other women in the Miranda stories are, at least at some time in their lives, as surely bound as Nannie to their society, to tradition, and to family. Porter makes Nannie's symbolic role explicit when she emphasizes that the slave Nannie and Miss Sophia Jane had been "married off" within days of each other—the passivity implied is chilling—and had started simultaneously "their grim and terrible race of procreation" (pp. 334–335). And the implication is clear when Porter says that even after Nannie was legally emancipated, she continued her life of service to the Grandmother, to her white "children," to her own offspring, and, during her childbearing years, to her husband.

However, Nannie does not serve Porter merely as a symbol. A realistic character in her own right, she is also a woman who manages to break her bonds and assert her honest self. In "The Last Leaf," the Grandmother dead, Nannie leaves the family she has served all her life, retreats to a cabin in the woods, takes off her neat servant's cap, dons the kerchief of her ancestral tribe, and sits on her doorstep, smoking, like "an aged Bantu woman of independent means ... breathing the free air" (p. 349). The identity that she finds most satisfying in the end is one that antedates her lifetime of slavery. Her children, black and white, had thought of her only in terms of their needs. Now she begins to reveal a self they had never suspected, and they are astonished "to discover that Nannie had always liked and hoped to own certain things, she had seemed so contented and wantless" (p. 349). Her final rejection of servitude and sacrifice takes place when Uncle Jimbilly, the husband whom she had long ago stopped living with, hints that he would like to share her cabin with her. She tells him pointedly, " 'I don' aim to pass my las' days waitin on no man. . . . I've served my time, I've done my do, and dat's all' " (p. 351).

But Nannie's spirited self-emancipation is not unequivocal. Her coming to her "honest self" is late; it is limited; and even in her total emotional self-sufficiency there is great irony. Others had always meant burdens for Nannie; now in rejecting those externally imposed burdens she rejects, too, their sources. She does not care, we are told, whether her children loved her or not; she wants only to be alone; she "wasn't afraid of anything" (p. 351). She is left finally only with herself. This reduction to the core of self—this recognition of one's ability to survive alone and of the validity of one's own desires—is a good starting point (it is the one Miranda discovers in "Pale Horse, Pale Rider"). But as a conclusion it is nihilistic, grim in its lack of connection with others, barren of emotions and of productivity. All Nannie has left to look forward to is restful night, both the immediate and the final one.

Death as liberator—perhaps the only one for those who can fight things as they are on no other terms—is also a theme in "Old Mortality" in the story of Amy Rhea Breaux. Owner of the original mare Miss Lucy (of which Miranda's bleeding winner is, significantly, only one in a long line of avatars), Amy has been dead over a decade at the beginning of "Old Mortality." In life she had been the victim of the weakness of her strengths. Had she been less perceptive she would, no doubt, have been happy as the belle of her day; had she been more perceptive she would have known what to do about her unhappiness. As it was, she sensed the emptiness of her life, but she had neither the understanding to define clearly what troubled her, the vision to see how she could successfully oppose it, nor the will or ability to effect that opposition, except fitfully. She cried out, " 'Mammy, I'm so sick of this world. I don't like anything in it. It's so *dull* ...' " (p. 188). But she possessed only the tools of the coquette to fight that dullness with: she had dangled the boring, spoiled Gabriel whom her family had chosen as her suitor; when he praised her long black hair, she snipped it off; after her father reprimanded her for her daring dress at a costume ball, she returned showing more ankle and bosom than before. Only once did her rejection of her empty life reach a serious level. After her brother Harry shot a man to save her "honor," she galloped off with him to the Mexican border in the one great self-willed horse ride of her life. But Amy had not had the strength to sustain her defiance. Passivity soon replaced action, literally and psychologically. She returned home in a state of collapse, nearly immobilized, unable even to dismount by herself.

Although Amy was unaware of it, a good part of what she struggled against so vainly and inarticulately was represented in the brotherly defense that occasioned her ride. Her great enemy was the monolithic family, the family as viceroy of society and tradition, which determines how the individual will act and which, indeed, squeezes individuality out and makes the person (and particularly the woman—Harry could, after all, ride to Mexico with impunity) just a unit expressing the larger whole. Porter's description of the Rheas' reaction to Amy's ride suggests a great spiderweb: "The rest of the family had to receive visitors, write letters, go to churches, return calls, and bear the whole brunt, as they expressed it. They sat in the twilight of scandal in their little world, holding themselves very rigidly, in a shared tension as if all their nerves began at a common center. This center had received a blow, and family nerves shuddered, even into the farthest reaches of Kentucky" (p. 189).

After the scandal subsided, Amy married Gabriel, whom she had been alternately enticing and rejecting for years. But that act itself, like almost all of her confused life, was at once an acquiescence to social pressure and a flaunting of it. She accepted Gabriel only after he had been disinherited and thus placed, in some measure, outside the familial pale. Her wedding, too, had the same strange combination of rebellion and surrender, of assertion of an independent selfhood and denial of it: " 'She would not wear white, nor a veil,' said Grandmother. 'I couldn't oppose her, for I had said my daughters would each have exactly the wedding dress they wanted. But Amy surprised me.... "I shall wear mourning if I like," she said, "it is *my* funeral, you know"'" (p. 182).

Even in marriage she struggled (without real understanding of what she wanted) to preserve something of her individual identity. In the first days of her honeymoon, the letter to her mother beginning with a playful description of herself as "'a staid old married woman,'" moved quickly to the plaintive announcement, "'I'm going to put on a domino and take to the streets with Gabriel sometime during Mardi Gras. I'm tired of watching the show from a balcony'" (p. 192). Except for her dash to Mexico, that was of course where she spent most of her life. The parties, the dancing, the flirtations—all had been only extensions of the balcony, because all had been essentially passive, not satisfying personal needs, but rather placating the demands and training of society. Marriage, she discovered, was only more of the same. She had planned after her marriage to follow the races in dizzying succession from New Orleans to Saratoga. Perhaps she realized now that this would have been merely another artificial escape, a substitute for the race she could not run herself.

Years later, her cousin Eva reminisced bitterly of Amy: "'She rode too hard, and she danced too freely, and she talked too much.... I don't mean she was loud or vulgar, she wasn't, but she was *too free*'" (p. 215). The truth, of course, is just the opposite: Amy had not been free at all, except in things that mattered little. Finally, unwilling to live on other people's terms and unequipped to alter the emptiness of her existence, she chose simply to make that emptiness final. There is little question that her death from an overdose of drugs was suicide. Only in taking her life could she condemn the life she had been meted. William Nance has pointed out in *Katherine Anne Porter and the Art of Rejection* how right Gabriel was, without realizing it, in the epigraph he wrote for Amy: she "who suffered life," it read, was "now set free..." (p. 181).[2]

Forgetting Amy's rebellion, her cries of boredom, the hints of a suicide motivated by a deep dissatisfaction with their kind of life, the family transformed her in their memories into the ideal belle. But there is more here. The family was involved in an ancient protective ritual. Like primitive people who worship what they fear and so regulate its powers, Amy's family reasserted its control over the woman who challenged it, by declaring her an "angel." They negated what her life and death really meant by worshiping what they said she stood for. By mythologizing her, they restored the woman to her "proper" place. The rebellious one was reintegrated; the spider web was whole once more—and Amy now became the pattern by which future generations of young girls could measure themselves and be measured.

If Amy's acquiescence to family and social pressure cloaked an inner defiance and desire for independence, the life of Cousin Eva Parrington reveals the reverse: that assertions of independence can just as easily hide real psychological bondage. Eva, the woman who accused Amy of having been too free, the old-maid without a chin who had endured in humiliation her mother's middle-aged flirtations while *she* sat a wallflower at all the parties—ugly Eva is the emancipated woman. She has taught Latin at a female seminary, fought for the franchise for women, and suffered imprisonment and loss of her job because of her stand. In terms of political action and professional and economic independence, Eva's emancipation is real. She speaks truly when she tells Miranda, " 'You'll live in a better world because we worked for it' " (p. 210).

But like the victories of all Porter's women, Eva's is ambiguous. Her problem is that she has never faced a source of restrictions on her liberty far more basic than being denied the right to vote. She does not perceive that what really bars her discovery of her honest self is her failure to achieve psychological freedom from her family. She is irrevocably bound to it by a strange mixture of hatred and need. In her work for women's rights she unconsciously transfers her fight for freedom from the arena of family —where she can never win because of her masochistic dependency on it—to that of society in general. Her lack of awareness of her motivations diminishes both the freedom and the personal validity of her libertarian activities. Their underpinning is self-delusion, not self-awareness. Eva can criticize the familial and social pressures which, she says, had turned the Amys of her time into sex-ridden, festering bodies; she can hiss, " 'Ah, the family ... the whole hideous institution should be wiped from the face of the earth. It is the root of all human wrongs...' " (p. 217). But she does not see that it has turned her into something festering, too. The very violence and exaggeration with which she avows her hatred show how strongly she still feels the family's influence and how severely it has warped her view of reality. And even while denouncing it, Eva is on a train, riding to the funeral of Amy's widower, Gabriel—that act itself a profession of the efficacy of family ties.

In Nannie, Amy, and Eva, Porter presents the terms of woman's fight for an independent and honest life. The opponents she faces are delineated: family, tradition, her own vacillation between desire for independence and need for others, her lack of preparation—philosophical, psychological, and practical—for establishing any relationship with others except the traditional ones requiring sacrifice of her own selfhood. The usual outcome of the fight has also been adumbrated: the emotional negativism, the defeat, the pain, and the delusion that are involved in even the smallest victories. These themes are repeated and elaborated in the stories about the Grandmother and Miranda.

In their youths both of these women suffered from what Simone de Beauvoir in *The Second Sex* has called being made other than self. Family, society, romantic mythology (including, for the Grandmother, the idealistic literature she was brought up on, and, for Miranda, the idealization of Amy)—all conspire to shape their attitudes, goals, and actions. But both Sophia Jane and Miranda manage somehow to preserve a secret self, an area of honesty within. For both women the process of moving toward an authentic life is one of unmasking that secret self and acting on the basis of inner rather than external motivations.

The double life from which the Grandmother emerged is described, largely in flashbacks, in the first two stories of "The Old Order." As a young girl, she appeared to be the belle of Southern stereotypes, "gay and sweet and decorous, full of vanity and incredibly exalted daydreams..." (p. 335). But in the rest of this sentence, in the rhetorical irony so typical of her, Porter reveals the hidden side of Sophia Jane. Those "incredibly exalted daydreams... threatened now and again to cast her over the edge of some mysterious frenzy." Dreams of loss of her virginity, envy of "the delicious, the free, the wonderful, the mysterious and terrible life of men," visions of the "manly indulgences" of her "wild" cousin—and future husband—Stephen: all these had filled her thoughts, giving evidence of her sense of the inadequacies of her life and offering compensations for its dullness. She had protected herself from her family's censure by memorizing high-minded poetry or bits of music to have on hand when they offered pennies for her thoughts. "She lived her whole youth so," Porter writes, "without once giving herself away..." (p. 336).

Her marriage to the dashing cousin had been, no doubt, motivated at least in part by the hope that it would grant access to the mysterious, exciting world that seemed to be his. Instead, marriage had revealed that the "wild" Stephen was spineless and self-indulgent, having neither ambition nor adhesiveness. Sophia Jane's true character began to develop as she tried to change his, her strength growing, for the most part secretly, in proportion to his weakness. To compensate for the sensual pleasure denied her in her marriage bed, she had begun, with her fourth child, to nurse her own children (and when Nannie was sick, her black foster child, too) in defiance of custom and her shocked husband and mother.

Yet except for this one overtly defiant act, Sophia Jane seems, on the whole, to have accepted the passive role in marriage. Even while despising her husband, she had been ruled by him. In fact, this must have been at least a partial cause for her hatred: her being forced by the conventions of marriage to submit to his decisions, while recognizing her own superiority. Many critics have pointed out the failure of love in Porter's women, overlooking the very good reasons for that failure. How can real love exist between people who know each other only by their false, public masks? How can a woman love when she is on all sides being forced to sacrifice that honest self from which, alone, love can come? How can she love when according to her training, love, for a woman, means exactly that sacrifice? Of Sophia Jane we are told: "She could not help it, she despised him.... Her husband threw away her dowry and her property in wild investments in strange territories: Louisiana, Texas; and without protest she watched him play away her substance like a gambler. She felt that she could have managed her affairs profitably. But her natural activities lay elsewhere, it was the business of a man to make all decisions and dispose of all financial matters" (p. 337).

However, just as the Grandmother's symbolic counterpart, the literally enslaved Nannie, won one type of emancipation during the war, so, after her fashion, did Sophia Jane. She found herself in one of those "epochs of social disintegration" during which, according to de Beauvoir, "woman is set free." It was in the war that Sophia Jane's husband received the wound from which he would afterwards die, allowing her "finally [to] emerge into something like an honest life. ..." Then "with all the responsibilities of a man but with none of the privileges," she had made her secret self (assertive, willful, self-conscious in the basic sense of the term) her public self (p. 336). She took charge not only of her own existence, but of all her family, both black and white. Her sense of responsibility extended finally to the fate of Nannie's soul and the color of the children born in the black quarters. And it is precisely this assumption of responsibility that indicates the true measure of the Grandmother's triumph. To take, by an act of will, the burden of one's world on one's own shoulders, to create obligations for oneself—that is the mark of the traditional hero. It is also the mark of the authentic self, which can be defined only in process, never in stasis.

Porter continually emphasizes the importance of action in the Grandmother's new life. Before her husband's death, her contact with the world of decision-making, planning, working—outside of her genteel wifely labors at home—had come only in her daydreams and in her usually unspoken criticism of her husband's failures in these areas. As a widow, however, she had set out for Louisiana with her nine children, repaired a house, planted an orchard, sold the house, moved on to Texas, built a house, had the fields fenced and crops planted, all the while driving herself as she drove her children and servants and horses.

But if she had achieved much, she had also suffered and lost a great deal. Independence had come to her only in what seemed an utter life-or-death dilemma. In such extremities, the one involved can scarcely appreciate the victory that results. For the hero the triumph is often only grim and ugly toil. For the Grandmother it meant realizing that she had driven her children too hard and fed them too little. It meant that her very strength had hardened her to enable her to endure: "griefs never again lasted with her so long as they had before" (p. 339). And it had meant weakening her children, probably because, feeling guilty about her own strength, she had begun to vacillate between firmness and indulgence, spoiling particularly her sons and making them unfit for effective living.

Nevertheless, the action to which she had been freed continued to characterize her life. Even in old age, when the reader first sees her, she cannot rest from her habit of doing. "The Source," a description of her yearly visit to the family farm, is dominated by the whirlwind of her activity: the flurry surrounding her arrival, her brisk supervisory walk through the house and yards, the uproar created by the soapmaking and washing and painting and dusting and sewing under her direction. Yet, to read this story is to see that something is wrong. The Grandmother's descriptions of what she plans to do do not jibe with what really takes place. She proposes going to the farm for "change and relaxation" instead of for work; she takes with her an elegant shepherdess hat "woven for herself just after the War"; she imagines "walking at leisure in the shade of the orchards watching the peaches ripen"; she speaks "with longing of clipping the rosebushes, or of tying up the trellised honeysuckle with her own hands" (pp. 321–322). But she never wears the hat; she put on instead a sensible chambray bonnet; and her work is more likely to be in the Negroes' cabins than among the fruit trees and flowers. Her vigor on horseback is also, significantly, diminished, but she does not speak of that either.

What we see happening to the Grandmother here is a reversion in mind, if not in fact, to the stereotype of the Southern lady. (Her actions are of a piece with those of other women of the postwar South one reads of, who, bereft of servants, rose before dawn to scrub their floors and do their laundry in secret, in order to maintain their society's myth of its ladies' delicate, indulged lives.) It is precisely in this self-deception that the Grandmother becomes a threat to Miranda and her generation. In spite of her own repression under it, she chooses to keep alive the myth that had contributed to the limitations of her selfhood in youth. The spider web of family, society, and tradition that made Amy its own after her death begins to ensnare the Grandmother as her life draws to a close.

"The Journey" (originally called "The Old Order") also deals with the Grandmother's retreat, in her last years, from significant action into a romantic evasion of reality. Even though the story makes clear that the Grandmother keeps busy literally until the day of her death (when she is working on moving a fifty-foot adobe wall), its imagistic emphasis is on lack of action. This apparent contradiction is resolved if one sees the imagery of stasis as underscoring the philosophical and psychological change that has taken place in the Grandmother in her old age. Her real passivity now lies in accepting the values and beliefs of the order she once chafed under. She and Nannie sit fingering the "material" of the past; making patchwork quilts of it; "gilding" each piece (with edgings of lemon-colored thread and linings of yellow silk); covering heirlooms with velvet and removing them—as she has, in effect, removed herself—from useful life. In re-ordering the past (or "carefully disordering" it, as she does the pieces in the quilts), the Grandmother idealizes it in spite of its bitterness, dreaming of a cessation of change and a return to the old ways. She overlooks her own life of hard work and censures her new daughter-in-law for "unsexing herself." (Porter suggests the daughter-in-law's participation in the race for integrity—the Grandmother describes her as "self-possessed"—by noting that her idea of a perfect honeymoon would have been riding on a cattle roundup.) She was, the Grandmother decides, "altogether too Western, too modern, something like the 'new' woman who was beginning to run wild, asking for the vote, leaving her home and going out in the world to earn her own living..." (p. 333).

How can we account for the Grandmother's forgetting the price of her own liberation and reverting to the prison of custom? The guilt the Grandmother felt toward her sons, with its suggestion of her early ambivalence concerning her strength, could itself have forced her back into the solace of traditional life patterns. Here at least there would be authority to blame if things went wrong; the other way, there was only self. Or maybe the Grandmother's reversion is more simply explained. Perhaps it is merely that freedom for women, in her time, could come only in moments of cultural chaos. When the talents that enabled her to survive and flourish were no longer so much in demand, after the re-establishment of the *status quo ante bellum*, society itself could have reclaimed her simply by no longer offering arenas for the exercise of her selfhood.

Whatever the reasons, by the time of "The Journey" she has fallen back upon a belief in "authority," and in "the utter rightness and justice of the basic laws of human existence, founded as they were on God's plans..." (pp. 328–329). So the cycle has come round full. The Grandmother, who, with Nannie, had wished that "a series of changes might bring them, blessedly, back full-circle to the old ways they had known" has, as in fairy tales, been granted the wish unwittingly asked for (p. 327). She has returned to her original dichotomized psychological state; she is once again playing a role; her secret self is once more hidden by the mask of her public face. It is as if Porter is suggesting that liberation is a non-transferable commodity and must be won anew by each individual.

But Porter's point is not so simple as that, for in sacrificing her real self—with its doubts, hesitancies, and social heresies—the Grandmother does give something of value to the next generation. We are told that the children "loved their Grandmother; she was the only reality to them in a world that seemed otherwise without fixed authority or refuge . . ." (p. 324). Porter's irony in all this is multi-layered, quite properly posing more questions than it answers. Must the freed woman of one generation inevitably become the oppressor of the next? Can order be established only at the expense of freedom? Is one—order or freedom—more valuable than the other? Or do they always exist in a dynamic relationship, one rising cyclically from the other? It is surely the Grandmother's very role as defender of order that, at least in part, makes possible Miranda's fight for freedom, by giving her a strong adversary to exercise her selfhood against.

Porter's awareness of the dialectic inevitably involved in establishing an identity is suggested in her essay on Willa Cather. She quotes approvingly Cather's comments on " 'the many kinds of personal relations which exist in any everyday "happy family" who are merely going on with their daily lives, with no crises or shocks or bewildering complications. . . .' " Even in such a stable household, Cather says, " 'every individual . . . (even the children) is clinging passionately to his individual soul, is in terror of losing it in the general family flavor. . . . the mere struggle to have anything of one's own, to be oneself at all, creates an element of strain which keeps everybody almost at breaking point.' " [3] Miranda's own early struggle against family control is presented symbolically in the opening of "The Fig Tree," where we see Miranda squirming as old Aunt Nannie grips the child tightly with her knees, brushes her hair back firmly, snaps a rubber band around it, and jams a freshly starched bonnet over her ears—a bonnet Miranda does not want to wear. Already, the story also reveals, Miranda wants to know where she is going and hates being taken some place by the family as a surprise.

A major part of what Miranda has to fight against in her attempts to save her "individual soul" is the romantic vision of reality represented by the Grandmother's mythology and perpetuated by all of her family. This is the problem she faces in "Old Mortality." Here Miranda finds previous generations' versions of reality contradicted on all sides by the evidence offered by her own senses. The picture of "lovely" Amy seems to Miranda not romantic, but "merely most terribly out of fashion..." (p. 173). Her father declares, " 'There were never any fat women in the family, thank God,' " in face of the plain fact of mountainous Great-aunt Kesiah (p. 174). And the dashing, impetuous Gabriel, Amy's "handsome romantic beau" turns out to be "a shabby fat man with bloodshot blue eyes, sad beaten eyes, and a big melancholy laugh, like a groan" (p. 197). But even as Miranda frets about the family's habit of making their own past into "love stories against a bright blank heavenly blue sky," she is beginning to gild her life in the same way (p. 175). She speaks with her sister Maria of being "immured" in their convent school, because "it gave a romantic glint to what was otherwise a very dull life for them..." (p. 194). Already her chances of discovering reality, exterior and interior, are threatened.

The problem reaches its climax in the final section of "Old Mortality," where Miranda, now eighteen and a year married, is confronted with two versions of the Amy story. As devil's advocate, she voices the family's romantic legend, while Cousin Eva Parrington gives the sordid, "Freudian," and ostensibly more realistic side. It is to Miranda's credit that she sees that Eva's tale is as romantic in its own way as the family's version. This awareness leaves her, however, with little certainty about what the truth really is. Her immediate reaction to this confusion is itself romantic and naive:

She was not going to stay in any place, with any one, that threatened to forbid her making her own discoveries.... Oh, what is life, she asked herself in desperate seriousness, in those childish unanswerable words, and what shall I do with it? ... She did not know that she asked herself this because all her earliest training had argued that life was a substance, a material to be used, it took shape and direction and meaning only as the possessor guided and worked it; living was a progress of continuous and varied acts of the will directed toward a definite end. (P. 220)

Miranda will never be able to escape the past completely. But there is strength in it as surely as there is weakness. From it had come the essentially Existentialist precept behind her question about life, the idea that life is a process defined by actions directed toward a goal. If she works from this premise given her by the past, while still acting, as she resolves here, from the basis of her own will and her own vision of reality, Miranda will be able to establish an authentic selfhood and avoid passively accepting a role or a view of reality created by others. She will, in Existentialist terms, become subject rather than object, and if she can sustain this identity derived from willed action, she will find all the freedom possible to her in this world.

At the end of "Old Mortality," Miranda's plans are vague, but she has at least decided to stop being like her Shakespearean namesake, watching in awe the phantom shows created by her forebears. Her name implies not only "the wonderer," but also "the seeing one." [4] True to the second implication, she has determined to discover reality for herself. Her mind, we are told, "closed stubbornly against remembering, not the past but the legend of the past, other people's memory of the past, at which she had spent her life peering in wonder like a child at a magic-lantern show" (p. 221). Since this is her determination, we are not surprised to learn in "Pale Horse, Pale Rider" that she has left her home and family and started a career. It may seem ironical, however, that she is still watching shows created by others, now as theater critic for a western newspaper (a "female job" to which she was relegated after compassion allowed her to suppress a news item about a scandalous elopement). By the end of the story, however, Miranda has become a critic of the *theatrum mundi*, a reviewer of reality, who will be, not just a passive "wonderer," but a creator. She is on her way to becoming, as Mark Schorer has said, Katherine Anne Porter herself, "the artist, who will proceed to write these stories and others with that ultimate clarity—clairvoyance—that only the true artist possesses." [5]

Perhaps the best internal evidence that the way Miranda will claim her "honest self" is through art lies in the title "Pale Horse, Pale Rider." It comes from the song that Miranda, sick with influenza, sings with Adam, the man she has known for ten days and is falling in love with. In the old spiritual, Miranda says, the pale horse of death takes away lover, mother, father, brother, sister, the whole family, but is always implored to "leave one singer to mourn." Miranda is left, after multiple remembered deaths of family members and after the death of Adam, as the one who will sing of the others. As she once wrote about the theater of the stage, she will now write of the theater of life. This interpretation is supported by the frequent comparisons of life to plays or to movies, occurring throughout the story. Bill, the city editor of the Blue Mountain *News*, behaves "exactly like city editors in the moving pictures, even to the chewed cigar" (p. 287); Chuck, the tubercular sportswriter, dresses his part from turtlenecked sweater to tan hobnailed boots; the restaurant next door to the newspaper, like all its cinematic counterparts, it seems, is nicknamed "The Greasy Spoon"; Miranda finds Liberty Bond salesmen in her office and on the stage of the theater; she and Adam talk to each other in the prescribed flippancies of the day as if they are role-playing; even the vision that comes to her when she is near death is couched in imagery of the theater: she sees that "words like oblivion and eternity are curtains hung before nothing at all" (p. 310).

Just as it took a war to release the Grandmother's true, subjective self in action, so it takes a war to free Miranda's to art. In her case, however, the war is clearly internal as well as external. As surely as Miranda fights against death from influenza at the end of World War I, she also fights—as a woman struggling for psychological and creative independence—against the death that comes from intellectual passivity, from the failure to act or to create, from the surrender of one's honest self. The story opens, significantly, with a description of an almost totally motionless Miranda, just beginning to feel the symptoms of her disease. She is half in a coma; "her heart was a stone lying upon her breast outside of her; her pulses lagged and paused..." (p. 269). It is not really very mysterious that, in this state, her mind should turn to her family, the cause of another kind of intertia in her life. She thinks: "Too many have died in this bed already, there are far too many ancestral bones propped up on the mantelpieces, there have been too damned many antimacassars in this house... and oh, what accumulation of storied dust never allowed to settle in peace for one moment" (p. 269). Only through a stubborn act of will, conscious refusal to die, will Miranda make it to the other side. In "Old Mortality" the child Miranda dreamed of being a jockey when she grew up, envisioning the day "she would ride out . . . and win a great race, and surprise everybody, her family most of all" (p. 196). Her victory will, like Miss Lucy's, be filled with suffering, but this is her day to ride. Although her pulse lags and her heart is almost lifeless, in her mind there is still action: she dreams of mounting her horse and riding to escape death—physical death and that other death, that sacrifice of self, associated with the spider web, or tangled fishing lines, of family.

But if the family was, in her past, the major source of temptations to passivity, other lures have presented themselves in her new life, calling on her to deny her integrity. Even though she believes the war "filthy," it takes all the strength she can muster to resist the intimidations of the men selling Liberty Bonds (the pun is perfect), who assert that she is the lone holdout in all the businesses in the entire city. She surrenders at least momentarily to social pressure when she puts in her time visiting hospitalized soldiers. And when an irate performer whom she has panned assails her, she is once again tempted to retreat from commitment. She wails: " 'There's too much of everything in this world just now. I'd like to sit down here on the curb, Chuck, and die, and never again see—I wish I could lose my memory and forget my own name . . .' " (p. 289). In treating Amy and Eva, Porter was concerned with the near impossibility of a woman's finding her true self under all the debris of psychological determinism, social pressures, acculturation. In Miranda's case, Porter turns—as she did by indirection in the story of the Grandmother—to the problems faced by the woman who, having discovered her own version of truth and the kind of life she wants to lead, must fight tooth and toenail to keep from denying them. Never again to see would be for Miranda, "the seeing one," the ultimate denial of self; it would be truly to forget her name. To lose her memory would be to abandon the very source of her art. Even Adam and the love she feels for him seem a threat to her free will—Adam who keeps her "on the inside of the walk in good American style," who helps her "across street corners as if she were a cripple," who would have carried her over mud puddles had they come across any, and whom she does not want to love, not now, but whom she feels forced to love *now*, because their time seems so short (p. 295).

There are, of course, more important reasons symbolically and thematically for Adam's death than just the fact that he would limit Miranda's independence. Described as "like a fine healthy apple," Adam is Miranda's Edenic self. He has "never had a pain in his life"—a "monstrous uniqueness" in Adam and, by symbolic transfer, in Miranda's own untested self. What pains she has suffered so far have given her, Porter says, only the "illusion of maturity and experience" (p. 280). The Biblical Eve invited Adam to partake of the tree of knowledge; Miranda's Adam, in effect, offers her escape from that knowledge. Perhaps there is a suggestion here of the archetypal offer of the male to "protect" the female, that protection, as it often turns out, effectively blocking creative participation in life, except on the biological level. It is significant that Adam "confessed that he simply could not get through a book" except for technical works, which deal with facts, but not with the truths that interest the artist (p. 285). And it is appropriate that Adam should stop Miranda in her prayer to Apollo, the god of poets—and of seers. Had Adam lived—or, on the symbolic level, had she accepted the kind of life he represented, the life of innocence, of avoidance of pain and reality— Miranda could never become the "singer" who would mourn for human suffering and loss. Adam becomes the "pure . . . sacrificial lamb" given in exchange for her new life (p. 295).

With Adam's death and her own delirious vision of oblivion, Miranda gives up all illusions, all hopes, all love. She is left with what Nannie had found only at the end of her life: that reduction to the very core of selfhood, that "hard unwinking angry point of light" that Miranda saw in her death sleep and heard say, " 'Trust me. I stay.' " She is left with the awareness of the power of her own will (strong enough to conquer death); of her ability to survive alone; and of an identity, a reality that is hers without dependence on any one else. But unlike Nannie, Miranda has the time and the emotional and practical equipment to make this center a starting point instead of a final station. As she returns from her race with death, she is not only a Lazarus come forth, but a "seer" in another sense now, a *vates*, who has looked into the depths and will, no doubt, be compelled to tell about it in certain seasons to come, when Pegasus replaces that other pale horse.

"The Grave" in "The Old Order" had revealed to Miranda that treasure can come from a tomb; her art will be another proof of the truth of this promise.

The likelihood that Miranda will express her selfhood in art may also suggest her superiority to her Grandmother in Porter's view. Porter once indicated her agreement with E. M. Forster's belief that "there are only two possibilities for any real order: art and religion." [6] The essential difference is significant: religion, the Grandmother's source of order in old age, has its anchor outside the self, in institutions, rules, dogmas. Art, on the other hand, has an interior source; the self becomes creator. Religion, as the Grandmother practiced it, means limitation of the self; art, expression of the self. For Porter it is the center that will hold. As she wrote in her introduction to *Flowering Judas and Other Stories*: "[The arts] cannot be destroyed altogether because they represent the substance of faith and the only reality. They are what we find again when the ruins are cleared away. And even the smallest and most incomplete offering at this time can be a proud act in defense of that faith."

And that is winning, too.

A Farewell to Arms:
Ernest Hemingway's "Resentful Cryptogram"

JUDITH FETTERLEY

I

Perhaps others were struck, as I was, when I first read Erich Segal's *Love Story*, by the similarity between it and Ernest Hemingway's *A Farewell to Arms*. Both stories are characterized by a disparity between what is overtly stated and what is covertly expressed. Both ask the reader to believe in the perfection of a love whose substance seems woefully inadequate and whose signature is death. "What can you say about a twenty-five-year-old girl who died?" asks Oliver Barrett IV on the opening page of *Love Story*. The answer is, as the question implies, not very much, because the investment of this love story, like so many others, is not in the life of the beloved but in her death and in the emotional kick which the hero gets from that death—Oliver Barrett weeping in the arms of his long-estranged but now-reconciled father. What one doesn't say is precisely that which alone would be worth saying—namely, that you loved her because she died or, conversely, that because you loved her she had to die.

While *A Farewell to Arms* is infinitely more complex than *Love Story*, nevertheless its emotional dynamics and its form are similar. In reading it one is forced to notice the distance between its overt fabric of idealized romance and its underlying vision of the radical limitations of love, between its surface idyll and its sub-surface critique. And one is also aware of its heavy use of the metaphor and motif of disguise.[1] When Sheridan Baker describes *A Farewell to Arms* as a "resentful cryptogram," he is essentially extending this metaphor to the form of the novel itself.[2] That deviousness and indirection are often the companions of hostility is no new observation, and feminists have always known that idealization is a basic strategy for disguising and marketing hatred. If we explore the attitude toward women in *A Farewell to Arms*, we will discover that while the novel's surface investment is in idealization, what stands behind that idealization is an immense hostility whose full measure can be taken from the fact that Catherine dies, and dies because she is a woman.

Such an analysis of necessity raises the question of Hemingway's "intention": the degree to which he is aware of the disparity between overt and covert, the degree to which he intends the one to make a comment on the other, the degree to which he intends the full meaning of the book to reside in the complex interrelation between them. The question of an author's intention is inevitably a complicated one and is perhaps finally unanswerable beyond the statement that if a certain reading is indeed supported by the text, then such a reading was "intended." It is possible, however, and valuable to make some distinctions. For instance, we might argue that Hemingway's insistent use of the metaphor of disguise is meant to be taken as a clue to our reading and to suggest that the novel's true content is different from its apparent content. Equally, we might explore the implications of Hemingway's choice of subject matter, his conjoining of the twin themes of love and war. While we are often told that love and war are "strange but time-honored bed-companions,"[3] and that "despite the frequency with which they appear in the same book, the themes of love and war are really an unlikely pair, if not indeed— to judge from the frequency with which writers fail to wed them —quite incompatible";[4] nevertheless many of those who have written on *A Farewell to Arms* have sought to provide a framework within which these apparently irreconcilable subjects do in fact make sense. We may, therefore, be justified if we pause for a moment to raise a question, and an eyebrow, at the remarks of Lewis and Young just quoted. Is it entirely accidental that both of them invoke a sexual metaphor to describe what they think can not be made to go together? If metaphor is indeed the ultimate cryptogram, may we not be justified in decoding thus: love and war appear together so frequently because romantic love is in fact a kind of war. Such a reading would seem to be invited by the title of the novel which suggests that the arms of war and the arms of love are one and the same.

But ultimately one is uncomfortable with such arguments. The similarity of *A Farewell to Arms* and *Love Story* returns with its consequent implications. For finally the point of view of *A Farewell to Arms* is Frederic Henry's; it is he with whom we are asked to identify, and it is his evaluations that we are asked to accept. At no place in the book can we locate a clearly articulated or clearly implied point of view which is separate from Frederic's and which has the function of putting Frederic's experience in perspective. The lump in the throat with which many readers greet the end of the novel is the signature of our identification with Frederic Henry and of Hemingway's intention to endorse Frederic's idealized view of his relation with Catherine. We are crying for the loss of something beautiful and, more specifically, for Frederic Henry's sense of loss. Had Hemingway any conscious awareness of the complex ways in which Frederic wants and needs Catherine's death, then the novel's ending would not ask for our tears.

We must also take into account the fact that as a war story *A Farewell to Arms* is anti-romantic. Certainly no one would argue that Hemingway intends in the novel to present an idealized view of war. In other words, Hemingway is aware of sentimentality and capable of exposing it when he sees it. And it is equally clear, if we look at some of his other work, that Hemingway is sensitive to sentimentality in love. Such a sensitivity is central to *The Sun Also Rises* in which Jake's romantic love for Brett and his "sickness" are made to connect intimately, so that by the end of the novel Jake recognizes that his attraction to Brett and hers to him are based on their mutual unavailability and that any other interpretation is simply a "pretty" thought. In short, Hemingway is immensely capable of anti-sentimentality when he wishes to be, and one can only assume that in this case he doesn't so wish because he doesn't so think. It is almost as if, by choosing a situation in which love can not be consummated, Hemingway protects himself against his romantic and sentimental impulses, for the greatness of *The Sun Also Rises* resides to a considerable extent in the tension between its gestures towards romance and its resistance to these gestures. When, as in *A Farewell to Arms*, love becomes "possible," it seems as if a crucial vantage point is lost and the gates to sentimentality are opened. Nevertheless the material of the novel, almost in spite of Hemingway's intention, pulls against this sentimentality. For Hemingway does know that love is a trap; he just doesn't know why. And that, of course, is precisely where feminist analysis enters in.

II

We may begin such an analysis by examining the attitude of the culture which surrounds Frederic and Catherine and which provides the background for their love. In the male world of the Italian front women are seen solely in sexual terms and are relegated to a solely sexual role. This attitude is made quite clear through the way in which the Italian doctors treat the British nurses they encounter: "What a lovely girl.... Does she understand that? She will make you a fine boy. A fine blonde like she is.... What a lovely girl." [5] Of doctors one asks if they are any good at diagnosis and surgery, will they make you a fine leg; of nurses one asks if they are sexually adequate, are they pretty, will they make you a fine boy. Rinaldi's one question about Catherine when Frederic returns to the front after his hospitalization in Milan is, "I mean is she good to you practically speaking," i.e., is she a good lay (p. 169). Rinaldi's inability to see women in other than sexual terms emerges quite clearly from a remark he makes to Frederic before the latter leaves for Milan: "Your lovely cool goddess. English goddess. My God what would a man do with a woman like that except worship her? What else is an Englishwoman good for? ... I tell you something about your good women. Your goddesses. There is only one difference between taking a girl who has always been good and a woman. With a girl it is painful.... And you never know if the girl will really like it" (p. 66). Any woman who wishes to think of herself in other than sexual terms is denying her humanness and trying to be superhuman, a goddess, for humanness in women is synonymous with being sexual.

The contempt and hostility for women which saturate Rinaldi's paradigm are equally clear in scenes like the one in which the soldiers watch their whores being loaded into a truck for the retreat. "I'd like to be there when some of those tough babies climb in and try and hop them. . . . I'd like to have a crack at them for nothing. They charge too much at that house anyway. The government gyps us" (p. 189). Herded like animals, they are seen by the men as so many pieces of meat whose price on the market is too damn high for what you get. Because after all, what do you get? "Over in half an hour or fifteen minutes. Sometimes less. . . . Sometimes a good deal less" (pp. 170–171). And the result? Syphilis and gonorrhea. This attitude toward women has its obvious correlative in an attitude toward sexuality in general. Coarse, gross, the subject matter *par excellence* for jokes whose hostility is hardly worth disguising, sex is seen as the antithesis of sensitivity, tenderness, idealism, and ultimately of knowledge. When the men in Frederic Henry's mess bait their priest with constant sexual joking, they are expressing their sense of his difference and their uneasiness in the face of it. For, by virtue of his asexuality, the priest has access to a certain knowledge and stature that the men who remain sexual do not have and secretly admire. "He had always known what I did not know and what, when I learned it, I was always able to forget" (p. 14). The priest who comes from the cold, white, pure mountainous world of the Abruzzi, where women are safely distanced and men relate to each other, knows that sex is a dangerous and wasteful commodity and that the best world indeed is that of men without women. The priest alone is able to carry out the implications of his culture's attitude toward sex.

The difference between what men deserve in the world which produces these doctors and soldiers and priests and what women deserve can be seen in the disparity between the treatment of Catherine's death and the treatment of the deaths of men at war. " 'You will not do any such foolishness,' the doctor said. 'You would not die and leave your husband' "; " 'You are not going to die. You must not be silly' " (pp. 319, 331). The tone here is one appropriate to a parent addressing a recalcitrant child and the remarks are at once a reprimand and an implicit command which at some level assumes that Catherine is in control of whether she lives or dies. Indeed, Catherine herself internalizes the attitude of her doctor and presents that *reductio ad absurdam* of the female experience: she feels guilty for dying and apologizes to the doctor for taking up his valuable time with her death—"I'm sorry I go on so long." No shadow of blame or responsibility falls on the two males who attend her as she dies. Catherine never questions Henry's responsibility for her situation, for she seems to operate on the tacit assumption that conception like contraception is her doing. And while Frederic is quick to smell incompetence when it comes to his leg, no doubts are raised about the doctor who performs the Caesarean on Catherine, though usually the need for such an operation is spotted before the child has strangled. Rather, the responsibility for both her death and the child's is placed on Catherine. In contrast, the soldier who, analogously, hemorrhages to death in the ambulance sling above Frederic Henry does not see himself as stupid, bad, irresponsible. Even more incongruous is the idea of a doctor referring to a dying soldier in such terms. Indeed, when Miss Van Campen accuses Frederic of the irresponsibility of self-induced jaundice, the results are quite different from those of the comparable scene between Catherine and her doctor. A soldier's primary responsibility is to himself, but a woman is responsible, even in the moment of her death, to men; as long as there is a man around who needs her, she *ought* not to die. Thus Catherine's death is finally seen as a childish and irresponsible act of abandonment. If we weep during the book at the death of soldiers, we are weeping for the tragic and senseless waste of their lives, we are weeping for them. If we weep at the end of the book, however, it is not for Catherine but for Frederic Henry abandoned in a cold, wet, hostile world. All our tears are ultimately for men because in the world of *A Farewell to Arms* male life is what counts.

III

On first consideration, Frederic Henry seems to be quite different from his companions at the front. His position as an American fighting in an Italian war would seem to be a metaphor for his larger role of outsider in this culture; he is sensitive and tender, capable of a sustained personal relationship with a woman, and of an idealization of love which appears to be the secular analogue of the priest's asexual spirituality. While he does not openly identify with the priest, neither does he join his mess-mates in their baiting. Catherine is for him a "sacred subject," and he resists Rinaldi's attempt to sexualize everything and to locate his feeling for Catherine in the genitals. At one point when Catherine is teasing Frederic, she refers to him as "Othello with his occupation gone" (p. 257). One is struck by the allusion because it seems to point out so clearly just how different Frederic is from the culture in which he finds himself. One can not imagine him strangling Catherine in a fit of jealous rage. But when one considers what in fact happens in the book, one is tempted to feel that the difference between Frederic and Othello is essentially superficial and rests only in the degree to which each is able to face his immense egocentrism and the fear and hatred of women which are its correlatives. If one is struck by the violence of the novel's ending, one is also struck by the abstract nature of that violence, its location in the biological trap which is the agent of an impersonal "they" who break the brave and beautiful. Yet the image of strangulation persists and nags us with the thought that Frederic Henry sees himself in the foetus which emerges from Catherine's womb and that her death is the fulfillment of his own unconscious wish.[6]

Frederic Henry's hostility to women is in some ways quite clear. In the course of the novel, he has a series of encounters with older women in positions of authority. In all of these encounters there is an underlying sense of hostility and while overt expression of this hostility is rare—such as the end of the novel when he shoves the two nurses out of the room in order to make his peace with the dead Catherine—it is implicit in the fact that in his mind these women appear as smug, self-righteous, critical, anti-sexual, and sadistic, and it is expressed by the nature of his reactions to them. Consider, for instance, Frederic's interchange with the head nurse at the hospital where Catherine first works. In response to his request for Catherine, he is informed that she is on duty and is told, "there's a war on, you know" (p. 22). By implication Frederic is defined as an egocentric insensitive non-combatant who expects to get his pleasure while other men are dying. This woman speaks from a position of moral superiority which in effect operates to diminish Frederic Henry.

The hostility between Frederic and this kind of woman, adumbrated in this early encounter, comes out in full force in his relation to Miss Van Campen, the head of the hospital in Milan where he is taken after his injury. Their dislike for each other is immediate and instinctual, as if each realizes in the other a natural enemy. The war metaphor would seem to be as neatly extended to the area of male/female relationships by the pun in Van Campen's name as it is by the pun in the book's title. Miss Van Campen defines the nature of their relationship as that of a power struggle when she describes Frederic as "domineering and rude," not the least bit interested in her authority or her rules. And, in fact, Frederic isn't interested because he thoroughly discredits her authority and pays no attention to her rules. "She was small and neatly suspicious and too good for her position. She asked many questions and seemed to think it was somewhat disgraceful that I was with the Italians" (p. 86). Like the earlier nurse, Miss Van Campen conceives of herself as morally superior to Frederic and is critical of him, implying that he is a selfish egotist, as insensitive to the concerns of others as he is to the larger issue of the war. But we discount Miss Van Campen's criticism because she is presented so unsympathetically and because of the implication that the basis of her hostility towards Frederic is his sexual relation with Catherine. She fits the stereotype, so comfortable to the male ego, of the frustrated old maid who, because she has never had sex, is jealous of those who do and persecutes them. Her hostility results from powerlessness while his is the product of power; she is hostile because of rejection and he is hostile out of a contempt whose ultimate measure can be taken by the fact that he sees rejection and powerlessness as the source of her hostility.

In the final phase of their struggle, Frederic employs the method by which men have classically sought to deny women who refuse to comply with the "feminine mystique" any possibility of power, authority, or credibility. He denies her ability to know anything by calling into question her sexuality and her status as a woman. All he need do to rout her utterly is remind her by implication that she is not a full woman, that she has had no sexual experience, that she knows nothing of the pain of the scrotum or the agonies of the womb. She is so insecure as a person because she has failed to be a woman that the merest mention of the sacred genitalia is enough to vanquish her.

If the Van Campens of this world threaten Frederic because of their pretensions to authority, other women challenge him because of their incompetence. There is the example of Mrs. Walker. Doing night duty in a just-opened and empty hospital, she is awakened from her sleep to deal with an unexpected patient and proves to be totally unable to handle the situation: "I don't know," "I couldn't put you in just any room," "I can't put on sheets," "I can't read Italian," "I can't do anything without the doctor's orders" (pp. 82, 83). Frederic ultimately deals with her incompetence by ignoring her and communicating with the men involved who, in spite of their position as mere porters, are able to get him to a bed. Mrs. Walker is one of a number of weepy women in the novel who appear to have no way of dealing with difficulty other than crying. The attitude towards them is one in which contempt is mingled with patronizing pity. Poor Mrs. Walker, poor Fergy, poor whores, poor virgins. Here, of course, is a classic instance of the double bind: women are pathetic in their inability to handle difficulty, but if they presume to positions of authority and, even worse, to execute the authority of those positions, they become unbearably self-righteous and superior. Damned if you do and damned if you don't. But ultimately less damned if you don't, because at least Walker is a Mrs.—no shadow here of not being a real woman—while it is Van Campen who bears the stigma of Miss. Frederic Henry is finally more comfortable with women who do not threaten his ego by pretending to authority over him. This is part of his attraction to whores: "'Does she [the whore] say she loves him?' ... 'Yes. If *he* wants her to.' 'Does he say he loves her?' ... 'He does if *he* wants to'" (p. 105—italics mine).

IV

While Frederic Henry is sometimes willing to evaluate his nurses in terms of skill, he certainly has as much of an eye for the body as his fellow war companions: "I heard the door open and looked and it was a nurse. She looked young and pretty"; "I heard it buzz down the hall and then someone coming on rubber soles along the hall. It was Miss Gage and she looked a little older in the bright sunlight and not so pretty" (pp. 84, 89). One can be quite sure that Frederic would never have fallen in love with Catherine if she were not beautiful. The idyllic quality of such love rests firmly on the precondition that the female partner be a "looker." And Catherine is, she most certainly is beautiful and so she is eminently lovable: "She looked fresh and young and very beautiful. I thought I had never seen anyone so beautiful.... When I saw her I was in love with her" (p. 91).

While Catherine's beauty is presented as a sufficient cause of Frederic's love, we are, of course, justified in taking a longer look at the basis of his emotion. Although one can explain his sudden falling in love on the basis of the trap metaphor which the novel develops so elaborately—things happen to you and all of a sudden you are in it and there is nothing you can do about it—it hardly seems fortuitous that the experience occurs when he is most in need of the loving service which Nurse Barkley appears so amply able to provide. Frederic has, after all, had several weeks of lying flat on his back with a blown up leg and little else to think about except the absurdity of his position in relation to the war, his isolation, and the essential fragility of life. Such thoughts might make one prone to accept affection and service even if they require the word "love" to get them. And Frederic, trapped as he is in a cast, in a bed, in a hospital, in a stupid war, seems only too willing to avail himself of Catherine's service. "Catherine Barkley was greatly liked by the nurses because she would do night duty indefinitely" (p. 108). Frederic greatly likes her for this, too, since it means she is available for his needs not only during the day but all night as well. While Frederic sleeps during the day, however, Catherine goes right on working. He is conveniently unaware of her exhaustion in the face of the double duty induced by his continual invitations to "play," until Catherine's friend, Ferguson, finally points it out to him and insists that he get her to take a rest.

The egotistic basis of Frederic's feeling for Catherine is clear from other vantage points as well. For instance, one can consider those few scenes in which Catherine would appear to be making demands on Frederic. During their second meeting, Frederic tries to seduce her. Because she feels that he is insincere, his gesture simply part of the routine which soldiers go through when they get a nurse on her evening off, she says no, and when that has no effect, she slaps him. Frederic responds to her initial refusal by ignoring it. Then, when she slaps him, he gets angry and uses his anger in combination with her guilt to get what he wanted in the first place. Jackson J. Benson describes the situation beautifully:

> In his early encounters with the British nurse Catherine Barkley, Henry is the casual, uniformed boy on the make, but down deep inside he is really a decent sort. In other words,

what makes Henry so sinister is his All-American-Boy lack of guile. He demonstrates an attitude and pattern of behavior that any Rotarian would privately endorse. He fully intends (he spells it out quite clearly) to take a girl, who is described in terms of a helpless, trembling Henry James bird, and crush her in his hands very casually as part of the game that every young, virile lad must play. It is a backhanded tribute to Hemingway's irony here that most readers don't seem to even blanch at the prospect.[7]

But if irony is so mistakable, one may be justified in questioning whether or not it is intended. And why should Hemingway in this instance be separated from the cultural norm of "any Rotarian" so brilliantly embodied in Frederic and Catherine's views of the affair? In both their eyes Frederic's anger is justifiable, the legitimate response of a male thwarted in his rightful desires by a maiden unduly coy (*vide* Catherine's reference to Marvell's "To His Coy Mistress": "it's about a girl who wouldn't live with a man"), whose posture of trembling helplessness is simply a way of disguising what she really wants or at least ought to want.

Richard B. Hovey's analysis of the scene in which Catherine announces her pregnancy is excellent for our purposes:

From any common-sense and manly point of view, Frederic is failing Catherine in this crisis. When she makes her big announcement and then confesses that she tried to induce a miscarriage, he makes practically no response. The lover-hero at this point reveals a startling lack of awareness, an unpleasing absorption in himself. Thereupon Catherine takes on herself all the blame for "making trouble"—and he allows her to do exactly that! ... So it is Catherine, the one who must go through childbirth, who does the comforting. A depth of pathos—or of downright absurdity—is reached toward the end of the scene when both lovers concern themselves with whether the pregnancy makes *Frederic* feel trapped.[8]

Later in the novel, in the hotel room which they have taken to spend a last few hours together before Frederic leaves for the front, Catherine has a sudden attack of depression. The idea of taking a room not for the night but for two or three hours, the quality of the hotel, the décor of the room all combine to make her feel like a whore. At the moment when Catherine is experiencing this feeling of alienation, Frederic is standing by the windows whose red plush curtains he has just closed, in a gesture which signals their possession of the room as another "home" and encloses the two of them in an inner world which reflects his sense of their closeness. Obviously they are at this moment poles apart in their feelings. Then Frederic catches sight of Catherine in the mirrors which surround the room and discovers that she is unhappy. He is surprised—for how could they be reacting so differently when they two are one and that one is he—and disappointed for this will upset his plans for their last evening together. "You're not a whore," he says, as if simple assertion were sufficient to cancel the complex sources of her sense of degradation. He then proceeds to register his own feelings of disappointment, anger, and frustration in unmistakable terms: he reopens the curtains and looks out, suggesting thereby that she has shattered their rapport and broken up their home. Quite literally, Frederic turns his back on Catherine. His meaning is clear; Catherine's unhappiness is something he can respond to only in terms of how it affects him; beyond that, it is her problem and when she gets herself together and is ready to be his "good girl" again, then he will come back. And if she doesn't? "Oh, hell, I thought, do we have to argue now?" (p. 252). In other words, either she does what he wants or he gets angry. Hostility and love seem very close indeed here, only separated by Catherine's ability to fulfill the demands of Frederic's ego. Catherine acts as if she knows quite well where Frederic's love is coming from. Hypersensitive to his ego, she is forever asking him, "What would you like me to do now"; and she continually responds to their situation in terms of his needs: I'll get rid of Ferguson so that we can go to bed, you must go play with Count Greffi, don't you want a weekend with the boys, I know I'm not much fun now that I'm big.

But there are other aspects of Frederic Henry's character that Catherine is made to respond to, that shape her character and form the basis of his love for her. Wyndham Lewis has amply commented on the essential passivity of Hemingway's protagonist, and others have concurred with his observations. Among "the multitudinous ranks of *those to whom things happen*," Frederic Henry lacks "executive will," a sense of responsibility and the capacity to make a commitment.[9] In contrast to Frederic's passivity, one is struck by Catherine's aggressiveness. How, after all, can a heroine be allowed so much activity and still keep her status as an idealized love object? On closer analysis, however, one notices that Catherine's aggressiveness achieves legitimacy because it is always exercised in the service of Frederic's passivity. Whenever Catherine acts she does so in order to save him from responsibility and commitment. It is Catherine who creates the involvement between herself and Frederic; it is she who constructs their initial encounter in such a way as to place them in a "relationship" almost immediately; it is she who shows up at the hospital in Milan so that he can fall in love with her. In addition, Catherine takes full responsibility for the pregnancy and for figuring out where and how she will have their baby and then, when she dies, she, in conjunction with certain ill-defined cosmic forces, takes the responsibility for this too. It is possible for Frederic to love Catherine because she provides him with the only kind of relationship that he is capable of accepting: he does not have to act; he does not have to think about things because she thinks for him ("You see, darling, if I marry you I'll be an American and any time we're married under American law the child is legitimate"); he does not have to assume responsibility; and he does not have to make a final commitment because both her facile logic to the effect that they are already married and her ultimate death give him a convenient out.

But Catherine relates to Frederic's need to avoid responsibility in an even deeper way. "You could not go back. If you did not go forward what happened? You never got back to Milan. And if you got back to Milan what happened?" (p. 216). So thinks Frederic as he is bogged down in the midst of the Italian retreat. The imagery of the retreat—thousands of people on a single road unable to move and unable to leave—is a perfect analogue for the form of Frederic's thought which turns back upon itself to leave him locked between two impossibilities. He is cut off from the past; he can not get to the Abruzzi, that idealized world of the past where God is not a dirty joke and where social relationships are exquisitely simple. He can not go back because it is clear that the aristocratic and chauvinistic world of the Abruzzi is responsible for the horror of this war, a war of kings and dukes which the peasants disavow and in so doing call into question the whole archaic structure which the Abruzzi represents. But he can not go forward either. His question is not, if you never got back to Milan what happened, but rather, if you *got* back what happened. His mind recoils in fear at the thought of the future. Indeed, he is able to relate to Catherine precisely because and as long as their relationship has neither past nor future, as long as, like the Italian retreat, it goes nowhere. When it threatens to go forward, it conveniently ends by Catherine's death in childbirth, that "cloud," as John Killinger puts it, "spread by the author as a disguise for pulling off a *deus ex machina* to save his hero from the existential hell of a complicated life." [10] Through Catherine's death, then, Frederic Henry avoids having to face the responsibilities incumbent upon a husband and father. Her death reflects his desire to remain uncommitted and it gives him a marketable explanation for so doing.

To say, however, that Catherine fulfills Frederic's need to avoid responsibility and to remain uncommitted is certainly at some level to say she has failed him. This is the burden of Robert Lewis' commentary on *A Farewell to Arms*. His sense of Catherine's failure is clearly carried in the following remark: "Her death carries the hope with it of the destruction of her destructive love that excludes the world, that in its very denial of self possesses selfishly, that leads nowhere beyond the bed and the dream of a mystical transport of ordinary men and women to a divine state of love through foolish suffering." [11] As the tenor of this sentence suggests, it would seem that Catherine's very adaptability to Frederic's need "to reduce life to its lowest denominator, to make it simple, to make it thoughtless, to destroy consciousness and responsibility in a romantic, orgiastic dream" is in itself a source of hostility towards her.[12]

But one can give the emotional screw of the novel one final turn. If Catherine finally fails Frederic, it may be that in so doing she is fulfilling his ultimate need, which is to feel betrayed. Frederic's mentality is saturated with the vision of betrayal. At one point, he jokingly refers to himself as Christ. Like all good jokes, this one reveals as much as it hides. And what it reveals in part is Frederic's instinctive affiliation of himself with one who was betrayed. The metaphor of betrayal also governs Frederic's war experience, for the only killings we ever see are those of Italians by Italians. In his view Catherine is finally betrayed by her own body, whose physical construction is in direct opposition to its biological function. Betrayal permeates Frederic's view of nature and is at the root of his view of the universe as one in which a "we" who are good and brave and beautiful are opposed by a "they" who wish to break us, precisely because we are good and brave and beautiful, so that once again we are betrayed by the nature of life whose ultimate treachery lies in the fact that it makes our selves the agents of our destruction.

V

The sense of betrayal which is so central to Frederic Henry's vision of Catherine and which provides such an important key to his attitude towards her is equally developed through another aspect of the novel's structure, and that is its use of spatial imagery. Very early in *A Farewell to Arms* a contrast is established between what I shall call, borrowing the terms of Erik Erikson, outer and inner space. Frederic is trying to explain to the priest why he never got to the Abruzzi "where the roads were frozen and hard as iron, where it was clear cold and dry and the snow was dry and powdery and hare-tracks in the snow," but rather had gone to smoke-filled cafés and dark rooms in the night (p. 13). The tension between these two kinds of space is central to Frederic's imagination. He essentially shies away from images of outer space, investing them with loneliness and fear, and he embraces images of inner space, investing them with an aura of security. The tension is further heightened by the fact that the images of inner space are developed against the background of a cold, dark, damp, unfriendly outer world.

This image of Frederic Henry inside—warm, dry, and secure—watching the world outside, isolated by light, struggle against the weather, is ever-present in the novel. It is this vision of inner space which he seeks equally in Catherine, loving as he does to let her hair fall over him like a tent and focusing incessantly on every room they inhabit and how they make it a "home." When Frederic arrives at the hospital in Milan, it is, significantly, empty. There is nobody in it, no patients, seemingly no staff, no sheets on the bed, and no room of one's own. By the time he leaves, the hospital has become a home from which he is ejected into the outer world of the war. The height of the creation of inner space with Catherine is, of course, their rooms in the house in the Swiss mountains with the big stove in the corner and the feather bed for the lovely dark nights and the air crisp and cold to define for them the security of being inside, snuggled and warm.

But while this archetypal image evokes feelings of warmth and security, it equally evokes feelings of immense vulnerability; it is but a momentary stay against the confusion of crowded troop trains where you spend the night on the floor with people walking over you, and of stalled retreats where, like a sitting duck, you wait to be picked off by planes coming in from Austria. It can at any moment be changed to simply an analogue for the outside world: "But after I had got them out and shut the door and turned off the light it wasn't any good. It was like saying good-by to a statue. After a while I went out and left the hospital and walked back to the hotel in the rain" (p. 332). The immense weakness of inner space is poignantly captured when Frederic and Catherine, on their way to the station for his departure to the front, encounter a soldier and his girl standing, in the mist and cold, tight up against a wet stone buttress, his cape pulled around them both. It is a posture which they consciously or unconsciously imitate a few moments later in sympathetic appreciation of their equal vulnerability. It is pathetic or ironic, or both, that Catherine, driven away in a carriage, her face lit up in the window, motions Frederic to get back in under the archway and out of the rain.

But the threat to inner space comes not only from outside but equally from inside, from its very nature. When Frederic is retreating from the retreat and trying to get back to Milan, he hops a train and dives in under the canvas of a flatcar where he is out of sight. In the process he hits his head against something and discovers, on feeling about, that what is sharing this world with him is a gun. This connection of the inner world with death is fully developed through Catherine. Her womb, nurturing an embryo, is an obvious analogue for the world which Frederic creates with her. At the end of the novel, however, we discover that Catherine's womb is in fact a chamber of horrors filled with blood and death. In an ironic reversal of expectations, the real danger to Frederic Henry turns out not to be the world of war, the outer world which seems so obviously threatening, but the world of love, the inner world which seems overtly so secure.

The connection of sex and death is incessant in Hemingway's writing. In *A Farewell to Arms* the association is made by the second page of the book: "their rifles were wet and under their capes the two leather cartridge-boxes on the front of the belts, gray leather boxes heavy with the packs of clips of thin, long 6.5 mm. cartridges, bulged forward under the capes so that the men, passing on the road, marched as though they were six months gone with child." The idea that pregnancy is death and the womb an agent of destruction could hardly be stated more clearly. Thus the real source of betrayal in the biological trap is not simply biology; it is, specifically, female biology. Women, who promise life, are in reality death and their world of inner space is finally nightmare. Conversely, the outer world of men which seems overtly to be given over to death, is finally the reservoir of hope and possibility: "If it is possible I will return to the Abruzzi" (p. 71). In the handling of these metaphors of space, then, we once again encounter the immense hostility toward women which underlies *A Farewell to Arms*. Perhaps the "they" of Frederic's philosophy can indeed be located in time and space. And perhaps that is why Frederic Henry is afraid of the numbers above two when, in a scene charged with unstated emotion, he stands over Catherine controlling the gas which could so easily, under the guise of easing her pain, kill her. So true to the end is this novel to the forms of disguise, a resentful cryptogram indeed.

Notes

ANNETTE BARNES

1. An adaption of Mailer's remarks in "The Prisoner of Sex," *Harper's Magazine* (March, 1971), p. 45.
2. Matthew Arnold, "The Function of Criticism at the Present Time," *English Literature and its Backgrounds*, ed. B. Grebanier (New York: Dryden Press, 1950), pp. 1201, 1191.
3. Irving Howe, "The middle-class mind of Kate Millet," *Harper's Magazine* (December, 1970), p. 110.
4. Frederick Crews, *The Pooh Perplex* (New York: Dutton, 1963), pp. 44, 20.
5. Sigmund Freud, "Analysis of a Phobia in a Five-Year-Old Boy," *The Sexual Enlightenment of Children* (New York: Collier, 1971), p. 80.
6. "The Avoidance of Love," *Must We Mean What We Say?* (New York: Scribner's, 1969), p. 286.
7. By citing certain criteria in virtue of which one ascribes correctness to an interpretation, I have not thereby given logically sufficient conditions for a satisfactory interpretation. I held that it was conceivable that an interpretation possess all the criterial features while not achieving correctness. How is this possible? If I ask doctors what criterion they use for establishing death, am I not, in effect, asking them how one conclusively decides the matter? Unless one has some bizarre responses to corpses one's behavior radically changes when the living become the dead. We want the criterion for death to guarantee that our judgments about people with respect to this property are correct. If permanent heart stop-

page is the criterion, then permanent heart stoppage seems understood by them to be a logically sufficient condition for death.
Sometimes when one asks for criteria it seems one is asking for
logically sufficient conditions.

One cannot always understand criteria, however, in terms of
logical sufficiency, for there are cases where one runs into difficulty doing so. Suppose you ask me what my criteria are in virtue
of which I ascribe pain to a person. How do I know when to say
that a particular person is in pain? I answer that if the person is
moaning, or clenching his stomach, or doubling up, or muttering
"I am in pain, get a doctor," then I know he is in pain. But you
might correctly point out that my criteria for ascribing pain are
in terms of behavior and that it is conceivable that a person
exhibiting such behavior may in fact not be in pain. The person
might be acting, or feigning pain. The behavior is evidence for
having pain; it is not, however, always conclusive evidence. The
pain situation is odd if one believes that criteria guarantee something. What I have called criteria for pain ascriptions are all one
has to go on, even though they are not logically sufficient.

I suggest that criteria for satisfactory interpretations are in this
regard like criteria for a person's being in pain; the relation between the criterion and what it is a criterion for is not one of
logical sufficiency. This is not to deny that there are obvious dis-
analogies between the two cases. Whereas it is possible in the pain
example for a person to be in pain without exhibiting pain behavior, it is implausible to suppose an interpretation that was inconsistent, limited, incoherent... was a satisfactory one.

8. Nelson Goodman, *Languages of Art* (Indianapolis and New York:
   Bobbs-Merrill, 1968), p. 264.
9. "Psychology Constructs the Female, or the Fantasy Life of the
   Male Psychologist," *Liberation Now* (1968), p. 272.
10. Stuart Hampshire, "Logic and Appreciation," *Art and Philosophy*,
    ed. W. E. Kennick (New York: St. Martin's Press, 1965), pp. 582,
    584.
11. Margaret Macdonald, "Distinctive Features of Arguments Used in
    Criticism," *Art and Philosophy*, p. 604.
12. Leo Tolstoy, "What is Art?" *Art and Philosophy*, p. 10.
13. In Joyce's brilliant parody, Gerty McDowell dreams of wedlock—
    "before he went out to business he would give his dear little wifey
    a good hearty hug and gaze for a moment deep down into her
    eyes"—while young Tommy Caffrey urinates. Bloom masturbates
    and comes, the scent of Gerty's perfumed handkerchief flimsier
    by far than the scent of Bloom's sperm. As both Gerty and the
    young man quoted above illustrate, the emotional fantasies pro-

vided by sentimentalizing the traditional roles need not be challenged by the mundane experiences of life. How one reads what goes on in one's life is affected by one's interests and needs—interests and needs all too frequently conditioned by commercial clichés.

14. Aristotle, *Politics* (Book I: Chapter 5,1254b ll. 12–13), *The Basic Works of Aristotle*, ed. Richard P. McKeon (New York: Random House, 1941), p. 1132.
15. Hilton Kramer, "Revival of Romaine Brooks," *New York Times* (April 25, 1971), p. 19.
16. Norman Mailer, "The Prisoner of Sex," p. 45. In all fairness to Mailer, he does allow that this might not be *the* reason.
17. "Orgasms," *New York Review of Books*, 19 (November 30, 1972), p. 29.
18. "The middle-class mind of Kate Millett," pp. 118–119.

MARCIA LANDY

1. Roland Barthes, *Writing Degree Zero* (New York: Hill and Wang, 1968), pp. 3, 5.
2. Ferdinand Toennies, "Gemeinschaft and Gesellschaft," *Community and Society* (East Lansing, Mich.: Michigan State Univ. Press, 1957), pp. 191–192.
3. Ibid., p. 192.
4. Christopher Caudwell, *Illusion and Reality* (New York: International Publishers, 1967), p. 28.
5. Walter Benjamin, *Illuminations* (New York: Schocken, 1969), p. 87.
6. Ibid., p. 95.
7. Boris Eichenbaum, "The Theory of the Formal Method," *Russian Formalist Criticism, Four Essays* (Lincoln, Nebr.: Univ. of Nebraska Press, 1965), pp. 138–139.
8. Kenneth Burke, *The Philosophy of Literary Form* (New York: Vintage, 1957), p. 262.
9. Ibid., p. 62.
10. Ibid., pp. 276–277.
11. Barthes, pp. 86–87.
12. Ibid., pp. 87–88.

LYNN SUKENICK

1. Georg Simmel, "Das Relative und das Absolute in Geschechter-problem," *Philosophische Kultur*, Leipzig, 1911. Quoted by Viola

Klein in *Feminine Character: A Study of Ideology* (London: Routledge, 1946), p. 82.

2. Mary Ellmann, *Thinking About Women* (New York: Harcourt, 1968), p. 187.

3. George Eliot, "Woman in France: Madame de Sable," in *Essays of George Eliot*, ed. Thomas Pinney (London: Routledge, 1963), p. 53.

4. Anaïs Nin, *The Diary of Anaïs Nin, II, 1934–1939*, ed. Gunther Stuhlmann (Chicago: Swallow Press, 1967), p. 234.

5. Joyce Horner, *The English Women Novelists and their Connection with the Feminist Movement, 1688–1797* (Northampton: Smith College Studies in Modern Languages, XI, 1, 2, 3 Oct. 1929, Jan., Apr., 1930), p. 37.

6. As Virginia Woolf points out in *A Room of One's Own* (New York: Harcourt, 1929), p. 127.

7. *A Room of One's Own* and *Three Guineas* (1938; reprinted, London: Hogarth, 1952).

8. Ellmann, p. 29.

9. William Hazlitt, *Works*, VIII (London, 1903), pp. 123–124.

10. Oliver Elton, *A Survey of English Literature, 1780–1830* (London: Edward Arnold, 1912), p. 174.

11. Quoted by Ellmann, p. 23.

12. Hugh Kenner, rev. of *Divorcing*, by Susan Taubes, *New York Times Book Review*, November 2, 1969, p. 4.

13. Harrison Smith, rev. of *Ladders to Fire*, by Anaïs Nin, *Saturday Review*, November 30, 1946, p. 66.

14. Quoted by Margaret Lawrence in *The School of Femininity* (New York, 1936), p. 63.

15. Kate Millett, *Sexual Politics* (Garden City: Doubleday, 1970), p. 139.

16. Sir Leslie Stephen, *History of English Thought in the Eighteenth Century*, 3rd ed. (New York: Peter Smith, 1949), p. 442.

17. Walter Jackson Bate, *From Classic to Romantic* (Cambridge: Harvard Univ. Press, 1946), p. 60.

18. Diana Trilling, "The Image of Women in Contemporary Literature," *The Woman in America*, ed. Robert J. Lifton (Boston: Beacon, 1964), p. 66.

19. Ashley Montagu, *The Natural Superiority of Women* (New York: Macmillan, 1957), p. 83.

20. Mary Wollstonecraft, *A Vindication of the Rights of Woman* (New York: Norton, 1957), p. 83. Pages for succeeding quotations are given in the body of the paper.

21. George Eliot, *Essays*, p. 334.

22. Ortega y Gasset, "Landscape With a Deer in the Background," *On Love: Aspects of a Single Theme* (New York: Meridian, 1957).

23. Klein, p. 42.

24. Havelock Ellis, *Man and Woman* (London: Walter Scott, 1896), p. 28.

25. John Stuart Mill, *The Subjection of Women* (London: Dent, 1929), p. 275.

26. Montagu, p. 140.

27. Helene Deutsch, *The Psychology of Women*, I (New York: Grune and Stratton, 1944–45), pp. 192, 136.

28. Mill, p. 273.

29. Henri Bergson, *An Introduction to Metaphysics* (1912). Quoted by Karl Stern in *The Flight from Woman* (New York: Farrar, Strauss, and Giroux, 1965), p. 43.

30. Stern, p. 86.

31. Ibid., p. 42.

32. Ibid., p. 26.

33. Germaine Greer, *The Female Eunuch* (New York: McGraw Hill, 1970), p. 100.

34. Frank Kermode, *The Romantic Image* (New York: Vintage, 1964), pp. 50, 53.

35. Stern, p. 21.

36. Norman O. Brown, *Love's Body* (New York: Random House, 1966), p. 80.

37. August Wilhelm von Schlegel, *Lectures on Dramatic Art and Literature*, Lect. xxii. Quoted by Bate, p. 31.

38. Ellis, p. 17.

39. Doris Lessing, *The Golden Notebook* (New York: Ballantine, 1968), p. 42.

40. *A Room of One's Own*, p. 140.

41. Wollstonecraft, p. 164.

42. *The Brontës: Their Lives, Friendships and Correspondence in Four Volumes*, ed. T. J. Wise and J. A. Symington (Oxford: Clarendon, 1932), III, 99; II, 180–181.

43. Ibid., III, 31.

44. *A Room of One's Own*, pp. 152, 181.

45. Anaïs Nin, *D. H. Lawrence: An Unprofessional Study* (Chicago: Swallow Press, 1964), pp. 49–50.

46. Mrs. Gaskell, *The Life of Charlotte Brontë* (New York: Harper, 1901), p. 160.

MAUREEN FRIES

1. See, for example, Robert B. Bechtel, "The Problem of Criseide's Character," *Susquehanna University Studies*, 7 (1963), 109–118; Joseph Graydon, "Defense of Criseyde," *PMLA*, 44 (1929), 141–177; Arthur Mizener, "Character and Action in the Case of Criseyde," *PMLA*, 54 (1939), 65–81; Constance Saintonge, "In Defense of Criseyde," *MLQ*, 15 (1954), 312–320. A recent and spirited defense is that of Neil D. Isaacs, "Further Testimony in the Matter of Troilus," *SLitI*, 4 (1971), 11–27. Controversy is not, of course, limited to the character of Criseyde but extends to interpretation of the poem as a whole, as Ida L. Gordon notes in *The Double Sorrow of Troilus* (Oxford: Clarendon, 1970), p. 3.
2. A typical comment: "Yet none who does not love her and wish 'to excuse hir yet for routhe' is seeing her as Chaucer meant her to be seen"—C. S. Lewis, *The Allegory of Love* (Oxford: Galaxy, 1970), p. 182.
3. For a good recent summary of changing attitudes toward Criseyde see H. R. Hays, *The Dangerous Sex: The Myth of Feminine Evil* (New York: Putnam's, 1964), Ch. 12, "As False as Cressid...."
4. *Chaucer and the French Tradition* (Berkeley and Los Angeles: Univ. of California Press, 1969), p. 164. Adrienne K. Lockhart, "Semantic, Moral and Aesthetic Disintegration in *Troilus and Criseyde*," *Chaucer Review*, 8 (1973), 100–118, sees Criseyde's so-called "ambiguity" as part of a structural pattern of debasement in moral meaning.
5. *The Crooked Rib* (Columbus: Ohio State Press, 1944), p. 5.
6. In "The *Doppelgängers* in Chaucer's *Troilus*," *NM*, 72 (1971), 732.
7. *The Works of Geoffrey Chaucer*, ed. F. N. Robinson (Boston: Houghton Mifflin, 1957). All references to this edition appear henceforward by book and verse number in the text.
8. *The Story of Troilus*, ed. R. K. Gordon, tr. R. K. Gordon (New York: Dutton, 1964), p. 48. All further references to *Il Filostrato* are to this edition and appear by page number in the text. For a recent look at Boccaccio's concept of love, see Robert P. apRoberts, "Love in the Filostrato," *Chaucer Review*, 7 (1972), 1–26.
9. Eugene A. Hecker, *A Short History of Women's Rights* (Westport, Conn.: Greenwood, 1971), p. 48.
10. Margaret A. Gist, *Love and War in the Middle English Romances* (Philadelphia: Univ. of Pennsylvania Press, 1947), p. 15.
11. *The Book of the Knight of La Tour Landry*, ed. Thomas Wright (rev. ed., London: EETS, 33, 1906), p. 25.
12. See Hecker, Ch. 2, "Women and the Early Christian Church."

13. Gist, pp. 37–38.
14. *Summa Theologica*, Part III (Supplement), Q. 46, Art. 1. This reference was suggested to me by Margaret Gist.
15. Saintonge, 314.
16. Hecker, p. 121; Gist, p. 16, n. 25.
17. Hecker, pp. 1–2.
18. *The Iliad of Homer*, tr. Richard Lattimore (Chicago: Univ. of Chicago Press, 1962), pp. 59–64.
19. Fear is one element of Criseyde's dilemma, but I cannot agree with C. S. Lewis' argument that it is the principal one (*The Allegory of Love*, pp. 185–187). For recent comment on fear as motivating Criseyde, see John M. Steadman, *Disembodied Laughter: Troilus and the Apotheosis Tradition* (Berkeley and Los Angeles: Univ. of California Press, 1972), p. 67 ff.
20. R. K. Root, "Introduction," *The Book of Troilus and Criseyde*, ed. Root (Princeton: Princeton Univ. Press, 1954), p. xxix.
21. Robinson, "Explanatory Notes," p. 828.
22. Gist, p. 116.
23. Tr. William Caxton, ed. Alfred T. P. Byles (London: EETS, 13, 1926), p. 29 (suggested to me by Margaret Gist).
24. *The Works of Sir Thomas Malory*, ed. Eugène Vinaver (rev. ed., Oxford: Oxford Univ. Press, 1967), I, 120: "and charged them never to do outerage nothir morthir, and allwayes to fle treson, and to gyff mercy unto hym that askith mercy ... and allwayes to do ladyes, damesels, and jantilwomen and wydowes [socour]; strengthe hem in hir ryghtes, and never to enforce them uppon payne of dethe."
25. Gist, p. 14.
26. See the beginning of Boccaccio's Canto VI, Gordon, p. 102.
27. Gist, p. 81.
28. Ibid., p. 82. For a comparison of the structures of Diomede's and Troilus's wooings, see Laila Gross, "The Two Wooings of Criseyde," *NM*, 74 (1973), 113–125.
29. *The Chronicles of Froissart*, tr. Sir John Bouchier, ed. W. E. Henley (London: D. Nutt, 1901), I, Ch. 89, 217.
30. Gist, p. 83. Two recent studies, John B. Maguire's "The Clandestine Marriage of Troilus and Criseyde," *Chaucer Review*, 8 (1974), 262–278, and Henry Ansgar Kelly's "Clandestine Marriage and Chaucer's 'Troilus,'" in the symposium "Marriage in the Middle Ages," ed. John Leyerle, *Viator*, 4 (1973), 435–457, argue that Chaucer meant to suggest seriously (rather than ironically) that Troilus and Criseyde had undertaken a clandestine marriage in Bk. III: that he surrounds their love with a "matrimonial aura" even while veering away "from calling their love a marriage in

explicit terms" (Kelly, 450). Kelly has enlarged upon this idea in his *Love and Marriage in the Age of Chaucer* (Ithaca and London: Cornell Univ. Press, 1975), in which the poem receives (in his words) "a lion's share" (p. 333) of the attention. I myself incline to the ironic view, however overused that word has become in speaking of Chaucer's poetry. Certainly no passage can be cited in which Troilus displays the "protective power" such a marriage, however clandestine, would imply.

31. *Crooked Rib*, p. 17. Images of imprisonment are used for Troilus as well, but since they have received much more attention than those associated with Criseyde I have chosen not to deal with them here. Stephen Barney, "Troilus Bound," *Spec.*, 47 (1972), 445–458, strangely interprets Criseyde's powerlessness as an advantage: "Criseyde receives more than she gives. She is acted upon by Pandarus, by the stunning sight of Troilus..., by the song of true love which Antigone sings, by her own dreams," etc. (445). A more accurate distinction is made in an interesting article which appeared after my own was completed, Georgia Ronan Crampton's "Action and Passion in Chaucer's *Troilus*," *Med. Aev.*, 43 (1974), 22–36, which suggests that "Criseyde's psychology ... [as] that of a doer, not a sufferer" appears only in "exceptional" interludes of the poem (34).

32. Pat T. Overbeck, "Chaucer's Good Woman," *Chaucer Review*, 2 (1967), 90.

33. For a discussion of how the Fathers' attitudes were reaffirmed by Canon Law, see Hecker, Ch. 6, pp. 106–119.

34. *Select English Works of John Wyclif*, ed. Thomas Arnold (Oxford: Oxford Univ. Press, 1871), III, "Of Weddid Men and Wifis and of Here Children Also," 193.

35. Giovanni Boccaccio, *Concerning Famous Women*, tr. Guido A. Guarino (New Brunswick: Rutgers Press, 1963), p. xxxiii.

36. Saintonge, 315.

37. Robert E. Kaske, "The Aube in Chaucer's *Troilus*," *Chaucer Criticism, II: Troilus and Criseyde & the Minor Poems* (Notre Dame, Ind.: Notre Dame Press, 1961), 167–179.

38. Gist, p. 13. See also nn. 12 and 13, same page.

39. Saintonge, p. 312.

40. Ibid., p. 317.

41. For instance, the lying Eve and the stubborn Noah's wife of the miracle/mystery cycles; aloofness begins—and reaches a pinnacle perhaps unscaled again—with the Guenevere of Chretien de Troyes' *Conte de la charette*.

42. Saintonge, p. 320.

43. Boccaccio, p. xxxvii.

44. Overbeck, p. 90.
45. Utley, pp. 63–64; Hays, p. 131.
46. Overbeck, p. 79.
47. Ibid., pp. 85–86.
48. Christopher Gillie, *Character in English Literature* (New York: Barnes and Noble, 1965), Ch. 2, "Women by Chaucer."
49. A somewhat different version of this paper was read on October 1, 1975, to faculty and graduate students at the University of Rochester's Medieval House.

ARLYN DIAMOND

1. From Douglas' translation of the *Aeneid*. Quoted in *Geoffrey Chaucer*, ed. J. A. Burrow (Baltimore: Penguin, 1969), p. 47.
2. "For . . . [the narrator] falls in love with Criseide so persuasively that almost every male reader of the poem imitates him." E. Talbot Donaldson, *Speaking of Chaucer* (New York: Norton, 1970), p. 9. "She is, in some ways, typically 'feminine,' but the femininity she represents was in Chaucer's day a philosophical rather than a psychological concept. That she still seems feminine to us is a tribute to the justness of the ideas which produced her." D. W. Robertson, Jr., *A Preface to Chaucer* (Princeton: Princeton Univ. Press, 1962), pp. 330–331. Or perhaps it is a tribute to the persistence of medieval notions in modern critics. Both statements are typical of responses to Chaucer's women.
3. Lula McDowell Richardson, *The Forerunners of Feminism in French Literature of the Renaissance* (Baltimore: Johns Hopkins Univ. Press, 1929), p. 12.
4. Francis Lee Utley's *The Crooked Rib* (Columbus: Ohio State Univ. Press, 1944) lists Middle English literature devoted to "the Argument about Women." Margaret Gist's *Love and War in the Middle English Romances* (Philadelphia: Univ. of Pennsylvania Press, 1947) begins with a very useful survey of medieval attitudes on the subject and their sources in early Christian teaching, etc.
5. For example, see Eileen Power, "The Position of Women," in *The Legacy of the Middle Ages*, ed. C. G. Crump and E. F. Jacob (Oxford: Clarendon, 1926), pp. 401–433; and Doris Mary Stenton, *The English Woman in History* (London: Allen and Unwin, 1957).
6. It is interesting to note that included in the *Magna Carta* is the provision that widows need not remarry if they do not wish to, providing they promise not to marry without the assent of their feudal lords.
7. *The Paston Letters*, ed. Norman Davis (Oxford: Clarendon, 1958).

Christine de Pisan's *Livre de Trois Vertus* discusses the noble-woman's need to be able to run a large estate in her husband's absence.

8. In *The Babees Book: Early English Poems and Treatises*, ed. Frederick J. Furnivall, (London: EETS, 32, 1868), 36–47.
9. Ibid., p. lxix.
10. See Power, "Position of Women," and Blanch Evans Hazard, "Mediaeval Women as Wage Earning Farm Hands," *Cornell Countryman*, 14 (1917), 300–309, 572–573, 600–602.
11. *Medieval Humanism and Other Studies* (Oxford: Blackwell, 1970), p. 25.
12. "The Letters of Cupid," *Hoccleve's Works: The Minor Poems*, ed. Frederick J. Furnivall, E.S. 61 (London: EETS, 1892).
13. Power, "Position of Women," p. 401.
14. *Piers Plowman*, C Text, Passus X, ll. 74–83.
15. The text used throughout is *The Works of Geoffrey Chaucer*, ed. F. N. Robinson, 2nd ed. (Boston: Houghton Mifflin, 1957).
16. Charles Muscatine, *Chaucer and the French Tradition* (Berkeley: Univ. of California Press, 1960), p. 223.
17. Robertson, *Preface*, p. 321.
18. Muscatine, *Chaucer*, p. 213.
19. In what follows I will inevitably make some of the same points that other critics have but from a rather different perspective. I would like to mention in particular an article by Daniel M. Murtaugh, "Women and Geoffrey Chaucer," *ELH*, 38 (1971), 473–492, which attempts somewhat the same thing as I do here, although with quite different conclusions.
20. Robert Pratt, "The Order of the *Canterbury Tales*," *PMLA*, 66 (1951), 1141–67.
21. R. M. Lumiansky, *Of Sondry Folk* (Austin: Univ. of Texas Press, 1955), pp. 105–112. The most extreme statement of this point of view is found in Arthur T. Broes, "Chaucer's Disgruntled Cleric: The Nun's Priest's Tale," *PMLA*, 78 (1963), 156–162. Broes seems to empathize strongly with Chauntecleer.
22. If we accept Lumiansky's argument that the Nun's Priest is a skinny and timid character, then we are looking at the revenge of Walter Mitty. Brawny or scrawny, no real man wants a lady boss, our sense of fitness tells us.
23. D. W. Robertson is useful in pointing out what is doctrinally incorrect about what the Wife says and is (see especially his discussion in *Preface*, pp. 317–331), but as note 2 above shows, his conclusions reinforce my point.
24. Maurice Hussey, in *Chaucer's World* (Cambridge: Cambridge Univ. Press, 1968), does not discuss the Wife "professionally" at

all, as he does the Shipman, et al., but concentrates on her physiognomy and her horoscope.

25. G. M. Trevelyan, *Chaucer's England and the Early Tudors*, rev., Illustrated English Social History, I (1942; reprinted Harmondsworth: Penguin, 1964), p. 82. A. R. Myers, *England in the Late Middle Ages*, The Pelican History of England, IV (Harmondsworth: Penguin, 1959), pp. 56, 136.

26. Murtaugh, "Women and Chaucer," is one among several who express this view.

27. Muscatine, *Chaucer*, pp. 190–197.

28. There is a good summary of the textual problems in Sister Frances Dolores Covella, "The Speaker of the Wife of Bath's Stanza and Envoy," *Chaucer Review*, 4 (1970), 267–283.

29. Paul E. Gray, "Synthesis and the Double Standard in the *Franklin's Tale*," *Texas Studies in Literature and Language*, 7 (1965), 213–224, who also sees the Franklin as a naive narrator, is an example.

30. Peter Beidler, "The Pairing of the *Franklin's Tale* and the *Physician's Tale*," *Chaucer Review*, 3 (1969), 275–279, condemns her for not killing herself. His model of femininity is Virginia, who finds suicide perfectly natural, and he is typical of those who find women most noble when they are dead or suffering. He also thinks the whole problem arises from the fact that Dorigen does not spend the two years of her husband's absence locked up in her room, as a good wife ought to.

31. Robert A. Pratt, "The Development of the Wife of Bath," in *Studies in Medieval Literature*, ed. MacEdward Leach (Philadelphia: Univ. of Pennsylvania Press, 1961), pp. 45–79.

COPPÉLIA KAHN

1. Robert Heilman, "Introduction," *The Taming of the Shrew* by William Shakespeare, ed. Robert Heilman, The Signet Classic Shakespeare (New York: New American Library, 1966), p. xxxii.

2. R. Warwick Bond, "Introduction," *The Taming of the Shrew* by William Shakespeare, The Arden Shakespeare (London: Methuen, 1904). Quoted by Robert Heilman, "*The Taming* Untamed, or, The Return of the Shrew," *MLQ*, 27 (1966), 147–161.

3. Here are four examples of this viewpoint:
   (a) "But 'taming' is only a metaphor. We can describe the action just as well by saying that Petruchio cures Kate of chronic bad temper.... more shrew than she, he 'kills her in her own humor.'" Richard Hosley, The Pelican Shakespeare (Baltimore: Penguin, 1964), p. 17.

(b) Muriel C. Bradbrook, "Dramatic Role as Social Image: a Study of *The Taming of the Shrew*," *Shakespeare-Jahrbuch*, 94 (1958), pp. 132–150, states: "Though at one point it is suggested that 'he hath some meaning in his mad attire,' no one seems to disagree when Bianca sums up at the exit of the pair [Kate and Petruchio], 'Being mad herself, she's madly mated.' The central point, the knot of the play, is here" (p. 142).

(c) In his *Shakespeare's Sexual Comedy: A Mirror for Lovers* (New York: Bobbs-Merrill, 1971), Hugh Richmond characterizes Kate's behavior before the wedding as "obviously pathological," produced by "a mind close to breakdown." Thus, "her disintegrating personality seems to justify almost any kind of shock therapy.... Petruchio's physical violence is only a figure for Katherine's, and 'kills her in her own humor'" (pp. 90–91).

(d) Heilman, "Introduction," p. xli: "Kate's great victory is, with Petruchio's help, over herself."

4. All quotations from *The Taming of the Shrew* are taken from the Signet edition, cited in note 1 above.

5. For a review of medieval shrew literature, see Katherine Rogers, *The Troublesome Helpmate: A History of Misogyny in Literature* (Seattle: Univ. of Washington Press, 1966), pp. 88–93. Muriel Bradbrook, "Dramatic Role," pp. 134–138, discusses Tudor treatments of the shrew. For an example of shrew literature contemporary with Shakespeare, see *Tom Tyler and his Wife* (ca. 1578), ed. Felix E. Schelling, *PMLA*, 15, no. 3 (1900), pp. 253–289.

6. Bradbrook, "Dramatic Role," p. 139.

7. Simone de Beauvoir, *The Second Sex* (Paris: Gallimard, 1949; reprinted New York: Bantam-Knopf, 1953), pp. 93–94.

8. George Hibbard, "*The Taming of the Shrew*: A Social Comedy," *Shakespearean Essays*, ed. Alwin Thaler and Norman Sanders, Special Number: 2, *Tennessee Studies in Literature* (Knoxville: Univ. of Tennessee Press, 1964), pp. 16–30. Hibbard's remarks on the financial aspects of marriage in the play are most helpful. He is more sensitive to Kate's position as woman and as marriage-commodity than any critic I have read.

9. In her first manifestation of violence, she torments Bianca only in response to Bianca's more underhanded treatment of her in the first scene, when she subtly lorded it over Kate by acting as though she were a martyr to her elder sister's failure to attract suitors. Actually, Bianca's confinement is not Kate's fault; it is the whim of their father. When Kate declares, "Her silence flouts

me," she means that Bianca intends her ostentatiously submissive attitude as a slap at her vocally rebellious sister. Kate responds to Bianca's slyness with blows, an "unfeminine" but understandable outlet.

After she breaks the lute on Hortensio's head, she strikes Petruchio, an outburst she could have avoided had she been able to think of an appropriately lewd rejoinder to his obscene remark, "What, with my tongue in your tail?" Invention fails her, as cunning later does when she fails to realize that Grumio, like his master, is only torturing her with the promise of food, and (in her last physical outburst) strikes him.

10. Northrop Frye, *A Natural Perspective: The Development of Shakespearean Comedy and Romance* (New York: Columbia Univ. Press, 1965; reprinted New York: Harcourt, 1965), p. 8.

11. Space does not allow me to compare the style and dramatic impact of Kate's and Petruchio's speech respectively. In quantitative terms, however, Petruchio speaks 564 lines in the play, Kate 207, less than half as many. In several scenes, notably IV. 1, Kate is conspicuously silent while her husband utters a volley of commands, oaths, and admonitory remarks.

12. Carroll Camden lists and summarizes the contents of such works in *The Elizabethan Woman* (Houston: Univ. of Texas Press, 1952), pp. 61–75, 77–82. Katherine Rogers, *Troublesome Helpmate*, pp. 140–151, reviews Puritan treatises on marriage. Of the latter, two of the most easily obtainable are *A Preparative to Marriage* (1591) by Henry Smith, in his *Works*, ed. T. Fuller (Edinburgh: J. Nichol, 1866), vol. I, and "The Marriage Ring," by Jeremy Taylor, in *The Whole Works*, ed. R. Heber, rev. ed. (London: Longman, 1862–65), vol. IV.

13. On this point I find myself in disagreement with Richard Henze, "Role Playing in *The Taming of the Shrew*," *Southern Humanities Review*, 4 (1970), 231–240, who sees Kate as playing a succession of "complementary" roles at Petruchio's direction, culminating in the role of obedient wife which has by then become "natural" to her.

Kate's pose of submissive wife is one of many instances in which characters assume roles or identities not their own. Christopher Sly, Tranio and Lucentio, Hortensio, and the Pedant all take on false identities, whereas Kate, Bianca, and the Widow behave so as to conceal their true natures. This common element of "supposes" (so named from one of Shakespeare's sources, Gascoigne's play *Supposes*) has long been recognized as a major source of meaning in the play. In the context of the play's treatment of marriage, the fact that not only Kate and Petruchio but also the other two couples assume sex-determined poses which their true personalities belie lends greater weight to the idea that masculine and feminine roles in traditional marriage are false.

MIRIAM LERENBAUM

1. *The Rise of the Novel* (1957; reprinted Harmondsworth: Penguin, 1963), p. 118. Watt repeats this view in "The Recent Critical Fortunes of *Moll Flanders*," *Eighteenth-Century Studies*, 1 (1967), 112. Only a few passing references to Watt's position have come to my attention. R. A. Donovan, for instance, writes, "In view of her lack of tenderness, Moll cannot very well be called womanly, but in her practical common sense, in her placing of expedience above principle, and in her unself-conscious vanity, she seems to me quintessentially feminine." *The Shaping Vision* (Ithaca: Cornell Univ. Press, 1966), p. 258, n. 11. For a more sympathetic and acute comment, see the quotation from Arnold Kettle, n. 31 below.

2. "Defoe," *Collected Essays*, Vol. I (New York: Harcourt, 1967), p. 64. This essay was written in 1919.

3. "In giving us the life-span, with its eager thrust from one experience to the next, Defoe robs life of its climactic structure." Martin Price, *To the Palace of Wisdom* (Garden City: Doubleday, 1964), p. 266. The book can indeed create this impression; on the other hand, the life-span provides its own climaxes, and Defoe is marvellously attuned to them.

Many critics take major account of at least one, but never all, of these episodes of depression in remarking upon the structural unity of *Moll Flanders*. Amongst the most perceptive treatments are Terence Martin, "The Unity of *Moll Flanders*," *MLQ*, 22 (1961), 115–124; Howard L. Koonce, "Moll's Muddle: Defoe's Use of Irony in *Moll Flanders*," *ELH*, 30 (1963), 377–394; John Preston, "Moll Flanders: 'The Satire of the Age,'" Chapter 2 of *The Created Self* (New York: Barnes and Noble, 1970); William J. Krier, "A Courtesy which Grants Integrity: A Literal Reading of *Moll Flanders*," *ELH*, 38 (1971), 397–410.

4. I follow the text of the Riverside edition, ed. James Sutherland (Cambridge: Houghton Mifflin, 1959).

5. Two critics make the same point in the course of pursuing other theses. See Robert R. Columbus, "Conscious Artistry in *Moll Flanders*," *Studies in English Literature 1500–1900*, 3 (1969), 422–423; Douglas Brooks, "*Moll Flanders*: An Interpretation," *Essays in Criticism*, 19 (1969), 46–48.

6. See Alice Clark, *Working Life of Women in the Seventeenth*

Century (New York: Harcourt, 1920). For this study, the author searched state papers, memoirs, the drama, and a variety of other available records to show that by the end of the seventeenth century, women's participation in professional life, business, and skilled trades had dwindled almost to nothing. Men were entering and beginning to dominate even so traditionally a female occupation as midwifery.

7. M. Dorothy George, *London Life in the Eighteenth Century* (1925; reprinted Harmondsworth: Penguin, 1966), pp. 229–230 (italics mine).

8. See George, pp. 178–196. All accounts of the needle trades show them to have been the least well paid. There was abject misery and starvation amongst the workers, and women as usual were the most poverty stricken.

9. *A Serious Call to a Devout and Holy Life* (1728; reprinted Everyman Edition, 1955), pp. 247–248. Some modern critics, notably Preston, op. cit., and Michael Shinagel, *Daniel Defoe and Middle-Class Gentility* (Cambridge: Harvard Univ. Press, 1968), pp. 145–148, make this observation about Moll's values.

10. The exception to this point—Moll's refusal to remain with her third husband—serves only to emphasize Moll's normal passivity. Although repelled by her discovery that she is committing incest, Moll vacillates three years before bringing herself to leave him.

11. George, p. 174.

12. See for example Michael Shinagel, "The Maternal Theme in *Moll Flanders:* Craft and Character," *Cornell Library Journal*, No. 7 (1969), p. 20: "As a mother she must be judged as culpably selfish, crass, insincere, and, although she rejects the epithet repeatedly, 'unnatural.'"

13. Not so many, however, as there were subsequently, for "the probability of death of the child after birth must have made termination of unwanted pregnancies less urgent than it is today, and it is believed that the incidence of abortion increased during the second half of the nineteenth century." Thomas McKeown and R. G. Brown, "Medical Evidence Relating to English Population Changes in the Eighteenth Century," *Population Studies*, 9 (1955), 132.

14. George, p. 55. See also William L. Langer, "Checks on Population Growth: 1750–1850," *Scientific American*, 226 (February, 1972), 92–99. Much of the rest of this paragraph is indebted to the same article, which is also relevant to Moll Flanders in describing such practices as "baby farms."

15. Langer, p. 98 (my italics). Langer's larger thesis is to account for the enormous *growth* in population that began around mid-

century. George's statistics make it clear that the same kind of *checks* on population growth obtained earlier than 1750.

16. *The Diary of John Evelyn*, ed. E. S. DeBeer (Oxford: Clarendon, 1955), II, 6–7 (my italics). For confirmation of the general practice, see also Philippe Ariès, *Centuries of Childhood: A Social History of the Family* (New York: Knopf, 1962), pp. 366, 368–369, 374, et passim.

17. Ivy Pinchbeck and Margaret Hewitt, *Children in English Society*, Vol. I (From Tudor Times to the Eighteenth Century) (London: Routledge, 1969), p. 301.

18. Shinagel, "Maternal Theme," p. 10.

19. See *Parenthood: Its Psychology and Psychopathology*, ed. E. James Anthony and Therese Benedek (Boston: Little, Brown, 1970) and Margaret Mead, "A Cultural Anthropologist's Approach to Maternal Deprivation" in *Deprivations of Maternal Care* (Geneva: World Health Organization, 1962).

20. See for instance Anna Freud, "The Concept of the Rejecting Mother," *Parenthood*, pp. 376–386; Therese Benedek, "Motherhood and Nurturing," *Parenthood*, pp. 153–165.

21. "The Development of Parental Attitudes During Pregnancy," *Parenthood*, pp. 214–216.

22. Ibid., p. 240.

23. "Biologic Considerations of Parenthood," *Parenthood*, pp. 23–24.

24. According to John Bowlby, Moll's own history of deprivation in early childhood would not only account for her deficient motherliness, but would also be a major cause of many (non-sexual) features of her personal history—superficial relationships, no real feeling, no capacity to care for people or make true friends, a history of deceit and evasion, stealing, etc. *Maternal Care and Mental Health* (Geneva: World Health Organization, 1952), pp. 31, 47, et passim.

25. *Rise of the Novel*, p. 114.

26. The major studies are Helene Deutsch, "The Climacterium," Epilogue of *The Psychology of Women: A Psychoanalytic Interpretation* (New York: Grune and Stratton, 1945), II, 456–487; Therese Benedek, "Climacterium: A Developmental Phase," *Psychoanalytic Quarterly*, 19 (1950), 1–27. A convenient short summary of these and other studies appears in Howard J. Osofsky and Robert Seidenberg, "Is Female Menopausal Depression Inevitable?" *Obstetrics and Gynecology*, 36 (October, 1970), 611–615.

27. Deutsch, p. 473. She continues, "While the active women deny the biologic state of affairs, the depressive ones overemphasize it." We have already remarked that Moll's account suggests that she is roused to energy by necessity rather than naturally energetic.

Amongst others, William J. Krier, op. cit., and Arthur Sherbo, Moll's Friends," in *Studies in the Eighteenth Century Novel* (East Lansing: Michigan State Univ. Press, 1969), pp. 168–176, both pursuing different lines of inquiry, take notice of Moll's essential passivity and dependency.

28. See for instance Benedek, p. 24.
29. Deutsch, p. 472; Benedek, p. 18.
30. Deutsch, p. 461; Benedek, pp. 22–23. Benedek continues, "It is as if these women, reassured that their main job is done, may draw on the emotional capital invested in that achievement so that they overcome feelings of inferiority and insecurity which inhibited them before."
31. Arnold Kettle sees the connection that eludes Watt: "Here Virginia Woolf's feminist preoccupations offer a more central and artistically relevant approach to the book than any other.... Moll becomes a criminal because she is a woman, and it is not at all by chance in the book's structure that she comes to her second career (that of a thief) by way of her first (that of a wife)." "In Defence of *Moll Flanders*," in *Of Books and Humankind: Essays and Poems Presented to Bonamy Dobrée*, ed. John Butt (London: Routledge, 1964), pp. 62–63.
32. "Defoe," p. 67.

KATHERINE ROGERS

1. Henry Fielding, *The Shakespeare Head Edition of the Novels* (Oxford: Blackwell, 1926), *Tom Jones*, I, 182, II, 88; Samuel Richardson, *The Shakespeare Head Edition of the Novels* (Oxford: Blackwell, 1929–31), *Clarissa*, I, 48; *Sir Charles Grandison*, I, 131. All references to the novels of Fielding and Richardson are to these editions.
2. Lovelace constantly voices aspersions on women from the misogynistic tradition, such as that they are foolish and perverse; they are so weak that he can subdue any one he wants; since they deceive and seduce men, they are responsible for men's deceptions and lust; they "have been the occasion of all manner of mischief from the beginning" (III, 357). Lovelace justifies the double sexual standard with the Pauline text "that the woman was made for the man, not the man for the woman" (III, 90). It is significant that Richardson placed this misogynistic but conventionally accepted text into the mouth of a rakish exploiter of women. All of Richardson's bad male characters are similarly exploitive: e.g., James Harlowe, Uncle Antony, and Sir Thomas Grandison.

3. Virginia Woolf, *A Room of One's Own* (New York: Harcourt, 1929), p. 86.
4. Ian Watt, *The Rise of the Novel* (Berkeley: Univ. of California Press, 1957), p. 224.
5. Among many examples, one might mention Mrs. Shirley's plea that women be addressed "on the common footing of reasonable creatures" and not be restrained by false modesty from "shewing themselves to *be such*" (*Grandison*, V, 407) and Pamela's comparison of a girl's struggle for knowledge to the efforts of a poor swaddled infant to stretch its limbs (IV, 320).
6. Compare the scene in *Amelia* where the admirable clergyman Harrison gleefully puts down Mrs. Atkinson for a small error in Latin (III, 67-70).
7. Jenny Jones is both plain and unchaste, and misuses her reading to justify common-law marriage; Mrs. Western proclaims her knowledge of politics and love, while actually knowing nothing of either; Mrs. Bennet (Atkinson), whose virtue is questionable, insists that women are as capable of classical learning as men but is caught out in two simple errors; Lady Bellaston is a feminist if not an intellectual, for she thinks "it the cause of my sex to rescue any woman who is so unfortunate to be under" the power of a tyrannical male like Squire Western (III, 208).
8. Selfish Lovelace, on the other hand, could not tolerate a wife who would "*condescend* to bear with" his follies (V, 13). Cf. *Selected Letters of Samuel Richardson*, ed. John Carroll (Oxford: Clarendon 1964), p. 108.
9. This seems to be the only possible justification for Charlotte Grandison's rude and wilful behavior to her innocent Lord G. She is a cruder reworking of Anna, similar in her rebellion against decorum and male authority, and in the sympathy with which Richardson presents her.
10. Harriet does not believe a man's extravagant passion will make his wife happy, and would rather put her faith in principles and love founded on reason. Charlotte Grandison derides Otway's *The Orphan*, a typical male-oriented tragedy in which two supposedly noble brothers treat the woman they claim to love as a passive sex-object. Mrs. Shirley ridicules her initial silly objections to Mr. Shirley because he was not like Oroondates. Sir Charles compliments women appropriately, not as angels (*Grandsion*, I, 164, IV, 252-253, V, 242, VI, 223-224).

292 · NOTES

MAURIANNE ADAMS

1. Charlotte Brontë, *Jane Eyre*, ed. Richard Dunn (New York: Norton, 1971), p. 236. All further references to the text will be taken from the Norton Edition and identified with parentheses.
2. Multiple puns revolve around Jane's surname, with the obvious allusion to *air* (for which *eyre* is an archaic spelling) and the French *aire* that Adèle calls attention to ("Aire? Bah! I cannot say it" [p. 89]), which means nesting place (for a bird of prey) as well as area or space. Interpretively, both puns are of value, the one with its obvious elemental and spiritual associations, the other with its reference to Jane's various retreats (window-seat, Thornfield arbor, the recesses of her own mind). There is further obsolete and archaic reference to *eyre* meaning the itinerant medieval circuit judges (Jane's peripatetic movements?). The primary pun on *air* reinforces the elemental imagery of other place-names: Marsh End, Moor House, Lowood, Thornfield, Ferndean) and of surnames (Burns, Rivers—the uncertain status of Reed seems interconnected peripherally with Rivers in an appropriately familial manner). On the elemental imagery in its own right, useful interpretations can be found in David Lodge, "Fire and Eyre: Charlotte Brontë's War of Earthly Elements," in *The Language of Fiction* (London: Routledge, 1966), pp. 114–143, and in Eric Solomon, "*Jane Eyre:* Fire and Water," *College English*, 25 (1963), 215–217. Jane's given name (plain Jane—how far back does the cliché go?) carries us to the class and status theme in the novel, contrasting markedly with the fancy foreign names of well-born women of "place" (Blanche, Eliza, Georgiana, Diana, Rosamond) as well as with the designation of foreign women of uncertain status (Céline and Adèle). Much is in a name and the name change required by marital status, Jane Eyre becoming Jane Rochester, invokes critical issues of identity and of status.
3. See Jane Millgate, "Narrative Distance in 'Jane Eyre': The Relevance of the Pictures," *Modern Language Review*, 63 (1968), 315–319, where all of the paintings, not merely the triptych shown at Thornfield, are discussed; and Thomas Langford, "The Three Pictures in *Jane Eyre*," *Victorian Newsletter*, *31* (1967), 47–48, the triptych here interpreted, wrongly I think, with reference to the structural divisions of Gateshead, Thornfield, and Marsh End. See also Jennifer Gribble, "Jane Eyre's Imagination," *Nineteenth Century Fiction*, 23 (1968–69).
4. Reminders of the psychic connection between Jane and Bertha recur in Jane's third-floor restless pacing and Bertha's maniacal grovelling; Jane's confinement after the outburst at John Reed and

Bertha's after flying at Mason; Jane, like Bertha, is compelled to
sleep "in a small closet by myself" (22); Jane fears she is "insane
—quite insane" (279) in her temptation to stay with Rochester,
the temptation characterized by "my veins running fire," "his
flaming glance" (279), "terrible moment: full of struggle, blackness, burning" (278). On the other hand, as elemental opposites,
Bertha applies fire and Jane water to Rochester's bedchamber, and
the two are compared by him (in an implicit parallel to the
Blanche/Jane contrasting portraits) as good angel to hideous de-
mon (277).

LEE R. EDWARDS

1. Virginia Woolf, *Mrs. Dalloway* (New York: Harcourt, 1925), p.
   182. All references are to this edition. Further references will be
   made parenthetically within the text.
2. See, for example, Margaret Blanchard, "Socialization in *Mrs. Dalloway*," *College English*, 34, No. 2 (1972), 287-305; O. P. Sharma,
   "Feminism as Aesthetic Vision: A Study of Virginia Woolf's *Mrs.
   Dalloway*," *Women's Studies*, 3, No. 1 (1975), 61-74; Jean Alexander, *The Venture of Form in the Novels of Virginia Woolf*
   (New York and London: Kennikat, 1974), pp. 85-104; Avrom
   Fleishman, *Virginia Woolf: A Critical Reading* (Baltimore and
   London: Johns Hopkins Univ. Press, 1975), 69-95.
3. In *Granite and Rainbow: Essays* (London: Hogarth, 1958), p. 81.
4. William Troy, "The Novel of Sensibility," *Literary Opinion in
   America*, ed. Morton Dauwen Zabel (New York: Harper, 1937),
   pp. 324-337, reprinted in *Virginia Woolf: A Collection of Critical
   Essays*, ed. Claire Sprague (Englewood Cliffs, N.J.: Prentice-Hall,
   1971), p. 27.
5. Fleishman, p. 80.

MARY COHEN

1. "Doris Lessing in the Sixties: The New Anatomy of Melancholy,"
   Contemporary Literature, 13, 1 (Winter, 1972), 15.
2. Ibid., p. 30.
3. Jonah Raskin, "Doris Lessing at Stony Brook: An Interview,"
   New American Review, 8 (January, 1970), 175.
4. In an interview with Florence Howe, "Talk with Doris Lessing,"
   Nation, 204 (March 6, 1967), 312.
5. " 'Only Connect': Form and Content in the Works of Doris Lessing," *Critique*, 11 (1969), 56.
6. P. 170.

7. *Declaration*, ed. Tom Maschler (New York: Dutton, 1958), p. 194.
8. *The Golden Notebook* (New York: Bantam, 1973), pp. 274–275. All page numbers will refer to this edition and will follow subsequent quotations in the text.
9. Tommy is used ambiguously. At the outset he is insightful, a truth-telling child. After his suicide attempt, he turns destructive; his mother and Marion become his victims. Then, rather abruptly, Lessing moves him to the background. Her treatment of Marion is similarly careless.
10. In 1966 in an interview with Florence Howe (p. 312), Lessing suggests her own intentions for *The Golden Notebook*: "You know, the Free Women section in *The Golden Notebook*—the envelope—I was really trying to express my sense of despair about writing a conventional novel in that. Actually that is an absolutely whole conventional novel, and the rest of the book is the material that went into making it." Of course, Lessing herself admits—insists—that the form of the novel says what it is about; that is, she was using the form of the novel to comment on both fragmentation and formlessness. By providing the notebooks, the various records of a welter of experience, she is able to suggest the complexity of life which it is the writer's responsibility to grapple with.

DAWN LANDER

1. Alice Marriot, *Hell on Horses and Women* (Norman, Okla.: Univ. of Oklahoma Press, 1953), p. 10.
2. Sarah J. Lippincott ("Grace Greenwood"), *New Life in New Lands: Notes of Travel by Grace Greenwood* (New York: J. B. Ford, 1873), pp. 62–63.
3. Caroline M. Kirkland, *A New Home—Who'll Follow?* ed. William S. Osborne (New Haven: College and University Press, 1965), p. 198.
4. Agnes Smedley, *Daughter of Earth*, rev. ed. (New York: Coward-McCann, 1935), p. 149.
5. Ibid., p. 102.
6. Leslie A. Fiedler, *The Return of the Vanishing American* (New York: Stein and Day, 1969), p. 109.
7. I will use the terms "garden," "pastoral," and "wilderness" almost interchangeably throughout this essay to indicate an essentially non-urban, non-civilized environment. "Pastoral" or "garden" might be used to invoke a literary tradition; "wilderness," however, is usually the more precise term in relationship to the particular American experience. See Leo Marx, *The Machine in the Garden* (Oxford:

Oxford Univ. Press, 1968), especially Chap. 1, for an elabora-
tion of the construct this essay assumes.

8. Francis Parkman, *The Oregon Trail*, ed. E. N. Feltskog (Madison:
   Univ. of Wisconsin Press, 1969), p. 57.
9. William Sprague, *Women and the West: A Short Social History*
   (Boston: Christopher Pub. House, 1940), p. 30.
10. Ibid., p. 37.
11. Ibid., p. 215.
12. Ibid., p. 107.
13. "Woman," in *Complete Works*, Vol. XI (Boston: Houghton Mif-
    flin, 1878), p. 409.
14. Emerson, p. 407.
15. Ibid.
16. Nathaniel Hawthorne, *The Scarlet Letter*, ed. William Charvat,
    Roy Harvey Pearce, Claude Simpson (Columbus: Ohio State
    Univ. Press, 1962), p. 199.
17. *Scarlet Letter*, pp. 197–198.
18. Henry David Thoreau, "Higher Laws," *Walden*, in *The Portable
    Thoreau*, ed. Carl Bode, rev. ed. (New York: Viking, 1969), p.
    459.
19. See Thomas Cole's "The Savage State," the first of five paintings
    in the series *The Course of Empire* (1833–36) for a representation
    of the same theme in American visual arts. On the left is the white
    hunter; on the right are Indian tepees. All the figures are very
    tiny in a wilderness which dominates all and which is softly illu-
    minated by the sun rising at the dawn of mankind. Of course there
    are no white women in the scene.
20. For Dickey, the only kind of sexuality possible in the wilderness is
    sodomy; thus, he makes explicit what Fiedler earlier suggested was
    implicit in American literature. At times the critic and novelist
    seem to dance after each other in a circle.
21. Ernest Hemingway, "Fathers and Sons," in *The Short Stories of
    Ernest Hemingway* (New York: Scribner's, 1938), p. 490.
22. Ibid., p. 497.
23. Ibid., p. 495.
24. A. B. Guthrie, Jr., *The Big Sky* (Boston: Houghton Mifflin, 1965),
    p. 177.
25. Ibid., pp. 177–178.
26. Ibid., p. 131.
27. Ibid., p. 219.
28. In *William and Mary Quarterly*, 2 (April, 1945), pp. 136, 137.
29. The slave society was a wilderness society and the patterns dis-
    cussed are also applicable to other areas of wilderness and frontier

America. In a population of about six million, there were only 48,000 city dwellers in the antebellum South, a predominantly rural and even wild region.

30. *Race Relations in Virginia and Miscegenation in the South, 1776–1860* (Amherst: Univ. of Massachusetts Press, 1970), p. 170.

31. The Virginia Act of 1662 reads as follows: "Whereas some doubts have arisen whether a child got by an Englishman upon a negro should be free or slave, be it therefore enacted by this present grand assembly, that all children born in this country shall be bound or free according to the condition of the mother." Quoted by Johnston, p. 167.

32. Johnston, p. 174.

33. Harriet Martineau, "The Morals of Slavery," in *Society in America,* quoted in Johnston, p. 287.

34. Johnston, p. 174.

35. Ibid., p. 257.

36. At the time of the Civil War a white Southern planter's wife wrote: "Like patriarchs of old, our men live all in one house with their wives and their concubines; and the mulattoes one sees in every family partly resemble the white children. Any lady is ready to tell you who is the father of all the mulatto children in everybody's household but her own." Mary Boykin Chesnut (Miller), *A Diary from Dixie,* ed. Ben Ames Williams (Boston: Houghton Mifflin, 1949), p. 21.

37. "I pity them for the stupid sameness of their most vapid existence, which would deaden any amount of intelligence, obliterate any amount of instruction, and render torpid and stagnant any amount of natural energy and vitality. I would rather die—rather a thousand times—than live the lives of the Georgia planters' wives and daughters." Frances Anne Butler Kemble, *Journal of a Residence on a Georgian Plantation in 1838–1839* (New York: Harper, 1863), p. 156.

38. As documented by Johnston, above, and other sources, e.g.: A woman who did not acquiesce and who taught a Negro child to read was, according to the ante-bellum indictment of the Commonwealth of Virginia, "guilty of one of the vilest crimes that ever disgraced society." Quoted by William Craft, "Running a Thousand Miles for Freedom," in *Great Slave Narratives,* ed. Arna Bontemps (Boston: Beacon, 1969), p. 288. "On the occasion of the examination of the guilty wife of a citizen of Powhatan county, in Virginia, this woman declared 'that she had not been the first nor would she be the last guilty of such conduct, and that she saw no more harm in a white woman's having been the mother of a

black child than in a white man's having one, though the latter was more frequent.'" Johnston, pp. 267–268.

39. David Hackett Fischer, *Historians' Fallacies* (New York: Harper, 1970), p. xvii.

40. George E. Hyde, *Life of George Bent, Written From His Letters*, ed. Savoie Lottinville (Norman: Univ. of Oklahoma Press, 1968), p. 98.

41. Hemingway, "Fathers and Sons," pp. 493–494.

42. James Bryce, *Relations of the Advanced and Backward Races of Mankind* (Oxford: Oxford Univ. Press, 1903), p. 23, as cited in Johnston, p. 165.

43. William Hepworth Dixon, a British traveler, wrote *New America* (Philadelphia: 1867), in which he criticized Denver severely, but in which he noted that due to the appearance of a few American and English ladies manners were beginning to improve. See Robert G. Athearn, *Westward the Briton* (Lincoln: Univ. of Nebraska Press, 1953), p. 66.

44. Athearn, p. 66. His source: William Shepherd, *Prairie Experience in Handling Cattle and Sheep* (New York: 1885), p. 72.

45. Athearn, p. 39.

46. Moller, p. 136.

47. Louis Ruchames, *Racial Thought in America* (Amherst: Univ. of Massachusetts Press, 1969), p. 12.

48. Fiedler, *Return*, p. 108.

49. Leslie A. Fiedler, "Leslie Fiedler Reintroduces Himself," *New York Times Book Review*, May 23, 1971, p. 2.

50. Fiedler, *Return*, p. 90.

51. Eliza W. Farnham, *Life in Prairie Land* (New York: Harper, 1855), pp. 270–271.

52. Fiedler, *Return*, p. 90.

53. Ibid., p. 91. I have seen this statue. "Raised aloft" to me implies over her head. Actually, the tomahawk is approximately waist-high, not quite the menacing image Fiedler invokes.

54. Fiedler, *Return*, p. 96. To "prove" this, Fiedler cites a narrative similar to the Duston narrative. He does not cite his source.

55. Again, Fiedler presents his materials selectively. He does not cite the case of Mary Jordan who reports that she saw her husband and six children partially buried, then burned alive by Indians, who then became drunk, which enabled her to escape: "With one of their tomahawks I might with ease have dispatched them all, but my only desire was to flee from them as quick as possible." Joseph Pritts, *Incidents of Border Life, Etc....* (Lancaster, Pa.: J. Hunt, 1841), p. 193.

56. Fiedler, *Return*, p. 92.
57. Ibid., p. 106.
58. A report in the *International Herald Tribune*, February 15, 1973, p. 1, taken from the *New York Times*, Febuary 14, 1973, entitled "Interracial Marriages in U.S. Show 63% Increase for '60's," concerning the 1970 Census returns, indicates that in the decade from 1960 to 1970 among "married American Indians, 33.4 percent had taken white wives." The number rose from 12,044 to 40,039. The article continues: "The more than tripling of the figure among Indians may be partially reflected by more complete methods of taking the census." The article seems to confirm that even the bare facts relating to a white woman's attitude toward race and miscegenation have had some trouble coming to light.
59. The motifs growing out of the image of white women in the wilderness assume significance in an urban society. Studies are beginning to identify the central city as the new American "wilderness." Nonwhites and the elderly are stranded in ghettos where decreased life expectancies due to slow starvation and exposure are hardly less common than they were on the Connecticut or South Platte Rivers. At the heart of these neo-wildernesses are nonwhite peoples among whom it is said white womanhood cannot safely venture. The social precepts and prohibitions have not changed. White women who were once confined to settlements or to the plantation house, away from the savages and slaves, are now cloistered in a suburban refuge away from the "savagery" of the inner city.

PATRICIA BARBER

1. Herman Melville, "Bartleby, the Scrivener: A Story of Wall-Street," in *Great Short Works of Herman Melville*, ed. Warner Berthoff (New York: Harper, 1969), pp. 39–74. All citations are to this edition and are included in the text.
2. We note here the rise of an idea that the differences between the sexes really matter very little, that psychologically we are all androgynous. Although so far as I know there is no evidence either to support or to refute this theory, the wish for it is strong, and strong, I think, for at least five reasons. First of all, most of the ideas about how women's minds differ from men's—they are not so logical, are prone to "hysteria"—are insulting to women and contrary to commonly observed fact. Second, we now generally believe in the principles of equal social and economic opportunity, and to say that men and women are importantly different from one another may seem to argue that real equality of opportunities

is impossible. In the third place, it is a common literary experience especially for feminist readers to notice that our literature is male-dominated, that female characters rarely attain the status of complex heroes, that they have a range of personalities and potentialities far more limited than in reality, and are rarely models of, say, courage, intelligence, and forthrightness: in order, then, to take literature seriously one has to believe that the supposedly "masculine" or "feminine" traits can be possessed by both sexes, so that the female reader may legitimately identify with Oedipus as well as Antigone, Antony as well as Cleopatra, Ahab as well as Hester Prynne. In the fourth place, we commonly believe in the importance of empathy for good human relations and if one is to believe that we are all able to experience and understand the concerns of both men and women, one is tempted to explain this ability with an idea that we all share in an androgynous universality of human experience. In the fifth place, there are many people who feel restricted by their own gender, who wish they could do and experience the things the other sex does, who, in short, wish they were androgynous and thus evolve a theory of psychological androgyny to make at least part of their wish come true. Still, given that androgyny is a rare phenomenon physiologically, and that it is infrequent in the social realm in that few social roles are equally open to both sexes, it is difficult to see how it could exist psychologically either, however strong the wish for androgyny might be. On the other hand, there seems reason to believe that if people struggle so that the social structure changes to permit women and men to share equally in a wider variety of roles, then perhaps a kind of psychological androgyny will come into being—for there is no principle in psychology which states that changes in psychological human nature are impossible.

3. There is a whole profession of business consultants devoted to these very difficulties of making human relationships in an office context. Their clients are businesses or other bureaucratic organizations who want to keep employees happy mainly in order to increase productivity or improve quality control. While earlier theories about employee satisfaction held that salary, physical working conditions, and good personal relations with supervisors and fellow workers were the main factors, a new school of "behavioralists" believe that these so-called "hygiene" factors only *prevent* dissatisfaction; in order to have actual satisfaction the work itself has to be challenging, creative, lead to new challenges, and in general give the worker a feeling of fulfilling his or her individual potential. See Frederick Herzberg, *Work and the Nature of Man*

(Cleveland: World, 1966); see also Clayton Reesor, "What the Behavioral Scientists Are Up To," *Machine Design*, October 5, 1972, pp. 96–101.

PRISCILLA ALLEN

1. The critics whose remarks on *The Awakening* will be considered here are the following: George Arms, "Kate Chopin's *The Awakening* in the Perspective of her Literary Career," *Essays in American Literature in Honor of Jay B. Hubbell*, ed. Clarence Gohdes (Durham: Duke Univ. Press, 1967), pp. 215–228; Werner Berthoff, *The Ferment of Realism* (New York: Free Press, 1965); Kenneth Eble, "Introduction," *The Awakening* (New York: Capricorn, 1964); Lewis Leary, *Southern Excursions* (Baton Rouge: Louisiana State Univ. Press, 1971); Per Seyersted, "Introduction," *The Complete Works of Kate Chopin*, Vol. I (Baton Rouge: Louisiana State Univ. Press, 1969); George M. Spangler, "Kate Chopin's *The Awakening*: A Partial Dissent," *Novel*, 3 (Spring, 1970), 249–255; Edmund Wilson, *Patriotic Gore* (New York: Oxford Univ. Press, 1962); Larzer Ziff, *The American 1890s* (New York: Viking, 1966). Eble is also author of an article entitled "A Forgotten Novel," which appeared in *Western Humanities Review*, I (Summer, 1956), 261–269, the same year as Robert Cantwell's "*The Awakening* by Kate Chopin," *Georgia Review*, X (Winter, 1956), 489–494. But neither article adds a dimension to the argument here.

2. Ziff contributes the sexual overtone to this mental image of Edna's. As it occurs in the novel (in the Grand Isle setting) it is devoid of sexual significance; it comes to Edna's mind as a programmatic gloss on a piece of music entitled "Solitude." The nakedness of the figure signifies his vulnerability before a cruel universe. That he is male, simply that he is generic man. Alas, poor females have the habit, until jolted out of it, of relating their feelings to those of mankind.

3. One other critic approaches the social question in an oblique formulation. Leary says, "Whether Edna is weak and wilfull, a woman wronged by the requirement of society, or a self-indulgent sensualist, finally and fundamentally romantic, who gets exactly what she deserves—these are not considerations that seem to have concerned Mrs. Chopin" (p. 174).

4. Edna is shocked and surprised by Robert's suggestion of such an outcome. In the same scene she has to tell him (1) "Then you must have forgotten that I was Léonce Pontellier's wife" and (2) "You have been a very, very foolish boy, wasting your time dreaming of impossible things when you speak of Mr. Pontellier's

possessions to dispose of or not. I give myself where I choose. If he were to say, 'Here, Robert, take her and be happy; she is yours,' I should laugh at you both." Robert's face turns white and he doesn't understand her meaning. He does not know that, many scenes before, Edna has resolved "never again to belong to another than herself" (p. 280 ff.).

The text used throughout is *The Awakening*, ed. Kenneth Eble (New York: Capricorn, 1964).

5. In the chapter "Phallic Criticism" of *Thinking About Women* (New York: Harvest, 1968) Ellmann quotes from Anthony Burgess' review of Brigid Brophy's *Don't Never Forget*. He tells of "an American professor friend who could never think of Brophy as an author after he had seen her in the flesh: " 'That girl was made for love,' he would growl" (p. 41). This is but one of Ellman's many examples of the phenomenon. It raises a question: would any of his colleagues and critics fail to take Ian Watt, for example, seriously because he was handsome?

6. "To Mrs. R." in *The Complete Works*, ed. Per Seyersted, V. II, 731.

BARBARA HARRELL CARSON

1. *The Collected Stories of Katherine Anne Porter* (New York: Harcourt, 1965), p. 199. All subsequent page references, given in the text, will be from this volume.
2. William Nance, *Katherine Anne Porter and the Art of Rejection* (Chapel Hill: Univ. of North Carolina Press, 1963), p. 118.
3. "Reflections on Willa Cather," *The Collected Essays and Occasional Writings of Katherine Anne Porter* (New York: Delacorte, 1966), pp. 31–32.
4. George Hendrick, *Katherine Anne Porter* (New York: Twayne, 1965), pp. 61–62.
5. "Afterword," *Pale Horse, Pale Rider* (New York: New American Library, 1965), pp. 61–62.
6. Quoted in *Katherine Anne Porter: A Critical Symposium*, ed. Lodwick Hartley and George Core (Athens: Univ. of Georgia Press, 1969), p. 162.

JUDITH FETTERLY

1. See, in particular, the documentation of Robert W. Lewis, Jr., in "The Tough Romance," in *Twentieth Century Interpretations of "A Farewell to Arms,"* ed. Jay Gellens (Englewood Cliffs: Prentice Hall, 1970), pp. 42–43.

2. *Ernest Hemingway: An Introduction and Interpretation* (New York: Holt, 1967), p. 73.
3. Robert W. Lewis, Jr., p. 45.
4. Philip Young, *Ernest Hemingway: A Reconsideration* (University Park: Pennsylvania State Univ. Press, 1966), p. 93.
5. Ernest Hemingway, *A Farewell to Arms* (New York: Scribner's, 1929). All further references are to this edition; page numbers will be indicated parenthetically within the text.
6. It is interesting in this connection to read Wyndham Lewis' essay on *A Farewell to Arms*, reprinted in *Twentieth Century Interpretations* (pp. 72–90) as "The Dumb Ox in Love and War." While he describes, and ultimately decries, the paralysis of the will which characterizes the Hemingway protagonist, he picks as his point of comparison and his representative of "passionate personal energy" Prosper Mérimée's Don Jose who dealt in a truly Othello-like way with his particular Desdemona, Carmen. In part, then, what Lewis' essay seems to be is a lament for the good old days when men's hostility for women could be openly expressed and socially justified. Indeed, the politics of this change are, as Lewis implies, immense.
7. *Hemingway: The Writer's Art of Self-Defense* (Minneapolis: Univ. of Minnesota Press, 1969), pp. 82–83.
8. *Hemingway: The Inward Terrain* (Seattle: Univ. of Washington Press, 1968), pp. 78–79.
9. Wyndham Lewis, pp. 73, 90.
10. *Hemingway and the Dead Gods* (Lexington: Univ. of Kentucky Press, 1960), p. 47.
11. Robert W. Lewis, Jr., p. 53.
12. Ibid., p. 52.

CONTRIBUTORS

MAURIANNE ADAMS is president of the Research Society for Victorian Periodicals and co-editor of *S. T. Coleridge: 1793–1899*, an annotated bibliography of criticism and scholarship.

PRISCILLA ALLEN has been teaching since 1945, most recently at the Free University of Berlin. She is now living in London and organizing a Women's Liberation School.

A short story writer and film maker, PATRICIA BARBER is also interested in American Studies.

A philosopher who has taught at Smith College and Amherst College, ANNETTE BARNES is currently working in an inter-disciplinary program at the University of Maryland.

BARBARA HARRELL CARSON has written on Ellen Glasgow and other southern writers, taught at Towson State College and the University of Massachusetts, and is presently living and teaching in Florida.

A member of the English Department at Temple University, MARY COHEN offers this anecdote: "I remember answering the telephone and having a friend demand: 'What's the matter?' 'Oh...I'm just reading *The Golden Notebook*.' 'But you said you would never read that book again.' 'When did I say that?' 'The *last* time you were reading *The Golden Notebook*.' "

ARLYN DIAMOND and LEE R. EDWARDS collaborated most recently on *American Voices, American Women*, a collection of short fiction by little-known women writers.

"*A Farewell to Arms*: Ernest Hemingway's 'Resentful Cryptogram'" is a chapter from JUDITH FETTERLEY's recently completed book, *Critical Karate: Perspectives on the Immasculating Imagination of American Literature*.

Medievalist MAUREEN FRIES has written on Ovid, Chaucer, and Malory, and is co-editor of *A Bibliography of Writings by and about Women Authors, British and American, 1957–1969*.

COPPÉLIA KAHN, who teaches English at Wesleyan University, is currently writing a book on Shakespeare and the feminine.

DAWN LANDER's "Eve among the Indians" is part of a longer study, *From Parlor to Teepee: The White Squaw on the American Frontier.*

Active in the Women Studies Program at the University of Pittsburgh, MARCIA LANDY has written extensively on women's language and education and has also published essays on Milton and Gide.

MIRIAM LERENBAUM is Assistant Dean of Arts and Sciences at the State University of New York at Binghamton, where she is also a member of the English Department. She has written articles on Defoe and a book, *Alexander Pope's Magnum Opus, 1729–1744.*

KATHERINE M. ROGERS' most recent book is *The Troublesome Helpmate: A History of Misogyny in Literature.* A member of the English Department at Brooklyn College, she is presently doing research and writing on women in the eighteenth century.

LYNN SUKENICK, author of *Houdini and Other Poems*, teaches creative writing and literature at the University of California at Irvine and is completing a book on women and fiction.